LINCOLN:

A Contemporary Portrait

LINCOLN:

A CONTEMPORARY PORTRAIT

EDITED BY

Allan Nevins and Irving Stone

1962
DOUBLEDAY & COMPANY, INC.
Garden City, New York

Library of Congress Catalog Card Number 62-7667
Copyright © 1962 by Doubleday & Company, Inc.
All Rights Reserved
Printed in the United States of America
First Edition

CONTENTS

INTRODUCTION

By Irving Stone

THIS BOOK has come into being because a group of friends and Lincoln enthusiasts living close to each other in Southern California, plus one or two friends of friends, wanted to do something to celebrate the Lincoln Sesquicentennial. We asked ourselves what could be more appropriate than to take a fresh look at the story of Abraham Lincoln, each of us in his own field, and see if we could not come up with interesting approaches to some of the facets of the president's many-sided nature.

The problem with still another book on Lincoln is, "What remains to be said?" None of us had any desire to rehash old materials. Neither could we claim to have unearthed long-hidden documents which would revolutionize existing knowledge about Lincoln or the Civil War. Yet if history is not a mountain, but a river, then it alters its bed with each new generation as modern ideas change the course of thinking and attitudes. Insights can sometimes be as revealing as new documents or hidden diaries.

What we hoped to achieve was a group portrait: Mr. Lincoln sitting for a dozen students who aspired to catch an authentic likeness, though each would be painting him from a different angle, in different lights, and against differing backgrounds. What would emerge, one Lincoln, or a dozen?

As the chapters began reaching our desks, Allan Nevins and I found something interesting to be happening: although the authors were addressing themselves to the reality of Abraham Lincoln rather than the substantial myth, and although none of them had consulted the others on the character, tone, mood, or conclusions of his essay, each chapter seemed to fit as an integral part of a design. Abraham Lincoln emerged as a man unified in mind, spirit, and action; we were tempted to title the book: *United He Stands*.

The contributors are all admirers of Mr. Lincoln, yet it is considerably more than admiration that binds together the separate contributions. No matter from what angle the portrait had been painted, it is the same, integrated man who gazes out at us, staggering under some of the cruelest burdens ever borne by one human being. What is revealed is a man of compassion and wisdom, a rare combination among famous historical figures.

A few years ago, while I was writing a biographical novel about Mary Todd and Abraham Lincoln, I went with Paul Angle, a Lincoln scholar, to spend an evening with Aldous Huxley. When the conversation came around to a discussion of Mr. Lincoln, I replied to a query of Mr. Huxley's that I found Mr. Lincoln the most complex human being I had ever tried to write about. Mr. Angle, who is ordinarily a mild-mannered man, cried out:

"Mr. Lincoln was one of the simplest men who ever lived. It is because his kind of simplicity has vanished from our world that we fail to understand him, and try to transfer our own ambiguities to his lucid mind."

Was Abraham Lincoln simple? Was he complex? Or is the proper descriptive word: *whole?*

And what direct meaning has he for today's troubled world?

His words then were, "Now we are engaged in a great civil war, testing whether that nation, or any nation so conceived, and so dedicated, can long endure." We are engaged in an identical task today, not to hold together the two halves of a nation, but the two halves of our planet. We have suffered the same series of seemingly endless defeats; the future looks dark. What may we learn from a fresh searching of Lincoln's mind and methods in the crisis of a century ago that can be of help to us today?

This book is, admittedly, a labor of love. But in writing history, must love be blind? Can there not be discernments?

If we, a baker's dozen of Lincoln students, shall have been able to send a few readers back to the historic record, to make observations and conclusions of their own, we will feel that our efforts have been richly rewarded.

LINCOLN:

*A Contemporary
Portrait*

ALLAN NEVINS

Lincoln's Ideas of Democracy

ঙ

IT IS AN incontestable fact that Americans in their first century of independence did little intensive thinking upon democracy. They accepted its existence and its beneficence upon faith. Our first formal treatise on the subject was a book published by Charles Camp in 1836 entitled *Democracy,* and he lamented this lack of intensive thinking.* Americans, he wrote, were content to live "in the rich experience and practical enjoyment of democratic freedom, but in entire and reckless indifference to its abstract principles." No native school of philosophers had arisen to combat the hostile European theorists then so numerous. Americans surrendered the field to Tocqueville, the first part of whose *La Démocratie en Amérique* appeared in 1835, and the second in 1840.

Why this neglect? For one reason, because the pragmatic bent of Americans made them satisfied with the "rich experience"; why theorize upon it? For another, noted by Harriet Martineau, the ideas of the Declaration of Independence took the place of an explicit rationale of democracy. This great document was the milk of the word. Its twin principles of faith in natural law, and faith in the indefinite perfectibility of man, underlay our scheme of government and society, and could be expanded to cover the whole American future. And finally, the history of party tenets was believed to furnish

* The author owes the quotation from Camp to a writer in the *New England Quarterly.*

a good theoretical framework for American political thinking. Study the party conflict, they said, and you would understand the nature of American democracy.

When Henry Adams wrote his novel *Democracy,* he too commented upon this vague, inarticulate attitude toward the subject. Early in the book that epitome of Congressional coarseness whom he calls Senator Ratcliffe, standing in a Washington drawing room, asserts his belief that the reform of government must wait upon the reform of the people. "Purify society and you purify the government. But try to purify the government artificially and you only aggravate failure." This sneer at reformers brings from a foreign member of the group, Baron Jacobi, a statement that he had never seen a society which possessed so many elements of corruption as the United States. Thereupon Mrs. Lightfoot Lee, the hostess, interposes to ask Mr. Gore, a historian, what *he* thinks of Ratcliffe's ideas about the people. "Do you yourself," she inquires, "think democracy the best government, and universal suffrage a success?" Poor historian! He wriggles hopelessly, for he, too, has never really thought about democracy. But he must answer, and he finally turns at bay with something like despair.

"These are matters," he says, "about which I rarely talk in society; they are like the doctrine of a personal God; of a future life; of revealed religion; subjects which one naturally reserves for private reflection. But since you ask for my political creed you shall have it . . . never to be repeated or quoted as mine. I believe in democracy. I accept it. I will faithfully serve it. I believe in it because it appears to me the inevitable consequence of what has gone before it. Democracy asserts the fact that the masses are now raised to a higher level of intelligence than formerly." Having floundered that far, he stopped; he had nothing more to say about democracy.

It must be admitted that, like his fellow countrymen, Lincoln made few and limited statements of an abstract character upon democracy; he took it on faith, without analysis.

Political democracy, to him, was the rule of the people; and he declared again and again that he believed in the virtue and strength of the whole people whenever they were properly instructed. God must have loved the people, he said, or he would not have made so many of them; you could never fool all of the people all of the time; government of, for, and by the people was not only the best government, but the hope of the world. In contradistinction to John Adams, whose sympathies were with an elite, he liked to speak of the plain people, meaning everyday citizens who were like himself in not having much property or much formal education.

Out of this deep regard for the common folk came Lincoln's seldom-erring instinct for popular sentiment; he divined how far and how fast he could go without losing touch with the majority. Out of it came his consistent refusal to talk down to the people, or to appeal to their passions. As Lowell wrote, he never played the Cleon—the demagogue. Instead, he presented the people with careful arguments, addressed to their reason and their loftier instincts. "I beg of you," he once said, after listing a certain set of arguments, "a calm and enlarged consideration of them." On minor questions he believed the people could err grievously; but on fundamental issues he would trust them, in the end, to decide aright. Perhaps the greatest decision they had to make in his time was that registered in the election of 1864, when they might have rejected him and his administration, and given up the Union in favor of immediate peace. He knew they would not flinch, and they did not. As he wrote just after the election:

The purpose of the people within the loyal States to maintain the integrity of the Union was never more firm nor more nearly unanimous than now. The extraordinary calmness and good order with which the millions of voters met and mingled at the polls give strong assurance of this. . . . There have been much impugning of motives, and much heated controversy as to the proper means and best mode of advancing the Union cause; but on the distinct issue of Union or no Union the politicians have shown their instinctive knowledge that there is no diversity among the people. In affording the people the fair opportunity of showing one to another and to the world this firmness and unanimity of purpose, the election has been of vast value to the national cause.

Instead of discoursing on the theory of democracy, Lincoln preferred to speak of its purposes, its significance, its perils, and its successes; that is, of the practical problems attending its course. Its main purpose, often obscure before the war, became plain during the conflict. "This is essentially a people's contest," he wrote. "On the side of the Union, it is a struggle for maintaining in the world, that form, and substance of government, whose main object is, to elevate the condition of men—to lift artificial weights from all shoulders—to clear the paths of laudable pursuit for all—to afford all, an unfettered start, and a fair chance, in the race of life. . . . I am most happy to believe that the plain people understand, and appreciate this." At an earlier period, and on various occasions, he declared that equality of rights and privileges was the central intent of democracy. As he put it during the discussion of the Kansas–Nebraska Act: "No man is good enough to govern another man without that man's consent." And he once gave the idea a still more emphatic statement: "As I would not be a *slave,* so I would not be a *master.* This expresses my idea of democracy. Whatever differs from this, to the extent of the difference, is no democracy."

The perils to democracy, in his view, were numerous. One was materialism, or selfish wealth, or what he called Mammon. "The plainest print," he said in 1857, after the Dred Scott decision, "cannot be read through a gold eagle." Another, to which he often adverted, was demagogy. He spoke scornfully of the troublemaking politicians who were more anxious to serve error than truth; that is, demagogues. These demagogues, he said, were enemies of the whole people: they "are subtle, and profound, on the rights of minorities. They are not partial to that power which made the Constitution, and speaks from the preamble, calling itself, 'We, the People.'" They were adroit in corrupting the electorate. The plotters of secession, for example, "commenced by an insidious drugging of the public mind. They invented an ingenious sophism, which, if conceded, was followed by perfectly logical steps, through all its incidents, to the complete destruction of the Union. This sophism is that any State of the Union may . . . lawfully and peacefully withdraw from the Union. . . ." The word *politician,* in Lincoln's vocabulary, usually had an unfavorable connotation.

As for the success of democracy, Lincoln was sure that this was two-thirds proved. He said this in almost so many words. "Our popular government," he wrote, "has often been called an experiment. Two points in it, our people have already settled—the successful *establishing,* and the successful *administering,* of it. One still remains—its successful *maintenance* against a formidable attempt to overthrow it." The question of maintenance did not concern the nation alone; it concerned the world. "And this issue," he declared, "embraces more than the fate of these United States. It presents to the whole family of man, the question, whether a constitutional republic, or a democracy—a government of the people, by the same people—can, or cannot, maintain its territorial integrity against its own domestic foes. . . . It forces us to ask: 'Is there, in all republics, this inherent, and fatal weakness?'" But he was confident of the outcome. When the war had endured three years, he told the Sanitary Fair in Philadelphia: "For the American people, so far as my knowledge enables me to speak, I say we are going through on this line if it takes three years more."

Lincoln thus gave something more than the two cheers for democracy that the novelist E. M. Forster has given it; say, two and a half cheers. Superior as it was to any other form of government, when bad men—politicians, demagogues—obtained an ascendancy, it worked badly. That is, it worked badly when deflected by an Aaron Burr, a James Buchanan, or a Vallandigham. It worked well when leadership was exercised by honest, sagacious men. Aberrations from the true path, however, would probably be brief, for the majority of the people would not be fooled very long. Lincoln would have applied to American democracy the apologue he once related of himself. "For such an awkward fellow," he said, "I am pretty sure-footed. . . . I remember the evening of the day in 1858 that decided the contest for the Senate between Mr. Douglas and myself . . . dark, rainy, and gloomy. I had been reading the returns, and had ascertained that we had lost the legislature, and started to go home. The path had been worn hogbacked and was slippery. Both my feet slipped from under me, but I recovered myself and lit clear; and I said to myself, 'It is a slip and not a fall.' " The American democracy was awkward but sure-footed; it experienced some bad slips, but it did not fall.

Thus repeating Lincoln's few formal statements upon democracy, or government by the whole people, we must confess that they do not carry us far into the subject. They would not have impressed Tocqueville or John Stuart Mill. They left Lincoln in Charles Camp's category of Americans who lived in the rich experience of democracy without analyzing its underlying theories. If we summarize his tenets under a half-dozen heads, as we can, this will perhaps make clearer both their values and their limitations:

Men may believe fervently in liberty but reject democracy. Lincoln's position was a pole apart from that of such thinkers as Burke, a passionate libertarian but no democrat. Burke wrote that he never addressed himself to the vulgar, nor to that which alone governs the vulgar, their passions. Lincoln pointedly addressed himself to the vulgar—the plain people— and to their reason.

Lincoln believed in a government by the whole people, without material restrictions. He did not share John Adams' opinion that a governing class was needed—an elite qualified by special mental and moral fitness. Neither did he share John Stuart Mill's fear of the tyranny of the majority, which led Mill to insist on special safeguards for minority rights, and finally made him a pioneer in the movement for proportional representation. Lincoln's faith in the whole people came near being absolute.

He believed emphatically in the egalitarian principle, telling the 164th Ohio in August 1864, that "every man has a right to be equal to every other man." But he believed with still greater emphasis that our society must be an *open* society, its members given full opportunity to apply their talents without hindrance and to rise to the height of their powers. Everyone should have "an open field and a fair chance." I am the temporary occupant of the White House, he told another Ohio regiment; and "I am a living witness that any one of your children may look to come here as my father's child has."

His pragmatic view of democracy was shaped largely by his special environment of the agricultural Middle West, where men were shrewd, well informed, full of common-sense sagacity, tinctured with idealism, and sufficiently homogeneous to be good-natured and tolerant. Had he seen more of the kind of population already filling much of the Eastern cities, he would possibly have shared Mill's fear that the stable agrarian elements in the democracy might not be strong enough to balance the more volatile urban and industrial elements. Had he seen the face of industrialism more clearly, he might have worried more.

He realized perfectly that the quality of democracy depends heavily on the quality of leadership. This was the exact converse of Senator Ratcliffe's theory that it is hopeless to do much about leadership until we improve the masses. Lincoln's position that democracy works admirably under a Washington or Jefferson, and fails to work under the Pierces and Buchanans, is not only borne out by history, but is supported by the instinctive feeling of the people. A democracy thirsts for nothing more than sagacious leadership, and is never so happy as when it appears.

In exercising leadership, Lincoln—as both his words and deeds show—always remained practical. He placed a heavy reliance on argument and logic; on the come-let-us-reason-together spirit. He used calm, dispassionate exposition. But he also used the practical tools of the politics of his day —patronage, pressure, conferences with legislative leaders which involved astute bargaining, and once or twice, such dubious steps as those he took to make sure that the House would pass the Thirteenth Amendment.

Springing from and guiding an optimistic people, he was always an optimist about democracy. He would have been the last man to sell America short.

The most remarkable of the features of his thought here enumerated is his optimism, for seldom if ever has American democracy offered more repulsive aspects than between 1830 and 1860. He believed in its virtues; but did they really outweigh its vices? Governor Thomas Ford, whom Lincoln knew, wrote a history of Illinois portraying the political life of the prairie state in lurid hues. He flayed his predecessors in the State House with merciless scalpel; he showed how petty were the men who governed Illinois in Lincoln's youth, how mean their motives, how sordid their acts. The Illinoisans of that generation cruelly maltreated Black Hawk and his Sac and Fox Indians; they brutally murdered Joseph Smith and his brother, and forced the Mormons at musket-point across the Mississippi. They indulged in wild extravagance during the internal improvements era, and wavered on the brink of debt repudiation later. The looser side of political morals was illustrated by the conduct of Governor Joel A. Matteson who, after almost gaining the Senate seat which Lincoln wanted, was proved guilty of theft from the state treasury, and compelled to restore to it nearly a quarter of a million dollars. The Alton riots and the murder of Elijah Lovejoy,

the abolitionist martyr, placed a sad blot on the shield of
Illinois.

On the national scene political democracy had even more
dismaying aspects. From Lincoln's point of view the Mexican
War was impossible to defend. The quarrel over slavery had
undermined the political integrity of the country, and a suc-
cession of presidential defectives—the commonplace Fillmore,
the forcible-feeble Pierce, the timid Buchanan—offered no
policy to meet the mounting crisis but evasion and postpone-
ment. Violence stained all political life. The House of
Representatives, said Thaddeus Stevens, when he entered it
in 1849 was a place of bowie knives, revolvers, and howling
demons. What a lurid light was thrown on the workings of
democracy by bleeding Kansas; by the assault of Brooks
upon Sumner in the Capitol itself; by the eclipse of civil
liberties throughout the South; and by the ideas of territorial
grabbing embodied in the Ostend Manifesto, and the filibuster-
ing raids on Cuba and Central America. The nation's descent
into civil war was by a series of episodes that indicted democracy, and the conflict itself seemed to mark its breakdown.
Punch published a cartoon which presented the shade of
George III poking the shade of George Washington in the
ribs and ejaculating: "What d'ye think of your fine republic
now? Eh? Eh?"

Lincoln had an ample firsthand experience of democracy
in its demagogic, reckless phases. As a young legislator he
had played his part in the internal improvement craze which
fastened a load of debt on his young state; he had been one
of the Sangamon delegation whose adroit lobbying removed
the capital from Vandalia to Springfield. He saw realistically
the vicious features of spoils-system government in the Jack-
sonian era. The Democratic Party had blindly followed Old
Hickory wherever he led it; or, as Lincoln put it, the hungry
Democratic ticks had stuck to the tail of the Hermitage
lion till his death. He thought the acts of the proslavery
administrations just before the war disgraceful. "Our Republi-

can robe," he said in the Peoria speech of 1854, "is soiled and trailed in the dust."

Lincoln in his wartime dealings with democracy experienced three painful failures. His passionate desire during his first month in office was to avert war, an end toward which he strove at any cost save the sacrifice of principle; but his labors were thwarted when passionate Southerners fired on Fort Sumter. His principal effort in the next seventeen months, second only to the prosecution of the war, was to persuade the border states to accept a plan of gradual compensated emancipation, joined with a program for colonizing the freedmen abroad. He put the utmost intensity of feeling into this effort. "Oh," he said to Isaac Arnold and Owen Lovejoy on July 13, 1862, "how I wish the border States would accept my proposition. Then you, Lovejoy, and you, Arnold, and all of us, would not have lived in vain!" He thought acceptance of his plan would soon lead to the end of the conflict; but Maryland and Delaware, Kentucky and Missouri, rejected it. In the next eighteen months, as the war dragged to its close, he signally failed to persuade the majority in Congress to adopt a moderate scheme of reconstruction; and in 1864 he had to veto the vindictive scheme embodied in the Wade–Davis bill. His own Cabinet so often opposed him that he said he hoped he would have more influence with the next administration. The policies on which he most set his heart, in short, broke down. Meanwhile, he might well have complained of public impatience, of the popular refusal to keep the armies sufficiently filled to avert a draft, of the widespread profiteering and cheating, and of such Congressional mischief as the attempt to dictate a new Cabinet just after Fredericksburg.

He never complained, and never lost faith. Why was it that during all his discouragements, amid all the demagogy, knavery, and selfishness of the time, he maintained an unyielding belief in the superior virtues of democracy? His best-trusted associate, Secretary Seward, sometimes lost faith in the people. We who bear the responsibility in Washington, Seward wrote his wife in 1862, see the war as a sad, painful, fearful reality. "To the public, who are not directly engaged in it, it is a novel, a play. . . . They weary and grow restive if the action of the war drags, or loses its intensity. They pronounce the piece a failure, and propose to drive the manager out of the theatre. Who could believe that nations could be made or saved in civil war, when the people act like this?" On another occasion Seward wrote that nothing preserved his sense of philosophy about the American democracy but reading history. "Selfishness crops out in everything, everywhere. It offends and alarms us constantly; but we learn from history that selfishness always existed. . . ."

Gideon Welles likewise lost faith. After watching the unprincipled antics of the defeatist Congressman Fernando Wood, he burst out: "But the whole city of New York is alike leprous and rotten." In such vicious communities, he thought, free suffrage was dangerous, and some outside control imperatively needed. During his youth Welles had believed that the popular voice was right; "but alas," he wrote, "experience has shaken the confidence I once had." In short, he doubted that democracy could succeed among what he termed "the strange materials that compose a majority of the population in our large cities." Thaddeus Stevens came to feel a yet deeper distrust. He was called the Great Commoner, and he was supposed to cherish a passionate attachment to democracy. Yet during the war and Reconstruction he came to a sardonic belief that misgovernment was chronic, and when near his death he commented: "With all this great struggle of years in Washington, and the fearful sacrifice of life and treasure, I see little hope for the republic."

An impulsive but equally caustic and pessimistic statement was expressed by William Tecumseh Sherman when he entered the war in the summer of 1861. He wrote home that he was in command of six regiments of volunteers called by courtesy soldiers, and that God alone could foresee the issue. He went on: "Our adversaries have the weakness of slavery in their midst to offset our democracy, and 'tis beyond human wisdom to say which is the greater evil." During his residence in Mississippi, Sherman had apparently been infected by the scorn which such Southern leaders as Robert Toombs, Howell Cobb, and Judah P. Benjamin always expressed for democracy. When Alexander H. Stephens, defending the Union before the Georgia legislature in 1860, asked what form of government could be preferred to America's, Toombs exclaimed "England's"—and England still had an aristocratic government.

A few years more, and during the Reconstruction period the voice of disillusionment filled the land. Henry Adams saw little hope for democracy. Ambrose Bierce, an Indianan sprung from the plain people, decided that popular government was a vast fraud. In *The Devil's Dictionary* he stated his conclusions: "Politics: The conduct of public affairs for private advantage." "Deliberation: The act of examining one's bread to see which side it is buttered on." Mark Twain was mordantly cynical about democracy in his novel *The Gilded Age,* and one of his paragraphs on the free, bold, egalitarian West in *Life on the Mississippi* was hardly a paean to its virtues. He wrote:

How solemn and beautiful is the thought that the earliest pioneer of civilization . . . is never the steamboat, never the railroad, never the newspapers, never the Sabbath School, never the missionary—but always whisky! Such is the case. Look history over; you will see. The missionary comes after the whisky—I mean, he arrives after the whisky has arrived; next comes the poor immigrant with axe and hoe and rifle; next, the trader; next the miscellaneous rush; next the gambler, the desperado, the highwayman, and all their kindred in sin of both sexes; and next, the smart chap who has bought up an old grant that covered all the lands; this brings in the lawyer tribe; the vigilance committee brings the undertaker. All these interests bring the newspaper; the newspaper starts up politics and a railroad; all hands turn to and build a church and a jail—and behold, civilization is established forever in the land.

To comprehend why Lincoln felt none of this cynicism, none of this disillusionment, we would look in vain in his writings. He often voiced his faith in democracy, but never gave explicit reasons—probably because he thought them unnecessary. And yet it is not true to say that he simply took democracy on intuitive faith. His policies, his acts, show that he had certain large bases for his confidence in its workings.

He founded this confidence largely upon what he saw of the people about him in the first fifty years of his life. That the inhabitants of the Old Northwest, from Ohio to Iowa, were then a folk of superior character and intelligence, is a fact attested by many observers. The second generation in that fertile area read the New York *Weekly Tribune,* founded colleges, and molded new communities with the tough idealism depicted by Herbert Quick and Hamlin Garland. Good studies of this society, founded on firsthand observation, may be found in Edward Eggleston's novel of Lincoln's younger days in Illinois, *The Graysons,* Clark E. Carr's picture of Galesburg entitled *The Illini,* and the letters of such leaders as Edward Beecher of Jacksonville and Josiah B. Grinnell of the Iowa town he named. Carl Schurz in epistle after epistle to German friends expatiated on Western intelligence, energy, and liberalism. Just after the election of 1856 he wrote from Wisconsin:

> The last weeks were times when public matters made more demands than ordinarily upon the American system. You over there in your decrepit Europe can hardly imagine how a great idea can stir up the masses of the people to their depths, and how an enthusiastic struggle for principles can thrust aside for a certain time all other interests, even the materialistic ones. . . . A general struggle of opinions among a free people has in it something unbelievably imposing; and you never see with greater clearness what a farreaching influence political freedom exercises upon the development of the masses.

Richard Cobden, the great English liberal, made an equally emphatic statement after he toured the Northwest in 1859.

Impressed by the high level of decorum, education, and interest in public affairs, he wrote home that his confidence in popular government had been quickened. "The concentrated earnestness," he remarked, "with which political parties were at work in the United States, inspired me with a full faith that the people of the country would, in spite of the difficulties and dangers of their political issues, work out their salvation." This earnestness likewise heartened Lincoln. He himself transcended the virtues of his time and section; as Herbert Croly later put it, he was more than an American. He was thoughtful where the frontier was thoughtless, studious where it was ignorant, magnanimous where it was vindictive. Still, he saw that the average was high. He founded his belief in democracy on the same rock as Whitman's, a sympathetic appreciation of the virtues of the common man.

This rock was fortified by a special set of principles expressed in the two basic American documents, the Declaration of Independence and the Constitution. Another reason for Lincoln's confidence was his belief that the spirit of these two documents had permeated the democratic mass. For both he felt a strong reverence. Of the Constitution he said in Congress in 1848 that it should not lightly be touched: "It can scarcely be made better than it is." For the Declaration he expressed a still deeper attachment, and whenever its spirit warred with the letter of the Constitution, he stood by its spirit. Every nation, he said in Chicago in 1856, needs a central idea. "The central idea in our political public opinion was, and until recently continued to be, the equality of man"—the idea of the Declaration. This was more than a purely national idea, however; it could and should be made world-wide in potency. Out of the Revolution, he told the New Jersey Senate in Trenton in 1860, had come something larger than American independence—"that something that held out a great promise to all the people of the world to all time to come." Faith in the American idea, faith in the American world mission—these two beliefs, Lincoln felt, had given our democracy a pervasive inspiration.

His confidence in the people, confidence in the inspiring charters the fathers of the nation had given them, and confidence in the world future of their central idea, he all summed up in a few sentences of his appeal to the Border State Representatives in July 1862. "You are patriots and statesmen," he said. "Consider this proposition, and at the least commend it to the consideration of your States and people." He went on:

> "As you would perpetuate popular government for the best people in the world, I beseech that you do in no wise omit this. Our common country is in great peril demanding the loftiest views and boldest action to bring it speedy relief. Once relieved, its form of government is saved to the world, its beloved history and cherished memories are vindicated, and its happy future fully assured and rendered inconceivably grand."

For all his faith and optimism, Lincoln did not expect too much of democracy, because he had a correct idea of its true nature. The men who grew cynical about it like Sherman, or discouraged like Thad Stevens, thought of it as an achieved state of political society, a goal, a terminal situation; hence its defects seemed to them horrible. Lincoln knew it was nothing of the sort. Democracy is a process, an unending struggle, a hard, grueling battle. Its best benefits are not the easy garlands found on arrival at a superior political position; they are the toughness, the heroic constancy, the stamina, developed during the desperate climb upward. Democracy is not a serene attainment; it is an incessant effort, marked by ignominious falls, heartbreaking defeats, and almost intolerable trials. Lincoln almost said this in so many words, telling some troops to gird themselves for the heavy postwar work ahead: "When you return to your homes rise up to the height of a generation of men worthy of a free Government." He said it in effect again and again. His writings cheered Americans

on to the struggle and the sacrifice. He would have endorsed
the crisp statement by Carl Schurz, who declared that the
revolutionary idealists of Europe might be startled by the
seamy side of American affairs. They would see:

> the most contradictory tendencies and antagonistic movements
> openly at work, side by side, or against one another, enlighten-
> ment and stupid bigotry, good citizenship and lawlessness,
> benevolent and open-handed public spirit and rapacious greed,
> democracy and slavery, independent spirit and subservience
> to party despotism and to predominant public opinion—all
> this in bewildering confusion. The newly arrived European
> democrat . . . without having had any practical experience
> of a democracy at work, beholding it for the first time, asks
> himself: "Is this really a people living in freedom? Is this the
> realization of my ideal?"

But, Schurz went on, democracy is essentially a struggle. The
acute observer would soon see this:

> He is puzzled and perplexed until it dawns on him that, in a
> condition of real freedom, man manifests himself, not as he
> ought to be, but as he is, with all his bad as well as his good
> qualities, instincts, and impulses; with all his attributes of
> strength as well as all his weaknesses; that this, therefore, is
> not an ideal state, but simply a state in which the forces of
> good have a free field as against the forces of evil, and in
> which the victories of virtue, of enlightenment, and of progress
> are not achieved by some power or agency outside of the
> people, for their benefit, but *by* the people themselves.

> Such victories of the forces of good may be slow in being
> accomplished, but they will be all the more thorough and
> durable in their effects, because they will be the product of
> the people's own thought and effort.

Seeing democracy as an incessant contest, a never-ending
battle, Lincoln's faith in it was buoyed by his sense that while
it was going hard, it was also going well. He had an increasing
conviction from 1848 onward that the masses were being

possessed by a stern moral conviction that would ultimately regenerate the country. They were rising to meet the demands of a cause larger than any they had known since 1789. Other men understood this ocean-heave of democratic idealism. William Cullen Bryant was one. When the presidential campaign of 1856 closed with a Republican vote for Frémont of 1,341,264 against 1,838,169 for Buchanan, Bryant was exultant. The party of freedom had swept New England, carried New York, Ohio, Wisconsin, and Michigan, and made great gains in Illinois and Indiana. Public opinion in these states, wrote Bryant, had shifted from indecision to resolution. "If we look back to 1848, when we conducted a Presidential election on this very ground of opposition to the spread of slavery, we shall see that we have made immense strides. . . . We were then comparatively weak, we are now strong; we then counted our thousands, we now count our millions; we could then point to our respectable minorities in a few States, we now point to State after State. . . . The cause is not going back—it is going rapidly forward; the freesoil party of 1848 is the nucleus of the Republican Party of 1856; but with what accessions of numbers, of moral power, of influence, not merely in public assemblies, but at the domestic fireside!"

Lincoln had felt the pulse of the great movement begin to beat with new energy when the Wilmot Proviso almost passed Congress. He felt the movement grow in urgency and strength as Mrs. Stowe published *Uncle Tom's Cabin,* as the Underground Railroad gave defiance to the Fugitive Slave Act, as millions of Northerners rose in wrath against what they deemed Douglas' betrayal of freedom in the Kansas–Nebraska Act, and as the Republican Party became a giant of crusading idealism. The North was presenting the impressive spectacle which gave the French liberal, Elie Gasparin, his title for the book he published early in the war, *The Uprising of a Great People.*

The war brought the upheaval to its climax. It did not

astonish Lincoln to find that depressing as were the confusion, cowardice, and meanness revealed by the conflict, far out-weighing these defects were the displays of heroism, devotion, and generosity.

The plain people rose to save the Union and vindicate the type of government which would elevate the condition of all men. Countless soldiers proved ready to give the last full measure of devotion. Countless mothers were proud to lay their costliest sacrifice on the national altar. Proud, in fact, was the word used by the mother of Robert Gould Shaw when she was told that Governor John A. Andrew had given her son the command of the famous new Negro regiment, the Fifty-fourth Massachusetts. She said, "I am nearly as proud as I would be to hear that he had been shot." Later she heard that also.

Countless fathers showed the spirit of Commodore Smith, who, said Hawthorne, uttered the finest short speech of the war. His son Jo commanded the frigate *Congress* in Hampton Roads when the Merrimac began battering her to pieces, and the old commodore knew that his boy would die before he hauled down the colors. When informed that the *Congress* had struck its banner he therefore said, with simple feeling, "Then Jo's dead"—and Jo *was* dead. He died before the flag came down.

There were countless public officers as devoted as the two Assistant Secretaries in the War Department who literally worked themselves to death; or as the much-tried Stanton himself, whom an aide once surprised with his head bowed on his desk, weeping and exclaiming over and over, "God help me to do my duty! God help me to do my duty!" These men and women were exponents of democracy as a never-ending proc-ess, a contest, an ordeal, toughening them by trials and defeats more often than it exhilarated them by victories. Lincoln knew that, as Schurz put it, democracy was not an ideal state, but an arena in which good had a free field against evil, and in which the people were made great by the fact that they achieved progress not as the gift of some outside agency, but by their own hard struggle.

One historian, unlike Henry Adams' Mr. Gore, knew what democracy was and what it could accomplish. When the war closed John Lothrop Motley wrote from Austria to tell a Boston friend how glad he was that the nightmare of blood and fire had ended. "Believing in no government but that of the people, respecting no institutions but democratic institutions," he declared, "I feel sure that the future of the whole world is in our hands if we are true to ourselves." He paid tribute to Grant as a master of the art of war—"What could be more heroic than his stupendous bashfulness?" Of Lincoln he wrote that he was reluctant to speak for fear of overenthusiasm. "But I am sure that through all future ages, there will be a halo around that swarthy face, and a glory about that long, lean, uncouth figure such as history only accords to its saints and sages." Lincoln would have shrunk from this as overenthusiasm indeed.

But the president would heartily have endorsed the statement which Motley sent at the same time to Thomas Hughes, the author of *Tom Brown's School Days*. "My dear Hughes," he wrote, "the true hero of the whole war—the one I respect and admire even beyond Lincoln and Grant . . . is the American people."

FAWN BRODIE

Lincoln and Thaddeus Stevens

ONE OF THE most enduring fictions in American history holds that Thaddeus Stevens was an enemy to Abraham Lincoln, an insistent and irritating thorn, deriding Lincoln's compassion and constantly pressing for a vindictive peace. It would be more accurate to say, first of all, that Lincoln and Stevens were neither friends nor enemies. There was a guarded mutual respect but no affection and very little personal communication. "Stevens never saw Lincoln during the war except when necessity required it," said Alexander McClure, who was friend to both. "It was not his custom to fawn upon power or flatter authority, and his free and incisive criticism of public men generally prevented him from being in sympathetic touch with most of the officials connected with the administration."

Temperamentally the two men were alien. John W. Forney, editor of the *Philadelphia Press,* pointed out that "no two men, perhaps, so entirely different in character, ever threw off more spontaneous jokes." But where Stevens used his stories as a weapon, Lincoln loved storytelling for its own sake, finding in it relief from tension as well as the chance to make a political parable. "Were it not for these stories, I should die," he once confided, "they are vents through which my sadness, my gloom and melancholy escape."

Where Lincoln's wit was usually droll and kindly, Stevens' was sardonic, sharp, and earthy. He could convulse the House by saying, "I yield to the gentleman for a few feeble remarks." And while most of his cloacal witticisms were edited out of the

Congressional Globe, it is on record that he once said in the House, "There was a gentleman from the far West sitting next to me, but he went away and the seat seems just as clean as it was before."

Justin Morrill, Stevens' colleague on the Ways and Means Committee, said in later years, "His wit was all his own, and he had no skill in working ores mined by others, failing even in the common art of story-telling . . . nor did I ever know him to reproduce or to give a new edition of the good things of which he was the constant and prolific author. Born in a jovial moment, often glowing with passion, they were foundlings never after to be nursed by parental solicitude." Carl Schurz wrote that Stevens "shot out such sallies with a perfectly serious mien, or at best he accompanied them with a grim smile not at all like Abraham Lincoln's hearty laughs at his own jests."

Lincoln, unlike Stevens, never used frankness as a weapon to deride and humiliate others. Where he was tactful and forbearing with many shades of political opinion, Stevens cut himself off from men whose principles did not largely coincide with his own. Where Lincoln's compassion was boundless as the sea, Stevens'—like that of most men—was channeled into estuaries of his own making. Both men were honest and incisive to a degree almost unknown among politicians. But Lincoln was incomparably abler as a statesman, and also shrewder as a tactician.

Stevens had one touchstone by which he tested his superiors and supported or abandoned his friends—the vigor with which they moved in the antislavery cause. This was his test for Lincoln. When he praised the president, it was because he had moved decisively in the direction of Negro freedom; when he attacked him, it was because he believed Lincoln dilatory in pushing emancipation, or in prosecuting the war.

"I am quite sure," wrote McClure, "that Stevens respected Lincoln much more than he would have respected any other man in the same position with Lincoln's convictions of duty.

He could not but appreciate Lincoln's generous forbearance
even with all of Stevens' irritating conflicts, and Lincoln
profoundly appreciated Stevens as one of his most valued
and useful co-workers, and never cherished resentment even
when Stevens indulged in his bitterest sallies of wit or sarcasm
at Lincoln's tardiness. Strange as it may seem, these two great
characters, ever in conflict, and yet ever battling for the same
great cause, rendered invaluable service to each other, and
unitedly rendered incalculable service in saving the Republic.
. . . Stevens was ever clearing the underbrush and preparing
the soil, while Lincoln followed to sow the seeds that were to
ripen in a regenerated Union."

Lincoln was, in fact, the driver of an eight-horse team. In
front were the Radical Republicans, galloping furiously forward, heedless of obstacles in the road. The second team were
the Conservative Republicans, headed in the same direction,
but less impulsive and often fearful. Behind them came the
War Democrats, leaping forward in a great co-operative lunge
in the beginning, and afterward doing their best to swerve
the lead team from its fixed goal of "the Union with emancipation," to "the Union as it was and the Constitution as it is."
Eventually they did their best to unhorse the driver. Finally,
there were the Copperheads, who wanted to do nothing but sit
on their haunches and stall. As could be expected, it was on the
Negro question that they pulled off in all directions.

Lincoln's skill and adroitness as a driver were certainly not
obvious to his contemporaries in harness, each of whom felt
that his direction and pace should be enforced upon all the
rest. Today much of the Radical Republican criticism of
Lincoln seems harsh. But one should not forget that Lincoln,
though often grieved by the hostility of these men, was not one
to lose sight of the difference between being damned for not
prosecuting the war vigorously enough and being damned for
prosecuting it at all.

Stevens' attitude toward the president was always distorted
by the fact that he was way out in front of him. "He and

Lincoln worked substantially on the same lines," McClure said, "earnestly striving to attain the same ends, but Stevens was always in advance of public sentiment, while Lincoln never halted until assured that the considered judgment of the nation would sustain him. Stevens was the pioneer who was ever in advance of the government in every movement for the suppression of the rebellion, whether by military or civil measures. Lincoln possessed the sagacity to await the fullness of time for all things, and thus failed in nothing."

The relations between Stevens and Lincoln started out badly when it became evident that Lincoln—who had been committed against his wishes—would appoint Simon Cameron of Pennsylvania as his Secretary of War. Stevens, with many others, believed Cameron to be unscrupulous and dishonest. And he was infuriated by Cameron's statement in late 1860 that he was willing to see slavery extended to California. Alexander McClure rushed to Springfield to fight the appointment, urging that Thaddeus Stevens or David Wilmot be selected instead.

For a time Stevens was led to believe that Cameron had not only declined the post but had even swung to his own support. What actually happened was that Lincoln revoked his offer to Cameron, but the Pennsylvania politician tenaciously refused to give it up. On February 3, 1861, Stevens wrote angrily to Salmon P. Chase: ". . . With Cameron to make whatever department he may occupy a den of thieves, I have but little hope that we shall be able to survive the next election."

When Lincoln arrived in Washington, Stevens with other Republicans went to him privately to protest the Cameron appointment. "We did not think that he was the proper person to go there," Stevens said later in the House, "nor did we think that he had the capacity. We gave other strong reasons why he should not be appointed. It is true that those reasons did not appear very strong, for the executive power treated them as I expect they deserved to be treated, with silent contempt."

During one interview Lincoln questioned Stevens pointedly: "You don't mean to say you think Cameron would steal?"

"No," said Stevens drily, "I don't think he would steal a red-hot stove."

Lincoln, partly as a joke and partly perhaps by way of delicate warning, repeated the statement to Cameron. He was not amused.

Stevens later returned to demand of Lincoln: "Why did you tell Cameron what I said to you?"

"I thought it a good joke and didn't think it would make him mad."

"Well, he is very mad and made me promise to retract. I will now do so. I believe I told you he would not steal a red-hot stove. I will now take that back."

For a time the press spoke of Stevens as a possible Attorney General, though it was the Treasury post he wanted. But after all the intrigue was over, Stevens was left out. McClure disclosed later that he felt "personally aggrieved, although few of his most intimate acquaintances had any knowledge of it."

Stevens was one of the few leaders in Washington who, from the beginning, urged Lincoln to resist secession by force. Before the inaugural he urged Lincoln to retake the "stolen forts," using "gentle means at first, and if those fail, then such as become necessary." After war broke out he became, as McClure described him, "the master spirit of every aggressive movement in Congress to overthrow the rebellion and slavery." He was never cowed, never dismayed or discouraged into retreat.

As chairman of the Ways and Means Committee, which at that time handled both appropriations and taxes, he held the most important post in the House. From the beginning he was out in front, badgering and demanding, months in advance of others, exactions that the cruel progress of the war made inevitable. Lincoln's first call for troops limited the service to three months, and Cameron so misunderstood the nature of the crisis that he actually turned back regiments eagerly offered by the state governors with the excuse that he had no place for them. Stevens, one of the few men in the North who did not underestimate the strength and tenacity of the South, urged enlistment for the duration of the war, or at least a term of three years.

When Lincoln roused public furor by suspending the privilege of the writ of habeas corpus in September 1862, Stevens introduced a bill expressly granting him the authority, and in what Nicolay and Hay described as an "energetic, not to say arbitrary, manner," succeeded in getting it passed the day it was introduced.

Both Lincoln and Stevens passionately desired to see an end to slavery. But Lincoln, a strict constitutionalist, who had always declared himself to be antislavery but not an abolitionist, could not for some time be persuaded that the outbreak of war had given him any special power to destroy it. He waited seventeen months, in fact, before issuing the Emancipation Proclamation. During this period, punctuated as it was by heartbreaking military defeats, Thaddeus Stevens in the House and Charles Sumner in the Senate led the struggle against widespread apathy and fear, pushing through Congress the limited emancipation measures that prepared the nation for general emancipation and the Thirteenth Amendment.

One of the reasons for their exasperation with the president was that he never caught up with them. And since he chose not to confide in them, they could never be certain that he would even follow in their direction. "Stevens, Sumner and Wilson simply haunt me with their importunities for a Proclamation of Emancipation," Lincoln complained once to Senator John B. Henderson of Missouri. "Wherever I go and whatever way I turn, they are on my trail; and still in my heart, I have the deep conviction that the hour has not yet come."

During the summer of 1862 it seemed to Stevens that Lincoln would never use his war power to destroy slavery. He believed Lincoln to be "as honest a man as there is in the world," but "too easy and amiable," and misled by Seward, Weed, and the border-state men, particularly Montgomery Blair. He described him with irony as "our very discreet Executive." But when the Emancipation Proclamation went to the world on September 24, 1862, Stevens sent an open letter to his constituents praising Lincoln's patriotism and promising him full support.

On the hotly debated issue of whether or not Negroes should be used as soldiers one sees the same pattern. Stevens introduced a bill as early as January 12, 1862, calling for 150,000 colored troops. When the president at first refused to consider arming Negroes, Stevens openly blamed William Seward. "I have accused the prime minister to his face for having gone back from the faith he taught us," he said, "and instead of arming every man, black or white, who would fight for this Union, withholding a well-meaning President from doing so." Lincoln eventually moved decisively over to Stevens' side. By March 1865 there were 178,000 colored troops. Thirty-eight thousand of these lost their lives during the war.

Lincoln and Stevens both treated others according to their measure as men, and not according to their color, status, or pretensions. When the famous ex-slave Frederick Douglass first visited the White House, Lincoln greeted him by saying, "Sit down; I am glad to see you." And later when he learned that Douglass was being turned away from a White House reception by the guards, he ordered that he be permitted to enter, and greeted him warmly by name in a frank gesture of friendliness.

In 1863 the Radical Republicans succeeded in passing a bill recognizing the republics of Haiti and Liberia, and immediately Washington society was distracted by the possibility of a black ambassador invading their drawing rooms as an equal. After listening to Representative Cox of Ohio express horror at the idea of a black diplomat in Washington, Stevens said ironically in the House: "I hope that we shall not be less liberal than a very rich colored merchant in Jamaica that I heard a gentleman from Boston, who had dined with him, speak of. He said to this gentleman . . . that he had no prejudices about color; that he would never prefer a man of color, and that he would just as soon dine with a man as white as his tablecloth."

On several critical issues Lincoln never came to agree with Stevens. From the beginning Stevens fought the idea of paying compensation for the slaves of the rebels. Lincoln, however, though he had no support in his Cabinet, toyed with the idea almost up to the day of his death. It seemed to him a conceivable measure for shortening the war. The most irreconcilable disagreement, however, concerned the confiscation of the Southerners' estates. Stevens was certain that the evils inherent in the political oligarchy of the South could not be eradicated unless the vast holdings of the aristocrats were broken up. For Lincoln, the confiscation of title to land "beyond the lives of the guilty parties" was a revolutionary excess to which he would not consent.

When confronted by the tough Second Confiscation Act of July 1862, he made it clear that he would veto the whole bill —which included confiscation and freeing of rebel slaves— unless the act was amended to state that confiscation did not include the rebel landowner's title. The change was made. It seemed to Stevens that Lincoln had knocked out the most important part of the bill, and he frequently growled about "the error of the President."

At a later date Lincoln permitted some of the captured estates to be sold for failure to pay taxes, and a few of these, notably on the sea islands around Port Royal, and the rice plantations along the coast, were broken up and sold in small parcels to the ex-slaves. But his insistence against confiscation of land titles in July 1862 knocked the teeth out of a movement which would have directed the Republican revolution into channels traditionally followed by revolutions of the past, with the thoroughgoing economic destruction of a privileged class. The slaves would be freed and granted suffrage, but the Southern aristocracy, except for certain changes wrought by the economic ravages of the war itself, would remain a powerful political force.

No other single act of Lincoln's served so efficiently to checkmate Stevens' essentially revolutionary intentions. By January 1864 the old Congressman had retreated so far on this point as to demand only confiscation of the estates of "the leading traitors."

The epithet Jacobin was repeatedly hurled at Thaddeus Stevens. It was a smear word, smelling of the guillotine. Even Lincoln was called Robespierre by irresponsible Copperhead journalists and Confederate editors, but most newspapers correctly styled the president a Conservative Republican, and never placed him in Stevens' radical camp. The word *conservative,* however, confused an already complicated semantic problem. Lincoln was a conservative leader when matched against Thaddeus Stevens, but when compared with War Democrat Horatio Seymour, Copperhead Clement Vallandigham, or Confederate Jefferson Davis, he could more properly be described as a radical or revolutionary leader in the tradition of Washington and Jefferson.

The distinction between the Conservative and Radical wings of the party was real and vital. It had something to do with timing and something to do with compassion. It had a great deal to do with the difference between devotion to principle and surrender to principle. The Radical Republicans had certain things in common with the Jacobins, but the guillotine was not one of them. Stevens was an agitator, delighting in the prickly and unpleasant truth, careless of personal popularity, reckless of his own reputation and capacity for vote-getting, compulsively intent on a political and social ideal. He understood thoroughly the revolutionary dynamics of the war. But unlike Robespierre, he never came to have more faith in killing than in conversion.

Like many of his Radical colleagues, Stevens had considerable faith in the indefinite progress of the human race. According to one associate, he "denied the power of time to sanctify injustice . . . he believed that the true end of government was to right all the wrongs men suffer." What detracted from the great strength of his moral position was his certainty of having a monopoly on political righteousness.

Nor did he ever escape the old Calvinist conviction that those who did not accept the truth must be cast out of the city of the saints. Like all true radicals, he hated the deviationist more than the enemy. He could never forgive William Seward for what he considered a betrayal of Radical principles. "It were a great blessing if Seward could be removed," he growled privately in a letter to Simon Stevens on November 17, 1862. "It would revive hope, now nearly extinct. But I fear it cannot be done. But Fessenden is not the man for his successor. He has too much of the vile ingredient, called conservatism, which is worse than secession."

In 1863–64 as decisive military results remained elusive, many Republicans came to lay the blame upon Lincoln. Among the Radicals there was a growing conviction that he could not possibly win the 1864 election, and they began intriguing over a possible successor. Late in 1863 it was no secret that Thaddeus Stevens favored Chase for president and considered Lincoln a "dead card" in the political deck. In November, when Lincoln and Seward left Washington to dedicate the Gettysburg cemetery, someone asked Stevens where the president and Secretary of State were bound.

"To Gettysburg," he replied.

"But where are Stanton and Chase?"

"At home, at work," he said curtly. "Let the dead bury the dead."

The story was carried to Lincoln, who wryly repeated it in a Cabinet meeting.

Stevens was not reluctant to contribute to the growing impression that Lincoln was without political support. In introducing a Pennsylvania editor to Isaac N. Arnold, congressman from Illinois, he said: "Here is a man who wants to find a Lincoln member of Congress. You are the only one I know, and I have come over to introduce my friend to you."

Arnold replied seriously: "Thank you. I know a good many such, and I will present your friend to them, and I wish you, Mr. Stevens, were with us."

Nevertheless, Stevens and other radical leaders remained remarkably reluctant to endorse Chase publicly for president. Henry Winter Davis, Senators Ben Wade, and Samuel Pomeroy, and J. M. Winchell, collaborated secretly devising a circular criticizing Lincoln for his tendency to compromise, and suggesting Chase for president, but Pomeroy was the only one who actually signed it when it was released in February 1864. The circular, a kind of trial balloon, collapsed before it was scarcely aloft.

There was no other significant Radical rival to Lincoln in the 1864 election save John C. Frémont, who was actually nominated by a group of Radical Germans in the West. But the Congressional party leaders, including Stevens, left Frémont severely alone. Still the intriguing persisted, as the Union armies failed to win a decisive victory in the East. In mid-August Stevens let it be known publicly in his home town of Lancaster, Pennsylvania, that he was no longer supporting Lincoln.

The moment, however, that George B. McClellan was nominated to oppose Lincoln on the Democratic ticket, Stevens and other Radicals, recognizing a real enemy, began to work feverishly for Lincoln's victory. As Charles Sumner put it privately, "Lincoln's election would be a disaster, but McClellan's damnation." Thaddeus Stevens quietly urged Carl Schurz to repair the split in the Republican Party by swinging the Frémont Radicals to Lincoln's side. And Zachary Chandler finally succeeded in getting Frémont to withdraw from the race. Stevens exacted a price for this, however— the Conservative, anti-Negro Montgomery Blair went out of the Cabinet. Stevens then campaigned vigorously for Lincoln in Pennsylvania, telling the voters that the president had risen above "the influence of Border State seductions and Republican cowardice." "Let us forget," he said, "that he ever erred, and support him with redoubled energy."

During the last year of Lincoln's life Stevens worked passionately to carry through Congress the legislation Lincoln wanted most—a Thirteenth Amendment abolishing slavery. When Lincoln in his first message to Congress after the 1864 election urged its passage and firmly repudiated the idea of a negotiated peace, Stevens called it "the most important and best message that has been communicated to Congress for the last sixty years." Stevens himself seldom gave prepared speeches on any issue; but when it was learned on Capitol Hill that he would speak on the amendment, senators and judges from the Supreme Court came to listen. It was in many respects the most reflective and moving speech of his life.

But Stevens, like Lincoln, was never so preoccupied with speechmaking that he lost sight of the necessity of counting votes. Both men had been counting and were disturbed lest the amendment be lost in the House by one or two defections. Lincoln quietly let it be known to several key congressmen that these votes must be procured regardless of cost. In later years there was talk about patronage, about a bargain over an odious New Jersey railroad monopoly, and about the release of Confederate prisoners who were kin to several Democratic congressmen. Thaddeus Stevens would never tell what happened, content to comment cryptically, "The greatest measure of the nineteenth century was passed by corruption, aided and abetted by the purest man in America."

The common misconception that Stevens was a vicious opponent of Lincoln's has resulted largely from exaggerated emphasis on their differences during 1864 over Reconstruction. Professor T. Harry Williams, in his *Lincoln and the Radicals,* went so far as to describe this as "a struggle to the death" against "cunning and implacable foes." Lincoln

wanted the seceded states back in the Union as soon as
possible after they had been conquered by the Union armies,
asking however that the new governments be set up by loyal
Union men, and that they repudiate slavery. His famous Ten
Per Cent Plan—providing that if ten per cent of the citizens
who had voted in 1860 would take a loyalty oath promising
to support the Constitution and respect the edict of emancipation, they would be permitted to set up a government—
specifically excepted all Confederate officials and military men
above the rank of colonel. This was not harsh enough for
Stevens, who wanted specific civil rights guarantees for the
newly freed Negroes written into the constitutions of the
Southern states before readmission. Lincoln favored a mild
loyalty oath, Stevens a stringent one.

When Lincoln insisted that no state had actually seceded
but had only tried to, Stevens called this reasoning absurd.
He insisted that the South had seceded and that the government by the laws of war could exact any terms it wanted
from the "conquered provinces." Actually the two were not
so far apart as appears on the surface, for Lincoln by many
acts had acknowledged the belligerent status of the Confederates and had acted decisively many times by virtue of his
"war powers." With consummate evasive skill Lincoln tried
to avoid the impression that he was handing down conqueror's
terms, but he was acutely conscious of the postwar problem
of political power, which he described to John Hay as the
problem of "how to keep the rebellious population from overwhelming and outvoting the loyal minority."

Those who believe that Lincoln would have welcomed
back the Southerners without sanctions generally forget that
he approved the Louisiana constitutional convention—organized under the Ten Per Cent Plan—though it disfranchised
rebel soldiers of high rank, Confederate officials, and wealthy
planters. Stevens advocated immediate Negro suffrage as the
only solution to the Negro's own safety problem, though he
recognized the appalling illiteracy problem and would have

preferred Negro suffrage after a five-year interval. It is generally forgotten that Lincoln too came to recommend suffrage for the Negro soldier and the educated Negro, and that near the end of his life he was seriously considering trading universal suffrage for universal amnesty. Stevens, on the other hand, always opposed universal amnesty.

As everyone knows, Lincoln was no man for hangings, and frankly hoped that the Confederate leaders would be frightened out of the country. "No one need expect me to take any part in hanging or killing these men, even the worst of them," he said in his last Cabinet meeting. It is not generally known that Stevens, who had many times demanded the hanging of the Confederate leaders, made an about face, near the end of the war, and insisted that they could not legally be hanged since Lincoln had granted the Confederacy belligerent rights. Later he even offered his services as a lawyer to defend both Jefferson Davis and Clement C. Clay against the treason charge. But where Lincoln's clemency stemmed from compassion, Stevens' was largely a weapon. This Davis realized perfectly. "I was aware of his line of argument," he wrote later, explaining why he declined Stevens' services. "It would have been that the seceding States were conquered provinces . . . therefore their property was subject to confiscation and the people to such penalties and conditions as the conquerors might impose. That would have been an excellent argument for me, but not for my people."

The last time Thaddeus Stevens talked to Abraham Lincoln seems to have been late in March 1865. The president was only fifty-six, seventeen years younger than Stevens, but his face was as haggard and deeply lined. Both men had suffered in the war, but Stevens had been stiffened through the years by his capacity to hate. Lincoln was bowed by the weight of a double burden, for he had, as he once himself admitted, suffered *with* the South.

William Crook of the White House staff later described what he remembered of their conversation. "Mr. Stevens was one of the ablest, as well as one of the most radical men then in Congress," he said, "but he was a very impatient man. The President listened patiently to Mr. Stevens' argument, urging 'a more vigorous prosecution of the war,' which was the watchword of those men of his own party who criticized the President, and when he had concluded he looked at his visitor a moment in silence. Then he said, looking at Mr. Stevens very shrewdly:

" 'Stevens, this is a pretty big hog we are trying to catch, and, to hold him when we do catch him. We must take care that he doesn't slip away from us.' Mr. Stevens had to be satisfied with the answer."

So Stevens left the president, as so many men before him, with the memory of a homely metaphor but no real certainty of having left so much as a thumbprint on Lincoln's policy.

Thaddeus Stevens was in Lancaster, Pennsylvania, when Lincoln was murdered, and we do not know how the death of Lincoln moved him. Two years later he said of Lincoln in a speech in the House: ". . . There is no danger that the highest praise that the most devoted friends could bestow on him would ever be reversed by posterity. So solid was the material of which his whole character was formed that the more it is rubbed the brighter it will shine." At this time Stevens was fiercely embroiled with Andrew Johnson in the fight over Reconstruction, and whatever troubles he had had with Lincoln must have seemed insignificant. In a thoughtful vein he went on to talk about Lincoln's death. It told much about Stevens' attitude that when he compared Lincoln with the heroes of the past he went far back to the Old Testament—to the imagery of Moses, and Elijah, and the Promised Land.

"All must regret the manner of his death," Stevens said, "yet, looking to futurity and to his own personal position, it may be considered happy. From the height of his glory he beheld the promised land, and was withdrawn from our sight. . . . Like the prophet of the Lord who knew not death, he was wrapt from earth to heaven along a track no less luminous than his who ascended in a chariot of fire with horses of fire. Would to God that some small portion of the mantle of our Elijah had fallen on his Elisha."

HAROLD HYMAN

Lincoln's Mars: Edwin M. Stanton

ॐ

ON HOT EVENINGS during the last three summers of the Civil War a plain open carriage could often be seen headed away from Washington toward the relative coolness of suburban Georgetown. There were usually two passengers, two tired men who talked in low tones and jotted notes on scraps of paper from the time they started the drive on Pennsylvania Avenue, but who visibly relaxed as they neared their neighboring residences on the shaded grounds of the Soldier's Home.

A troop of cavalry flanked the carriage, and the soldiers stole curious glances at the men they were convoying—the President of the United States and his Secretary of War. Even while slouched in his seat, Abraham Lincoln appeared tall and lean, his lank height magnified by the high hat he wore at a careless angle over the dark, bearded face which fell easily into familiar lines of warm laughter. Next to him Edwin M. Stanton seemed squat and short, although he held his heavy body stiffly erect as though to prove that it was of good average height. Like Lincoln, Stanton wore a formal frock coat and tall beaver hat but he was far better groomed than his companion. Lighter than Lincoln in complexion, Stanton's long chin whiskers, protuberant eyes behind heavy spectacles, and square, rigid facial features gave him a belligerent appearance.

When the vehicle stopped, the cavalrymen moved on to a nearby camp, where they stayed until reassembled the next morning for the return trip. A group of shouting, jostling, importunate children, the sons and daughters of both men, replaced the soldiers as an escort, and dragooned their un-resisting fathers into a game of mumble-the-peg, or showed off their equestrian prowess on the Stantons' patient white pony. On one occasion the youngsters reported the dreadful news that some pet peacocks had entangled their leg ropes in the branches of a tall tree. In the bright, warm twilight the President of the United States and the Secretary of War convened with the worried children in a solemn council, evolved strategy, confiscated a nearby ladder, and while Stanton held it firm to the ground, Lincoln, still in his formal attire, ascended into the foliage, loosened the snarled lines, and retrieved the birds. Both men then gravely accepted the cheers of the appreciative audience and offered short speeches to celebrate the victory.

While he and Lincoln walked toward their residences, Stanton smoked a last cigar, its spark marking their slow progress through the peaceful dusk. From these pitifully brief interludes of tranquillity each man gained part of the strength he needed to face the day to come. For Lincoln and Stanton, so different from each other in temperament and appearance, were more than official associates. They were close personal friends.

A few men—telegrapher David Homer Bates, Provost Marshal William Doster, Adjutant General E. D. Townsend, War Department clerk Charles Benjamin, Stanton's secretary, A. E. H. Johnson, and Senator Henry Wilson, among others—who observed Lincoln and Stanton together almost every day for three years, came to understand the nature of this cordial relationship. In their published reminiscences these men agree that the President and War Secretary worked together in official harmony and treasured each other in reciprocal amity. Stanton's sister, Pamphila, and his young nephew, William Stanton, concurred that Bates's description of the War Secretary's character was the most accurate one in print. Although this is by no means a flattering portrayal of the man, it correctly asserts that a fruitful co-operation rather than friction existed between the White House and the War Department.

Careful examination of the endless memoranda, inquiries, and reports passing between Lincoln and Stanton bears out the logical assumption that Bates's estimate is a true one. If it were not, there was no reason why Lincoln should have kept Stanton on. The President was a consummate political manipulator. He ousted Simon Cameron, Montgomery Blair, and Salmon P. Chase from the Cabinet when it was propitious for him to do so, and nothing could force him to take these steps earlier than he did or prevent him from acting when he was ready. Yet each of these men was a potent political chieftain in his own right, with strong backing from factions in Congress, and able to sway public opinion and votes through well-organized supporters and subservient newspapers. Stanton, on the other hand, had no ambitions for office. His only support came from Lincoln; his only defense against the bitter attacks directed against him all through the war from Congress, from Democrats in general, and from some Republican factions, lay in the President's conviction that Stanton was serving him, and through him the Union. Lincoln not only kept him on in the War Department but made clear that he was the right man for the job in hand.

The nature of that job inevitably involved Stanton in controversy. John Hay, Lincoln's private secretary and later his biographer, wrote to Stanton soon after the tragic night at Ford's Theatre: "Not everyone knows, as I do, how close you stood to our lost leader, how he loved you and trusted you, and how vain were all the efforts to shake that trust and confidence, not lightly given & never withdrawn. All this will be known some time of course, to his honor and yours." Hay noted that ". . . you generally care very little about what people say or think about you," and recalled the ". . . many meddlers whose knuckles you had rapped, many thieves whose hands you had tied, and many liars whose mouths you had shut for a time by your prompt punishments, who had occupied themselves in traducing you, so as to shake the faith of many decent people in you."

But Hay's confidence that history would place Stanton in his true light as a faithful servant and deserving confidant of Lincoln has proved illusory. Ninety-five years after Hay wrote this letter, its recipient is popularly thought of in opposite terms. Stanton is most often described as a Uriah Heep in a position of great power; cruel and oppressive when dealing with subordinates and the helpless public, but obsequious and covertly insulting toward his superiors. A recent writer has gone so far as to intimate that Stanton was implicated in the murder of Lincoln.

The first strokes of this unpleasant portrait were painted by men who hated Stanton personally and who fought against the policies which the War Secretary supported. Jeremiah Sullivan Black, a former friend and legal associate of Stanton, who served with him in the Buchanan Cabinet's tense lame-duck weeks, but who remained static in his political views while Stanton moved ahead, was the initiator of this low estimate. In a series of magazine articles published the year after Stanton died in 1869, Black left the impression that the contributions of his subject to the salvation of the Union in 1860 had been inessential and that his services as War Secretary after 1862 had retarded rather than forwarded the winning of the war. Stanton's colleague in Lincoln's Cabinet, Navy Secretary Gideon Welles, is even more important in degrading the stature of the war minister. Like Black, Welles published a series of periodical pieces on wartime policy matters. In these articles "Neptune" Welles based his assessment of Stanton, as a wartime minister, on the tortuous events which followed Appomattox, and misconstrued the nature of the Lincoln–Stanton relationship because of the controversy surrounding Stanton's relationships with Lincoln's successor in the White House, Andrew Johnson.

Welles's real impact on historical attitudes came in 1911 with the publication of his three-volume *Diary,* one of the great sources for information on the inner workings of the Lincoln and Johnson administrations. After reading it Lincoln's old friend Jesse E. Weik wrote to Horace White that "It has completely upset my notion of Seward, Stanton, and Grant. I have always been such a profound admirer of all three that I sometimes regret that I ever read Mr. Welles' estimate." Since then the *Diary* has served historians George Fort Milton, Claude G. Bowers, and James G. Randall, as well as many others, as the basis for their evaluations of Andrew Johnson's stature. While the pendulum of historical estimation ascended for Johnson, it inevitably fell far down for Stanton.

That descent, regardless of its adequacy for the postwar years, does not fit the facts of Stanton's role in Lincoln's administration. Welles normally observed Lincoln and Stanton only at Cabinet assemblies. John Hay, A. E. H. Johnson, General Townsend, David Bates, and Charles Benjamin were better reporters than Welles. They were with Lincoln or Stanton constantly and were close by when the President and War Secretary were together, as they so often were. Almost daily Lincoln made his way from the White House through the rickety turnstile leading to the War Department in order to visit the military telegraph center in Stanton's office, and to wait with him for news of victory or defeat, or to enjoy intimate conversations with his war minister regarding the qualities and defects of civil officers and military commanders. Welles rarely shared in this aspect of Lincoln's life or thoughts.

Unfortunately for Stanton, none of the men who really knew him kept diaries. Their thin body of writings is largely forgotten. Stanton never troubled to put his own case before the public or posterity; as Hay recognized, the man just did not care for popular plaudits. There has been no substantial collection of Stanton manuscripts for historians to examine, and gathering together a more representative array is an exhausting and frustrating task. Stanton's few literary defenders—George C. Gorham in 1899, Frank A. Flower in 1905, and Fletcher Pratt in 1953—wrote uncritical book-length praises of their subject or else produced inadequate and incomplete biographical essays. It has been such a one-sided historical combat that the man who edited the Welles *Diary,* John T. Morse, bemoaned the fact that Stanton had not kept an opposite record. "At present," Morse wrote in 1911, "it is too much like sitting in a prize ring and seeing only one pugilist."

The real casualty resulting from this inequity is our understanding of Lincoln as well as of Stanton. For both men, the war was the major experience of their lives. They shared for three years the nation's agony and directed its efforts toward survival. The war dominated Lincoln's thoughts. He understood little of public finance and was willing in the main to let Seward direct foreign affairs. Lincoln thought of himself primarily as the commander in chief of a nation threatened with disruption, but which deserved to endure and was worthy of the sacrifices men were making that it might survive. Stanton, in his own way, shared this view. He knew that the Union needed to exert efforts far greater than history recorded of any previous nation. If it was to live, the Union required a man able to be the director—the secretary—of a war.

Only the cataclysm of war could have brought Lincoln and Stanton together. To be sure, their lives had certain parallels and had even touched at one point before 1862. The paths that brought one man to greatness in the White House and the other to unprecedented responsibilities in the War Department began in the same western region that stretches from the Appalachians toward the mighty rivers which divide yet knit together the imperial expanse of the frontier.

Lincoln, five years older than Stanton, spent his childhood

in a rural environment one step advanced from a wilderness. Stanton lived in relatively urban centers of commerce and industry fronting on the Ohio; knew merchants and lawyers rather than trappers or farmers; and attended school regularly rather than haphazardly. Sickly as a child where young Abe was strong, dominated by the ideals of an acquisitive, middle-class family, Stanton even as a youngster expressed his goals in materialistic terms. Both youths transcended the poverty of their early years. They learned to love books and decided to become lawyers. For chubby, asthmatic, emotional Eddie Stanton, the lawyer's life was a narrow avenue leading only to the accumulation of wealth. He married young and knew that, in addition to his growing family, he would always have to support his widowed mother and divorced sister. Stanton single-mindedly set out to achieve financial security.

Balancing his own pursuit of wealth with a far wider range of interests, Lincoln plunged into Illinois politics and set his legal life to the leisurely pace of the old rural circuit courts. Stanton, on the other hand, opened his office in a town and stayed in one place until success beckoned him on to a larger metropolitan practice. He had no time to waste. Eschewing public office for himself, restricting his participation in politics to the lowest levels of county work, Stanton exploited Ohio politics primarily for the legal business that it helped to bring him. But Lincoln the Illinois Whig and Stanton the Ohio Democrat were in basic agreement on one transcendent issue; they abhorred the institution of slavery, resisted in their respective parties the advocates of its further extension, and detested the increasing number and vociferousness of Northern abolitionists as well as of Southern extremists.

By the early 1850s Stanton had achieved a much loftier professional success than Lincoln; he was widely known as an indefatigable, resourceful, and skillful attorney. The new industrial and technological wealth of Pittsburgh drew Stanton to the Golden Triangle, where he represented prominent textile and metal fabricators and telegraph, railroad, and steamboat operators. His briefs were based on exhaustive research, his oral arguments were cogent, relentless, and, unlike Lincoln's, utterly devoid of humor.

Their first encounter came when Stanton was a junior member of a staff of lawyers in the famous McCormick Reaper case. Stanton's superior in the case, George Harding, decided to employ an Illinois attorney in order to assist his staff if necessary in the intricacies of that state's law, a common practice of the time. He chose Lincoln, in default of men with better reputations who were unavailable. When it was decided to hear the case in Ohio and not in Illinois, Stanton and his colleagues realized that they did not need the assistance of the gawky country lawyer who had come to them with a lengthy brief and who presumptuously assumed that he was the professional and social equal of the sophisticates from the East. Lincoln got his fee, and his brief was thrown away. Stanton followed the lead of his legal superiors in snubbing and insulting Lincoln, the rural nonentity.

Such snobbery was standard practice in the strict hierarchy of the lawyer's world. In a similar instance Stanton was pleading before Judge Grier in the federal district court at Pittsburgh. The opposition counsel were "country lawyers," young William Stanton remembered, and it ". . . was hard to tell which was the most haughty, severe, domineering, and rude in his treatment of these lawyers—Stanton—or . . . Grier." If Lincoln had remained as anonymous as the two lawyers of this reminiscence, Edwin Stanton would be accounted only as an insensitive snob, but no worse than most others in his status. But Lincoln became great, and Stanton's treatment of him in the Reaper case has come, therefore, to seem like an insult to the Lincoln of a decade later. Stanton may not have been discerning concerning Lincoln's future but he was not alone in this error.

Stanton progressed on the road he had chosen. By 1860 he was living in Washington and earning fees as large as those of any lawyer of the day from his practice before the Supreme Court. After the election of Lincoln, Stanton was pessimistic concerning the nation's prospects for survival, and like many others, considered the unknown President-elect as an unlettered and inadequate choice for the White House.

Accident and patriotism then brought Stanton into the political limelight which he had sedulously avoided. The Buchanan administration in its last weeks in office was taking no effective steps to halt the secession process. Stanton accepted a place in the Cabinet, and with Jeremiah Black and John A. Dix helped to pressure panicky old Buchanan into a sterner attitude toward the defiant South. Then, after Lincoln's inaugural, Stanton returned to his private law practice, expecting never again to hold office. He had already done a great service for the Union.

Less than a year later, Lincoln asked him to become Secretary of War. The President explained to him that military reverses had underscored the inadequacies of the War Department's administration. The army had to have more men, supplies, and money than anyone had anticipated, and a Secretary was needed who could correlate a thousand different problems, find solutions, and let the President concentrate on policy while the generals took on the rebels.

Stanton accepted. This man who wanted wealth above almost all else closed his law office, knowing that his income would drop from more than $60,000 in 1861, with promise of much more to come, to a Secretary's fixed salary, $8000. He also knew that he was taking on a responsibility which no Secretary before him had faced, and that he was assuming an office that up to this point had been a symbol of weakness rather than a source of strength.

In the developments of the national government's institutions before 1861, the office of the Secretary of War had become an annoying obstacle or an insignificant clerical convenience for the senior army officers. A few Secretaries had tried to alter this and were crushed or evaded by the uniformed galaxy. Years earlier, for example, in contempt of the nominal superiority of the incumbent Secretary, ranking General Winfield Scott had moved his headquarters away from Washington altogether. He returned only because of the secession crisis; this did not mean, however, that the civilian Secretary thereby regained control over the military arm.

Lincoln's first appointee to the war office, Simon Cameron, might have been acceptable as a Secretary of War if there had been no war. The corruption and confusion that centered in his lax administration lessened the prestige and power of an institution that had none to spare. Under Cameron, the army commanders remained as independent as they had been in prewar years. But the Civil War required that men and arms be amassed in quantities no earlier Americans had ever commanded. If civilian authorities could not learn how to control this martial might, which they were creating in order to crush the South, then democratic government could collapse in the North.

In this war, unlike the short, cheap, simple conflict against Mexico, men from every loyal state were coming under arms, grain and cattle from Midwestern farms and metals from Appalachian mines were being fabricated into food and guns in Eastern factories, tens of thousands of draught animals were to be purchased and shipped. A knowledgeable central authority was needed to assemble the men and supplies and to train the one to use the other, and then to move them to where they were needed. The new communications technologies of the railroad, steamship, and telegraph could, if understood and properly exploited from Washington, provide a new kind of mobility for the conduct of war.

Great expenditures of money were necessarily involved. If the contracts were tainted with corruption, as had been occurring under Cameron, Lincoln feared that soldiers would come to despair of the purposes for which he was asking them to die. For the same reason the President needed someone to do a better job than Seward and Cameron had done in suppressing home-front subversion. Forthright prevention of disloyalty rather than punishment for treason was the best way, Lincoln was convinced, to sustain the soldiers' efforts and the loyal civilians' faith.

The civilian authorities had to find solutions for these problems and apply them with great sensitivity yet with unrelenting strength. Lincoln had simultaneously to infringe upon traditional civil liberties and yet retain enough popular support to win elections. The mere passage of time, the development of war-weariness in the North and of cynicism among Union troops, could give victory to the rebels. In the last analysis the fate of the nation depended upon the President's and War Secretary's ingenuity, skill, and determination to find the leaders, men, and material for the battle fronts while keeping unity on the home front.

Since the days of Andrew Jackson, Presidents of the United States had let slip the reins of executive initiative which he had held so firmly. Lincoln as President, like Stanton as War Secretary, had to repair the diminished power and dissipated prestige of their respective offices. They brought to their work the best possible combination of talents.

Lincoln brought patience. He had a limitless capacity to endure whatever outrageous fortune might bring so long as eventual success seemed attainable through pursuit of a policy or support of a general. Democratic party spokesmen condemned him as a ruthless tyrant because of the internal security measures; members of Lincoln's own party flayed him as being excessively tender toward traitors. Lincoln shrugged off the criticisms. He continued suspending the habeas-corpus-writ privilege and authorizing the arrests and trials of civilians by military officials even in the face of a blast from Chief Justice Taney. As Lincoln correctly saw it, disloyalty was not a theoretical threat but a distressingly clear and present danger. He wanted to prevent disloyalty from developing into treason in the North; the arbitrary arrests were primarily for prophylaxis rather than punishment. Suspicious persons and mild offenders suffered only brief imprisonments and were released after swearing to be loyal in the future. It was an essentially patient, moderate, middle way, considering the harshness which some more radical Republicans advocated and the dangerous formalistic inaction which many Democrats supported.

His patience permitted Lincoln to stand by McClellan and to take the insults of the immodest officer until failures on the battlefield provoked the President into removing him from command, a step which Stanton had impatiently advocated for weary months. The President sifted through McDowell, Hooker, Burnside, and Meade, and relieved each in turn. Patiently, he kept the "political generals" in uniform, and, along with Stanton, suffered the incapacities of the Ben Butlers because they commanded important segments of public opinion and votes and so must be permitted to command troops.

Stanton's impatience complemented the President's forbearance. To the creaky old War Department building a few hundred feet away from the White House, Stanton brought his unresting energy, his unstable temper, and his harsh insistence that everyone from clerks to bureau heads shake off the leisurely habits of prewar procedures. Impediments or objections triggered him into fierce rages. "Mr. Stanton was a passionate man," a clerk recalled. "A word or a gesture would set him aflame in an instant. He would dash the glasses before his eyes far up on his forehead, . . . the muscles of his face would become agitated, and his voice would tremble and grow intense, without elevation." Then, quickly, the rage would pass and be succeeded by his normal icy demeanor.

His intemperate bullying hustled the Department's staff into unwonted activity, and some officials yearned for the "good gone days of Cameron." But more important, the War Department began to provide the necessary supplies and manpower in a growing and unceasing flow. Contractors and manufacturers learned that the "carnival of fraud" was ended,

that the volcanic Secretary was ready to throw the vendor
of shoddy boots or tainted meat into prison along with bridge-
burners or alleged sympathizers with rebellion.

Stanton also took on the task of maintaining home-front
security. His orders to rear-area army commands put teeth
into Lincoln's proclamations concerning suspensions of civil
liberties; his name more than Lincoln's became associated
with the arbitrary arrests of civilian suspects who filled the
"American Bastilles." Lacking Lincoln's patience and hiding
his own merciful predilections, Stanton built up and reformed
the chaotic mélange of police agencies which Seward and
Cameron bequeathed to him. He forced civil and military
officers, and federal, state, county, and municipal officials,
into a responsible and efficient security system, adapting it to
the needs of combat units in the field and making it useful
for enforcing the conscription apparatus in the North. True,
his security mechanism failed to prevent draft riots or dangerous Copperhead plots. But nothing short of a totalitarian
secret-police force could have done so.

Stanton was determined to create security and inspection
systems so strong that ordinary political dissenters would refrain from acting against the war, and so complete that the
word *shoddy* would disappear from the soldier's vocabulary.
Politics, patience, and mercy were Lincoln's business. He and
the President had agreed before Stanton accepted the war
office that he would have a free hand in all army matters up
to the point where political factors intruded. Stanton was
to be able to criticize and to contradict Lincoln's suggestions
until they became orders; then he would obey. Until this
point was reached Stanton was his own master.

And so Stanton suppressed his normal sensitivity to basic
human distress in favor of the more important needs of the
Union. His normal superficial inconsiderateness was accentuated by the accumulating effects of overwork, worsening
health, and unceasing worry. When it was pointed out to him
that he was unfair, rude, or needlessly cruel, he was sur-

prised, and tried to make amends or to apologize. If he could not, then he forgot the incident. Men were dying by the thousands. He was responsible for them, he felt, far more than anyone else. The Union, which the soldiers served, was his new client, and he offered her the same thoroughness and dedication which had brought him such success at the bar. Provost Marshal Doster realized that there was nothing mysterious about Stanton. He understood that Stanton saw the War Department as another, larger, law office, where "he could abuse his client as much as he chose, provided he won his case," and that "he knew, no matter what he did, all would be right, if he secured the verdict. One thing was mandatory, he must not throw up the case—that no good lawyer does."

Lincoln's patience and Stanton's impatience combined in a productive symbiosis which helped finally to realize the verdict of victory. Stanton was impatient with any person or institution that stood in the way; he did not have the temper to temporize or the time to excuse errors, forgive duplicity, or accept excuses. Lincoln, the only man in the country with wider responsibilities than Stanton's, and possessing qualities of greatness which Stanton lacked, found the time and had the patience and wisdom to repair at least some of the injustices produced by his War Secretary's unswerving devotion.

Time after time Lincoln canceled penalties imposed on deserters by Stanton's courts-martial, forgave misguided civilians and released them from prison merely on their word to be loyal in the future, insisted that slow-starting generals keep their commands a bit longer. Stanton raged, fumed, and at times publicly damned the President as an utter fool. Stories concerning his pithy criticisms of Lincoln are legion, and they have misled many persons into accepting the fury for the fact. For what happened, always, was that Lincoln's will prevailed if he felt that the case at hand was important enough to warrant his intervention. In less worthy instances Lincoln justified his decisions not to intervene by asserting to petitioners that he was helpless to alter Stanton's policies. Thus the Secretary became the President's convenient buffer against competing political factions, sectional pressures, and individual claims for special consideration, commissions, contracts, or commands. Stanton was willing to perform as the ogre because it was necessary to his job and because, knowing and respecting Lincoln, he was content to bear as much of the President's burden as he could.

Like almost all Americans, Lincoln and Stanton knew nothing of the techniques of conducting a major war. But both men were intelligent enough to understand their own limitations, and to seek professional advice. At the same time, however, they were wise enough never to forget that the President must remain superior to all military personnel and that political needs often had prior claims over the soldier's simpler strategical views.

Stanton created a war council—Quartermaster General Meigs, Adjutant General Townsend, retired General Ethan Allen Hitchcock, and, later, Provost Marshal General Fry, supplemented by any officer visiting from the battle fronts— and used it to hammer out the infinite details of strategy and logistics. This council served as a general staff. Its "decisions," combined with the communications monopoly Stanton maintained over the military telegraph and the co-operation he wrested from railroad operators, made possible the mass movements of men and material on a scale heretofore unknown in the history of warfare. Stanton never presumed to create political policies; this was Lincoln's task. To be sure, the Secretary urged the removal of McClellan, favored a proclamation of emancipation, and advocated the use of troops to insure Republican victories in New Hampshire, Maryland, Indiana, and Missouri elections. But it was Lincoln who decided in each instance if, when, and how Stanton's suggestions were to go into effect. The President could usually deflect the resulting hullabaloo away from the White House and let it concentrate on Stanton, the executor, not the initiator, of scores of controversial policies. Stanton took the abuse and never faltered.

Ingenuity and resourcefulness were characteristics of the President and his War Secretary. Force, both men realized, was the only solvent corrosive enough to crack the Confederacy in time to save the Union. Lincoln's concept of the limitless powers of a wartime President were put into daily practice at the War Department. Neither man, however, ignored the realities of American government. They worked with, rather than against Congress when they could. Stanton co-operated with Congress' Joint Committee on the Conduct of the War; if he had refused to do so, the legislators could have hamstrung the army. But he was human enough to resent it when Lincoln, obeying similar imperatives, canceled or modified War Department policies on behalf of congressmen, state governors, or powerful individuals. Stanton had to go along, for example, with the vexing, demoralizing cotton-traffic policy which Lincoln authorized for the Mississippi Valley out of deference to Salmon Chase and Northern textile interests. But he did go along, grumbling, muttering imprecations at Lincoln as well as at Chase, sounding to uninformed auditors like a man ready to quit in disgust. But he never quit. Beneath the grumbling he realized that perfection was not the goal. Victory was.

Lincoln brought his fine and earthy sense of humor to lessen the strains and soften the tragedy that each day brought. He irritated Stanton time after time by reading from popular comic writers and by referring to him publicly as "Mars" as he addressed his Navy head as "Neptune." Humor was Lincoln's safety valve from the galling uncertainties with which he had to live. Stanton did not know how to relax. He never learned the trick of coming out of himself and indulging in anything but a task at hand. Only his family was capable of taking his attention away from his responsibilities. He found no comfort in the theater which Lincoln loved and on one occasion when he was attending a theatrical performance at

Mrs. Stanton's suggestion, he rose during the performance, pushed his way to the presidential box where Lincoln was enjoying the play, and commenced a discussion of current war policy.

The President's humor let him slough off the stories which indignant talebearers and would-be troublemakers sometimes told of how Stanton had traduced him. "Did Stanton say that?" Lincoln asked an informant on one such occasion, and then he concluded that Stanton must have been right, for the fiery Secretary usually was. Lincoln's cousin, Dennis Hanks, told Lincoln after meeting Stanton, "Abe, if I's as big as you, I would take that little feller over my knee and spank him." Lincoln replied, laughingly, that in some ways Stanton was bigger than he. "I asked Abe," Hanks recalled of another occasion, "why he did not get rid of Stanton. I told him he was too fresh altogether." The President answered, "If I did, Dennis, it would be difficult to find another man to fill his place." And there was the key to the Lincoln–Stanton official relationship. Lincoln needed Stanton.

Twenty years after the war ended, Stanton's son, Lewis, admitted that his late father never met a man who did not become either a friend or an enemy, and the latter result was by the far the most common. There can be no doubt that in many ways Edwin Stanton was not a great man. But in partnership with Abraham Lincoln he performed greatly. The success of the Union army, the survival of the Union, must in no small measure be credited to his work. To say that Stanton was rude, insensitive, and humorless is to pit minuscule defects of character against gigantic achievements. Conversely, to assert the truth that he was incorruptible and that not a penny of the millions of dollars which he disbursed ever stuck to his hands, that when the war ended he was a poor man by relative standards, does not alone suffice to rehabilitate his reputation. Stanton's claim to his rightful place in the history of the war and in the preservation of this nation is based on more substantial stuff. Under his skillful administrative manipulation the Union amassed enough military power to crush a great rebellion. Yet, when it was over, the nation emerged from its trial of arms with its essential democratic forms and federal organization intact. The Union carried on its effort with moderation when excess was the easier way. Under Stanton the armies were not merely well supplied, fed, and transported; they were also well-controlled.

That control emerged from the partnership which Lincoln and Stanton worked out in friendship together. As in all things in the past, only the broad outlines of this story are yet fully apparent even after nine decades of efforts to re-create the whole. But historians are a sticky breed, and they will continue to try. Stanton, as Hay admitted to John Nicolay when the two men were preparing their monumental study of Lincoln, "is going to be a nut to crack." The kernel is worth the effort.

WILLIAM E. MARSH

Lincoln and Henry W. Halleck

To STUDENTS of the military history of the American Civil War, General Henry Wager Halleck remains a mysterious person. Sadly neglected by historians, he has never been the subject of proper biographical treatment. In fact, he receives scant mention in the vast literature of this critical period of disunion and rebellion, although his influence runs throughout its entire story.

As nominal general in chief of the armies beginning July 11, 1862, he was generally condemned by contemporaries as incompetent, and was charged with partial responsibility for some of the worst of the military failures—particularly the failure of Meade to pursue Lee after Gettysburg. In spite of this, President Lincoln continued to retain him in nominal command until March 1864, when Grant was made lieutenant general, and Halleck took the title of chief of staff. This was in the face of bitter criticism from members of his Cabinet, members of Congress, and practically every political personage in Washington at the time.

During Abraham Lincoln's presidency, no one was more intimately associated with him than Halleck, yet no written record of this association exists. Historians have often asked why Lincoln kept Halleck in high command, but have lacked adequate material to explore the relationship between them.

Fifty years ago it was frequently said that the true story of the Civil War would never be told, for the reputations of many prominent men, military heroes and statesmen alike, would be destroyed thereby. Some partisan histories of this period are highly prejudiced and unreliable.

General Halleck's enemies bitterly assailed him for his incompetence. "Never did a general in chief before make up in so short a time so sad a record. That the President retained him in power so long, under such an accumulation of disasters, filled the country with surprise." This was the opinion held by the Radical Republicans in particular, attacking Halleck as "slow."

Today, every unprejudiced student knows that the military genius of Robert E. Lee, the valor and fortitude of his Army of Northern Virginia, the delays of McClellan, and the stupidities of Burnside and Hooker, were chiefly responsible for the prolongation of the war. Not wishing to dignify his detractors by answering their calumnious charges, Halleck steadfastly remained silent and went to his death without leaving any known written attempt to vindicate his official conduct. A fair appraisal of Halleck would make an important contribution to a more accurate interpretation of the military and political history of the War between the States.

Henry Wager Halleck was born in Westernville, Oneida County, New York, on January 16, 1814, the eldest of thirteen children, a descendent of Peter Hallock, who emigrated from England in 1640.

Little is known of his early life. His father, Joseph Halleck, one of the early settlers of this section of the Mohawk Valley, was obliged to wrest a precarious living from the soil. Young Halleck was forced to spend his youth at hard labor on the farm with few opportunities for schooling. A sensitive and shy boy, he bitterly resented the harsh treatment given him by his father, who had the reputation of a strict disciplinarian. Running away from home at fifteen, he was brought back by his favorite uncle, David Wager, a resident of Utica, for whom he felt a strong affection. With compassionate understanding of the young boy, Wager assumed the responsibility of guardian to Halleck and generously agreed to arrange for his education.

His first schooling (1829) was at the Hudson Academy, Fairfield, Herkimer County, New York, where he proved to be an apt student, eager for knowledge. His education was continued at Union College, Schenectady, but he left before completing the course of study. Uncle David Wager had decided to send him to West Point and a military career. Procuring an appointment, Halleck entered the United States Military Academy as a cadet on July 1, 1835. When he became homesick and indicated a desire to leave, Uncle David told him in no uncertain words to attend strictly to business. He took heed of this advice, for he was graduated third in his class of thirty-one, and appointed second lieutenant, Corps of Engineers, July 1, 1839. Generals James B. Ricketts, Edward O. C. Ord, and Edward R. S. Canby were classmates.

His marked ability having been observed by the Superintendent, he was retained as assistant professor of engineering at the Academy until June 28, 1840. Thereupon he was assigned as an assistant to the Army Board of Engineers in Washington. In the capital he had the advantage of knowing the family of the Secretary of State, and often called on President Tyler at the Executive Mansion. During this tour of duty, he prepared a treatise on *Bitumen, Its Varieties, Properties and Uses,* which included all that was then known of the use of asphalt in military structures.

He was then detailed as an assistant engineer to help in the construction of fortifications in New York Harbor. He was in charge of the rebuilding of Fort Wood on Bedloe's Island until July 1846.

In November 1843, however, he was temporarily relieved from duty in New York and ordered by the Secretary of War to depart immediately for France and "study and report on the fortifications and sea-coast defenses of the principal European military establishments." He accompanied Napoleon's favorite field marshal, Bertrand, who had been on a visit to America.

A letter to his mother, dated Paris, France, January 28, 1844, tells of the progress of his mission: "I am impatient to finish my business here, so as to return again to the United States. I have now been in France about a month. I expect to stay here two or three weeks longer, and go to Italy. I shall return here again in about a month and leave for home sometime in April. My time has thus far been very profitably spent in visiting fortifications and places of historical interest. I was in the Palace of the King [Louis Philippe] about two weeks ago, and was presented to both him and the Queen. The King talked with me in English, which he understands very well, but the Queen spoke French altogether, so that I was obliged to answer her questions in French. I learned this language at West Point, so was able to get along with it without any difficulty."

Soon after his return to the United States in the spring of 1844, his report to the Secretary of War was published by authority of Congress under the title *The Means of National Defense*. Following its appearance, a committee representing the Lowell Institute of Boston invited him to deliver a course of twelve lectures on the science of war. They proved so popular that he published them in 1846, under the title *Elements of Military Art and Science,* with an introductory chapter called "Justifiableness of War." Lippincott and Company published a second edition in 1861, with additional notes on the Mexican and Crimean Wars. This treatise, regarded then as the best in the language, was much in demand by military officers and was used as a textbook at West Point. During the war a revised edition was adapted for use in training officers of the volunteer army.

Halleck's correspondence with his family during these early years shows him to be a young man of high ideals, conscientious and deeply religious, and endowed with qualities of loyalty, resolution, and determination. It also discloses the deep anxiety he felt concerning the welfare of his younger brothers and sisters. He generously took the responsibility of contributing toward their education from his meager salary. On January 1, 1845, he was promoted to first lieutenant, Corps of Engineers.

Soon after the outbreak of the war with Mexico he was detailed by the War Department as engineer for operations on the Pacific Coast. He sailed from New York on July 14, 1846, accompanying Battery "F," Third U. S. Artillery, officered by Lieutenants William T. Sherman and Edward O. C. Ord, on the U. S. Storeship *Lexington,* destination Monterey, California. During the tedious seven months' voyage around Cape Horn, Halleck, partly as a military study and partly as a means of keeping himself occupied, translated from the French Baron Jomini's *Vie Politique et Militaire de Napoléon.* In 1864, with the aid of a friend, he revised this work in four octavo volumes, with notes and an atlas.

After arrival in Monterey on January 28, 1847, he was engaged in helping fortify the bay as a base for the Pacific fleet. He accompanied several military and naval expeditions, and served with Colonel Henry S. Burton in operations in Lower California. Besides engineering duties, he was aide-de-camp to Commodore William B. Shubrick in operations along the Pacific Coast, including the occupation of Mazatlán, of which place he was lieutenant governor. From August 1847 to December 1849 he served in California as secretary of state and auditor in the military governments of Generals Richard B. Mason and Bennet Riley. He was brevetted captain, Corps of Engineers, May 1, 1848, for gallant and meritorious services during the California campaign.

As secretary of state, it became obligatory for him to codify the Mexican laws still in effect in California concerning the sale of public and mission lands and private property. This he soon accomplished, publishing a digest and translation of the Mexican Political and Judicial Laws of 1837, for the use of the courts. Anticipating the rush of land-hungry Americans who were soon to overrun the country, Halleck began a systematic collection and study of California land records. His comprehensive report on land titles, published as House Ex. Doc. No. 17, Thirty-first Congress, First Session, was largely responsible for the creation of the first Board of Land Commissioners, which President Fillmore sent to California in 1851 to settle the tangle of title claims.

In 1848 Halleck was proffered an appointment as professor of engineering at the Lawrence Scientific School of Harvard University but declined the offer.

California was admitted as a state on September 9, 1850. In the formation of the first state government, Halleck, the real head of Riley's military government, was undoubtedly the central figure. While others of more prominence received all the credit, historians are generally agreed that Halleck first initiated the movement for state organization, and was a conspicuous member of the Constitutional Convention and the committee that drafted the constitution.

In a speech to the Constitutional Convention, Riley paid high tribute to Halleck: "My success in the affairs of California is mainly due to the efficient aid rendered me by Captain Halleck, the secretary of state. He has stood by me in all emergencies. To him I have always appealed when at a loss myself, and he has never failed me." The Rev. Mr. Samuel H. Willey, member of the convention from Monterey, was equally complimentary. "It takes more than a soldier of ordinary qualifications," he wrote, "to guide civil affairs through the confusion incident to a change of flag. Such work calls for a lawyer and statesman. It was the good fortune of the army and the country to have a man here just at that time combining in himself these qualifications, as Captain Halleck did. He was really the ruling spirit of both the administrations of Governors Mason and Riley. He was well read as a lawyer and had enjoyed the then rare opportunity of foreign travel and study abroad. At the same time, he was a man of practical sense and balanced judgment."

During this turbulent period the youthful statesman apparently held the confidence and respect of everyone, and his name was prominently mentioned as a candidate for the Senate. But he was unwilling to relinquish his military career for one so uncertain as politics. He also refused an appointment to the bench of the California Supreme Court. Undoubtedly, no one more than Halleck himself realized his entire unfitness for the strenuous game of politics; an ungenial disposition and a scholarly, reserved personality disqualified him for such a career.

Halleck remained secretary of state until December 1849, served as inspector and engineer of lighthouses from December 21, 1852, and was a member of the Board of Engineers for Fortifications on the Pacific Coast from April 11, 1853.

Like his friend Captain William T. Sherman, who resigned his commission to become president of Lucas, Turner and Company, a San Francisco banking house, Halleck decided to seek a lucrative business career. For years it had been his ambition to engage in the practice of law. Besides one of the best legal minds in California, his most valuable asset was his familiarity with the Spanish language and a comprehensive knowledge of land titles and land laws. His opportunity came when two young lawyers who had recently opened an office invited him to join their firm. For a month the following business notice appeared on the front page of the San Francisco *Alta California:*

Halleck, Peachy and Billings, Attorneys and Solicitors, San Francisco. Office, the room at present occupied by Peachy and Billings, on the north side of Sacramento Street, between Kearny and Dupont Sts. Mr. Billings, Commissioner for New York, Massachusetts and Connecticut. H. Wager Halleck, Arch'd Carey Peachy, Frederick Billings, January 1, 1850.

Halleck, Peachy and Billings came to be known as the ablest law firm on the Pacific Coast. In addition to the general practice of law, it specialized in procuring confirmation of

Spanish land grants for claimants before the Board of Land Commissioners, and within a year it had acquired as clients such prominent men as Robert F. Stockton and George W. Aspinwall. Its land-claim business assumed enormous proportions, becoming the largest and most profitable in a city famous for its legal talent and its costly, protracted litigation.

In 1853 Halleck built the famous Montgomery Block, a four-story brick office building that was for years the largest and most imposing on the Pacific Coast. Of Italian design, it housed twenty-eight basement and ground-floor stores and 150 upper rooms, with all the conveniences of that period. Built on securely anchored piles, it occupied a filled-in site on Montgomery between Washington and Merchant streets that had been partially covered by the waters of San Francisco Bay as late as 1849. This old building still stands, unharmed by the earthquake and fire of 1906.

During this busy period Halleck remained on active duty with the army, and was promoted to the rank of permanent captain, Corps of Engineers, on July 1, 1853. He did not resign until August 1, 1854. It is interesting to note that although he was not admitted to the bar until 1853, since January 1, 1850, he had been senior member of a prominent and rapidly growing law firm, was engaged in several business enterprises, and was on duty with the army. By 1860 he was one of the most distinguished citizens of San Francisco, a man of affluence. His home was on Rincon Hill at the corner of Second and Folsom streets. The city had already named a street for him and later erected his statue in Golden Gate Park. He had been director-general of the New Almaden (Quicksilver) Company since 1850, president of the Pacific and Atlantic Railroad Company since 1855, and a director of the banking house of Parrott and Company. He was also a member of the first board of directors of the State Historical Society of California in 1852, and of the Society of California Pioneers, 1850–54. He invested heavily in San Francisco real estate, the land records showing his acquisition of several city lots as early as July 1847; and he was also the owner of the 30,000-acre Rancho Nicasia in Marin County. That he was eminently successful in business cannot be disputed, for at his death his estate showed a net value of $474,773.

His active mind meanwhile found time for the preparation of several valuable legal works: *A Collection of Mining Laws of Spain and Mexico* (1859); a translation from the Spanish of *De Fooz on the Law of Mines* (1860); and a 907-page treatise on *International Law, or Rules Regulating the Intercourse of States in Peace and War* (1861). He also wrote about seven hundred pages of a history of California, never published, and as a hobby studied heraldry.

While on a business trip to the East in 1854, he met Elizabeth Hamilton, daughter of the New York attorney John Church Hamilton, son of Alexander Hamilton. It was a complete surprise to his friends when the reserved, unromantic Halleck married the girl, seventeen years his junior, on April 11, 1855. They soon left for San Francisco, where a son was born to them in 1856.

On December 16, 1860, Governor Downey of California appointed Halleck a brigadier general of militia and assigned him to command a division then being organized for possible service in the event of civil war. Early in April 1861 the law firm of Halleck, Peachy and Billings was dissolved by mutual consent. Peachy was a Virginian. Frederick Billings had been requested by John C. Frémont to accompany him to Europe on business connected with his great Mariposa estate, while Halleck wished to arrange his private affairs in anticipation of his return to active service with the army. The firm's extensive law library, advertised as the largest in San Francisco, was sold at public auction on April 22.

When the news of Fort Sumter reached California, Halleck was ready to resume his old profession. He immediately offered his services to General Winfield Scott in Washington. Discouraged over the resignation of many of his most competent officers, Scott determined to have Halleck appointed to high command. Three major generals of the regular army were to be appointed, and Scott had every reason to believe that President Lincoln would follow his recommendations. However, powerful political forces were at work to circumvent the plans of the ailing old general.

On May 14, 1861, George B. McClellan, thirty-five-year-old ex-army captain, was appointed a major general of the regular army. The preliminary step in his advancement had been his appointment as a major general of militia by Governor Dennison of Ohio. The next move was to secure the active support of Secretary of the Treasury Chase, Ohio's representative in the Cabinet. On May 11, 1861, Governor Dennison telegraphed Chase: "Can McClellan get a commission for three years at once, so as to make him rank over all others, and make sure of his holding the chief command here? Ohio must lead throughout the war." Chase replied on May 14: "We have today had McClellan appointed a major general in the regular army." While Halleck patiently waited orders in San Francisco, Lincoln delayed making his second appointment pending the return of John C. Frémont from a business trip to Europe. Frémont, the "Pathfinder," Republican candidate for president in 1856, received his commission on July 1, 1861, as a major general of the regular army to date from May 14, 1861.

Halleck, meanwhile, promoted to the rank of major general of state militia, was engaged in preparing California troops for service in the East. Early in May 1861 he issued a proclamation calling on citizens in the counties to form themselves into companies, battalions, and regiments, and promising arms should they be called into service. Importuned by Scott, Lincoln finally appointed Halleck a major general in the regular army on August 19, 1861. However, it was not until September 17 that he received his commission and orders to report for duty at Washington. He sailed from San Francisco October 10 on the *St. Louis,* accompanied by his wife, child, and two servants. The *Alta California* commented: "California will lose one of her most patriotic and useful citizens." In Washington old General Scott delayed his retirement awaiting the arrival of Halleck, whom he wished to succeed him as general in chief of the army.

General McClellan, desiring the position for himself, was fully aware of General Scott's intentions. On October 19 he confidently wrote his wife: "General Scott proposes to retire in favor of Halleck. The President and Cabinet have determined to accept his retirement, but not in favor of Halleck." This intention Lincoln, on November 1, 1861, carried out. Halleck arrived in Washington to find that he must take a subordinate position.

President Lincoln decided to send Halleck to St. Louis to relieve General Frémont, whose administration of the Department of Missouri was coming to an end. Elated by the prospect of an independent command, Halleck set about selecting the members of his staff. Major George W. Cullum, distinguished engineer and aide to General Scott, was promoted to the rank of brigadier general of volunteers and made chief of staff and chief engineer. Schuyler Hamilton, grandson of Alexander Hamilton, West Pointer and veteran of the War with Mexico, was named assistant chief of staff, with the rank of colonel. Captain James B. McPherson, whom Halleck had met in San Francisco several years previously, was selected as aide-de-camp and promoted to the rank of lieutenant colonel.

Repairing to St. Louis, Halleck took command of the Department of Missouri on November 18, 1861. His written instructions from General McClellan graphically describe the task he faced: "In assigning you to the command of the Department of Missouri it is probably unnecessary for me to state that I have entrusted to you a duty which required the utmost tact and decision. You have not merely the ordinary duties of a military commander to perform, but the far more difficult task of reducing chaos to order, of changing probably the majority of the personnel of the staff of the department, and of reducing to a point of economy consistent with the interests and necessities of the State a system of reckless expenditure and fraud perhaps unheard of before in the history of the world."

He entered upon his difficult duties of administration and reorganization with characteristic energy. The effectiveness of his work is described in somewhat exaggerated terms by General Cullum: "Around him was a chaos of insubordination, inefficiency and peculation. Hardly had Halleck assumed command before his remorseless juggernaut of reform began to crush out every abuse and scatter all opposing obstacles. Fraudulent contracts were annulled; useless stipendiaries were dismissed; a colossal staff hierarchy was disbanded; composite organizations were pruned to simpler uniformity; the construction of fantastic fortifications was suspended; and in a few weeks order reigned in Missouri."

The loyal citizens of St. Louis got to know General Halleck very well during his stay in that city. His tall portly figure was a familiar sight on the street in the vicinity of the Planter's House. Many people remarked his resemblance to a country parson—a parson attired in full regimentals and wearing a wide-brimmed black felt hat on the back of his head. Cleanshaven, sallow-faced, his bearing was that of a quiet, self-sufficient man distrustful of everyone else. His stern, expressionless countenance was an effective mask for his own thoughts and emotions. A prominent forehead and large dark eyes gave him an owlish appearance, while his piercing gaze bored through people with searching thoroughness.

During the winter of 1861–62 General Halleck organized and equipped his armies for the spring advance. The value of professional training was again demonstrated in his preparations for the campaign that followed. General William Tecumseh Sherman, then under Halleck's command, is authority for the statement that the idea for breaking the Confederate center at Fort Donelson originated with Halleck. He relates: "I remember one night sitting in his room on the second floor of the Planter's House with him and General Cullum, his chief of staff, talking of things generally, and the subject then was of the much talked of 'advance' as soon as the season would permit. Most people urged the movement down the Mississippi River. General Halleck had a map on his table, with a large pencil in his hand and asked 'Where is the rebel line?' Cullum drew the pencil through Bowling Green, Forts Donelson and Henry and Columbus, Kentucky. 'That is their line,' said Halleck; 'now, where is the proper place to break it?' And either Cullum or I said, 'Naturally the center.' Halleck drew a line perpendicularly to the other, near its middle, and it coincided nearly with the general course of the Tennessee River, and he said, 'That's the true line of operations.' This occurred more than a month before General Grant began the movement and as he was subject to General Halleck's orders, I have always given Halleck the full credit for that movement, which was skilful, successful, and extremely rich in military results; indeed it was the first real success on our side in the Civil War."

Actually, a number of people had seen the necessity of an advance up the Tennessee River, and the idea for the movement had nothing like the impromptu origin suggested by Sherman. But Halleck was only too glad to claim the credit, and to use Grant's success as a basis for demanding promotion. Immediately upon the capture of Fort Donelson by Grant, Halleck telegraphed Washington: "Make Buell, Grant, and Pope major generals of volunteers and give me command in the West. I ask this in return for Donelson and Henry." Lincoln issued on March 11, 1862, his War Order No. 3, creating the Department of the Mississippi, and placed General Halleck in command. This same order relieved General McClellan as general in chief of the army.

Soon after Grant's battle at Shiloh, Halleck arrived at Pittsburg Landing and took personal command of the armies in the field. When full details of the battle reached the North, not even an apparent victory could shield General Grant from general condemnation. The president was urged to remove him from command. Several Senators, among others, waited on General Halleck and insisted that the incompetent, intemperate general should not again be trusted with an army. But Halleck, though fully realizing that Grant had committed a gross blunder in placing his army on the west bank of the Tennessee without means of retreat in case of disaster, and had exposed himself to attack while waiting for Buell's army to arrive, declined to remove him from command. Undoubtedly he recognized in the unpretentious Grant a soldier of uncommon military talent and stubborn tenacity. As a military man, he knew that Grant's neglect of the simple military precaution of intrenching his army at Shiloh was attributable to inexperience and not incompetence, and therefore pardonable. In the army reorganization which followed, General Grant was retained as General Halleck's second-in-command.

General Halleck has been severely criticized for his cautious advance on Corinth, which consumed over a month. However, his critics have perhaps given insufficient weight to the fact that when he arrived at Pittsburg Landing he found the army demoralized by its frightful losses and the shock of battle. Many of the troops were green, for General Sherman records: "My division was made up of perfectly new regiments, all having received their muskets, for the first time, at Paducah. None of them had ever been under fire before."

Only two weeks were spent in reorganizing the army and bringing up reinforcements, supplies, and ammunition. When the forward movement began, Halleck determined that his untrained troops and inexperienced officers should receive an intensive field training. For four weeks, over a country of rolling ridges covered with forest, but with little underbrush on the high land, his compact columns slowly dug their way to Corinth. The impatient Sherman complained that "Halleck moved on Corinth with pick and shovel," for each night found the army completely intrenched and the camps fully guarded against a surprise attack. Grant later wrote contemptuously that there was no time after Shiloh "when the enemy would not have left if pushed," and implies his censure of Halleck's timidity in noting that he cautioned all commanders "that it would be better to retreat than to fight." But Halleck's defenders maintain that the army which appeared before Corinth—however exasperated by the delays—was better disciplined and trained than the one that started out from the banks of the Tennessee, and that the training and experience thus received was to prove of lasting benefit.

Many years later, after writing that Halleck had used all of May, "the most beautiful and valuable month of the year for campaigning in this latitude," in what was simply "a magnificent drill," Sherman added: "General Halleck was a man of great capacity, of large acquirements, and at the time possessed the confidence of the country, and of most of the army. I held him in high estimation, and gave him credit for the combinations which had resulted in placing this magnificent army of a hundred thousand men, well equipped and provided, with a good base at Corinth from which he could move in any direction."

President Lincoln, at the beginning of the conflict, assumed the responsibilities of a military commander, his prerogative as constitutional commander in chief. He found himself far too busy, however, to take full responsibility as director of military operations. Every emergency compelled him to consult with the Secretary of War or directly with the generals in the field. After McClellan's Peninsula fiasco he was at a loss to know what to do and badly needed military advice from someone in whom he had confidence. Advised by old General Scott that Halleck was the most competent military strategist then in the field, Lincoln decided to bring him to Washington as his military adviser. Knowing that the general was reluctant to leave his independent command in the field for Washington, he sent two Assistant Secretaries of War and a senator to persuade Halleck to accept the assignment.

General Halleck declined the offer and told the president's emissaries that he would not go to Washington unless positive orders were issued him. The president, meanwhile, left for a visit to the Army of the Potomac at Harrison's Landing on the James and a consultation with General McClellan and his corps commanders. Immediately upon his return to Washington he issued on July 11, 1862, a clear directive: "Ordered, that Major General Henry W. Halleck be assigned to command the whole land forces of the United States as general in chief, and that he repair to this Capital as soon as he can with safety to the positions and operations within the department under his charge."

Lincoln later explained to Senator Sumner: "My mind became perfectly perplexed, and I determined right then and there to appoint a Commander in Chief who should be responsible for our military operations, and I determined further that General Halleck should be the man. Accordingly, as soon as I arrived in Washington, I telegraphed him to come here and assume the responsibilities of that office."

Halleck reached Washington on July 23, 1862; and thus began the close and lasting relationship between Lincoln and the scholarly, reserved Halleck, a relationship that passed through several distinct phases, and that has seldom been clearly understood. In his early months in Washington, Halleck gave great disappointment to Lincoln; later, after Grant came East to take command in Virginia, Halleck took a position in which his very real talents found better expression.

Undoubtedly, at first, Lincoln hoped that Halleck would decide the general strategy for all the main armies in the field, would help the president find commanders able to execute this strategy, and would issue his orders decisively. In this hope, Lincoln conferred upon Halleck the title of general in chief. It was an unfortunate title in that it deluded many people into thinking that the general would exercise, whenever advisable, an active field command. The fact was that Halleck, a master of military texts and a closet or study general, had

neither taste nor capacity for directing an army in the field—
and for that matter, almost no experience. Moreover, neither
in selecting the best men for high command, nor in devising
strategic combinations, did he show keenness of judgment
or firmness of decision. Had he possessed the traits of a
Wellington or Grant, in July 1862 he could have taken command of McClellan's army on the James, united it with
Burnside's force at Falmouth on the Rappahannock and with
Pope's troops covering Richmond, and led the whole command against Lee. It appears that Lincoln expected just this;
certainly Pope expected it. But as the advance to Corinth had
shown, Halleck lacked decision in the presence of the enemy,
and abdicated all responsibilities for generalship in the field.
He left the fighting to McClellan and Pope; and Pope, failing
to get the reinforcements he needed, bungled Second
Manassas.

By the date of that defeat, which ended September 1, 1862,
Halleck had lost his opportunity for active field command;
lost it willingly and perhaps happily, for he knew that his
usefulness lay elsewhere. Inevitably, some men attacked him
for not using his generalship-in-chief vigorously. Hooker
sneered that he held the position of a man who married with
the understanding that he would not sleep with his wife. But
General Jacob D. Cox puts the matter more kindly and
accurately when he writes that Halleck "had become, what
he remained to the close of the war, a bureau officer in
Washington." Cox might have added that as a bureau officer
he did sterling service.

Lincoln's disappointment was naturally keen. He continued
for a time to expect that Halleck would show the characteristics
of command and decision which any great general possesses.
At the least, in Lincoln's opinion, this eminent strategist should
give sound advice on the choice of generals, and on the
movements for field officers to follow. Burnside, after his
terrible disaster at Fredericksburg, contemplated another forward thrust farther up the Rappahannock (the thrust that

broke down at the outset in the "mud march"), whose wisdom Lincoln strongly doubted. The president thought that Halleck should boldly assume responsibility for endorsing it, modifying it, or countermanding it. When the irresolute Halleck did nothing, Lincoln on January 1, 1863, wrote him a tart letter:

> My dear Sir: Gen. Burnside wishes to cross the Rappahannock with his army, but his Grand Division commanders all oppose the movement. If in such a difficulty as this you do not help, you fail me precisely in the point for which I sought your assistance. You know what Gen. Burnside's plan is; and it is my wish that you go with him to the ground, examine it as far as practicable, confer with the officers, getting their judgment, and ascertaining their temper, in a word, gather all the elements for forming a judgment of your own; and then tell Gen. Burnside that you *do* approve, or that you do *not* approve his plan. Your military skill is useless to me, if you will not do this. Yours very truly A. Lincoln.

After Halleck protested that he did not have the view of his relation to generals in the field which Lincoln held, and that Lincoln's attitude was harsh, the president withdrew his letter. It nevertheless expressed the sense of disappointment he had come to hold; disappointment over Halleck's refusal to do more than advise. Halleck on January 7 did send a letter of counsel—and nothing more decided—to Burnside. Lincoln saw that he must make other use of the general's undoubted brains and learning.

That during his first year in Washington Halleck was fully aware of the embarrassing position he held as a general in chief who would not take the field or issue orders is clearly indicated in his letter to General McClellan written July 30, 1862: "You are probably aware that I hold my present position contrary to my own wishes, and that I did everything in my power to avoid coming to Washington. But after declining several invitations from the President, I received the order of the 11th instant, which left me no option. I have always had strong personal objections to mingling in the politico-military affairs of Washington. I never liked the place, and I like it still less at the present time. I greatly feared, whatever I might do, I should receive more abuse than thanks. There seems to be a disposition in the Press here to cry down anyone who attempted to serve the country instead of party. This was particularly the case with you, as I understand, and I could not doubt that it would be in a few weeks the case with me. Under these circumstances I could not see how I could be of much use here. Nevertheless, being ordered, I was obliged to come."

General Halleck's prediction that he would be the subject of abuse was soon realized. Repeated disasters in the field were charged to his incompetence, and he was continually compelled to assume the responsibility which belonged to others. It was not long before he became one of the most thoroughly despised officials in Washington. In a letter to his wife at about this time, he wrote that he was in a "political hell."

Many men in high administrative positions in the government took part in the attack. The most outspoken censure came from members of the president's Cabinet. Secretary of the Treasury Chase told Secretary Welles: "Halleck was good for nothing, and everybody knew it but the President." Welles continually vented his spleen upon Halleck. He was not far astray when he wrote: "Lincoln's own convictions and conclusions are infinitely superior to Halleck's, even in military operations more sensible and most correct always; but yet the President says, 'It being strictly a military question, it is proper I should defer to Halleck, whom I have called here to counsel, advise and direct in these matters, where he is an expert.' I question whether he should be considered an expert. I look upon Halleck as a pretty good scholarly critic of other men's deeds and acts, but as incapable of originating or directing military operations." In September 1863, however, Welles was much more unfair: "Halleck originates nothing, anticipates nothing; takes no responsibility, plans nothing, suggests nothing, is good for nothing. His being at headquarters is a national misfortune. In this whole summer's campaign I have been unable to see, hear or obtain evidence of power, or will, or talent, or originality on the part of General Halleck. He has suggested nothing, decided nothing, done nothing but scold and smoke and scratch his elbows. Is it possible that the energies of the nation should be wasted by the incapacity of such a man?"

General McClellan added his voice to the chorus of condemnation: "Of all men whom I have encountered in high position, Halleck was the most hopelessly stupid. It was more difficult to get an idea through his head than can be conceived by anyone who never made the attempt. I do not think he ever had a correct military idea from beginning to end." And General Ben Butler once burst out against Halleck, the translator of Jomini, as a trifler and idler. What, he asked a knot of officers, does he really do? "At a moment when every true man is laboring to the utmost, when the days ought to be forty hours long, General Halleck is translating French books at nine cents a page; and sir, if you should put those nine cents in a box and shake them up, you would form a clear idea of General Halleck's soul."

One recent historian, the late Clarence E. Macartney, echoed the opinions of Halleck's enemies when he wrote: "The strange thing is not that Lincoln should have chosen Halleck for commander-in-chief in the summer of 1862, for many of the best military minds and the sentiment of the people at large approved the choice. The strange thing is that after his incapacity had been so strikingly demonstrated Lincoln should have kept him in command and constantly deferred to his judgement. Originating nothing, taking no responsibility in time of danger or crisis, letting the burden rest on the shoulders of other men, afraid to make use of the powerful weapon that Lincoln had placed in his hands when he made him the supreme commander of the armies of the Union, Halleck is a contemptible, almost ridiculous figure.

. . . Selected by Lincoln and kept in power by Lincoln, Halleck did more injury to the cause of the North than any other man."

All this was decidedly unfair; and the reason why we must pronounce it unfair was crisply stated by Halleck himself in a letter to Sherman: "The great difficulty in the office of General-in-Chief is that it is not understood by the country. The responsibility and odium thrown upon it do not belong to it. I am simply a military adviser of the Secretary of War and the President, and must obey and carry out what they decide upon, whether I concur in their decisions or not. It is my duty to strengthen the hands of the President as Commander in Chief, not weaken them by factious opposition. I have, therefore, cordially cooperated with him in any plan decided upon, although I have never hesitated to differ in opinion. I must leave it to history to vindicate or condemn my own opinions or plans. They will be found at some future time on record."

This was precisely the fact: Halleck was never a generalissimo, never a field general after leaving Corinth, never a man of authority. He was not even a chief of staff in the modern meaning of the term. He was an adviser, an intermediary between the president and the generals, and to some extent a co-ordinator of the various commands; in Cox's phrase, "a bureau officer." But he should not be depreciated. As a writer on strategy, he knew all the accepted rules for conducting a war, and his emphasis on them was salutary. He kept insisting on the importance of military concentration, and the folly of dividing forces into a number of commands; precisely the rule that he and Washington between them violated when they scattered the great army at Corinth in 1862, which might have taken Vicksburg or Chattanooga, to the four quarters of the compass. He insisted equally on the fact that the objective in Virginia was not the capture of the cities, but the destruction of armies; the Union should aim at smashing Lee, not at taking Richmond. He insisted also on the superiority of West Point officers to "political generals," a principle he sometimes carried too far, but which in the main was sound. While he had failed to rise to the high potentialities before him, on the lower plane which he occupied he was a very useful officer indeed.

This was particularly true when the greatest of the Union field officers came East. Stanton's General Order No. 98, dated March 12, 1864, relieved Halleck from duty as general in chief and assigned Lieutenant General Grant to the command of the armies. Halleck was assigned by the same order to duty in Washington as chief of staff of the army, under the direction of the Secretary of War and the lieutenant general commanding.

In creating for Halleck this entirely new position President Lincoln acted for the purpose of retaining him as military consultant, official intermediary, and co-ordinator of Grant's military operations. He remained in Washington until the end of the war, performing much the same duties as those imposed upon him theretofore. Nobody knows who suggested this new office; possibly Lincoln invented it himself. In any event, Halleck was the perfect choice for it. He could facilitate communication between Lincoln and Grant, and between Grant and the various departmental commanders. It is significant that neither Lincoln nor Stanton, who knew him best, ever spoke critically of him.

Chief of Staff Halleck, as T. Harry Williams writes, "had the happy faculty of being able to communicate civilian ideas to a soldier and military ideas to a civilian and make both of them understand what he was talking about." His reports and letters are models of lucid, businesslike English. He could convey to Grant the broad strategic concepts in Lincoln's mind, and convey to Lincoln the full import of Grant's pregnant military phrases. Thus when Grant, holding Lee at bay before Petersburg in 1864, wanted Sheridan sent to drive the Confederates under Early out of the Shenandoah Valley and destroy that source of supplies, he sent his wishes to

Halleck. The general talked with Lincoln; the president grasped the situation at once, and telegraphed Grant to "force it"; and the result was Sheridan's prompt and fateful devastation of the Southern granary. Meanwhile, Halleck helped Grant manage and co-ordinate the seventeen different commands with more than a half-million men under his control. All dispatches of departmental generals went to Halleck to be forwarded or summarized, and most of Grant's own orders to commanders were routed through Halleck's office. That office, in short, became a grand clearing house in the final year of the war.

Victory came, and after victory, Lincoln's death. Terribly shaken by the assassination of the president, and feeling lonely in the new administration, Halleck asked permission to leave the capital. Secretary Stanton promptly granting his request, he was assigned to command the Military Division of the James, with headquarters in Richmond, where he remained from April 22 to July 1, 1865. Then, wishing to see his beloved California once again, he requested a transfer to the Pacific Coast. After a short stay with his father-in-law, John Church Hamilton, in New York, he left for San Francisco and assumed command of the Military Division of the Pacific on August 30, 1865.

Four years later, to relieve the ailing General George H. Thomas, he was transferred to command the Military Division of the South with headquarters at Louisville, where he arrived March 16, 1869. While helping to administer the government's plan of reconstruction in his department, he died suddenly in that city on January 9, 1872.

In his own lifetime Halleck got more abuse and less credit than he merited. He can never be placed on such a pedestal as that occupied by the great field generals—Grant, Sherman, and Thomas; Lee, Stonewall Jackson, and Forrest. But history will give him his reward, for it is impossible to write of Lincoln without emphasizing Halleck's indispensable if modest services in 1864–65. Sir Frederick Maurice has sketched one little scene, which must have had many parallels. "We can picture the President taking his usual morning stroll after breakfast from the White House across to the War Department, and, on arriving in Halleck's room asking for any messages from Grant. That of the fifteenth [of August 1864] is handed to him, and he is told that it has just come in. He would naturally have asked to see the dispatch which had evoked this reply. When he had read both messages, he must at once have scribbled the answer: 'Hold on with a bulldog grip and chew and choke as much as possible.' " Who could ask for a better place in history than to have played a role in such a scene?

NORMAN CORWIN

Lincoln and Douglas: The Tangled Weave

❦

ONLY A MAPMAKER could be expected to know that Vladivostok, Siberia, is actually farther south than Venice, Italy. And only walking memory machines could be expected to reel off the order of the cities and towns in which Lincoln and Douglas staged their joint debates. For there is a shadowy zone in the back of the head where one files away miscellaneous impressions based on knowledge, half-knowledge, and misinformation; and perhaps the average American's idea of the Lincoln–Douglas debates has been stored in this zone.

Most people are only vaguely aware of their ignorance about Douglas. They know that he was a short, dynamic man, who tangled with Lincoln in two vital contests. The rest is oversimplification. Few have any idea of Douglas' rank in his own time—a rank not nearly indicated by his office. One tends to classify him among various enemies of progress, simply because he was an enemy of Lincoln.

The stature of the man becomes apparent not so much through the debates, as through the events in his life which preceded and followed the canvass of 1858; his role as what has been called a "nation-builder"; his services to the expansion of American railroads; his untiring efforts to strengthen the educational system of Illinois (he donated the land on which the University of Chicago was built, and for the rest of his life "looked to it to light the lamp of learning for the West").

Before the debates Douglas completely overshadowed his adversary. Lincoln was strictly local stuff; Douglas was the most conspicuous figure in national politics; his prestige was beyond the reach even of the then president of the United States, the uninspired James Buchanan; the home that his second wife, Adèle Cutts Douglas, made for him far outranked the White House as the social cynosure of Washington. Indeed, never was a man more clearly indicated for the highest office in the land. Lincoln was not being sardonic or coy when he said, during one of the debates:

> Senator Douglas is of world-wide renown. All the anxious politicians of his party have been looking upon him as certainly, at no distant day, to be President of the United States. . . . On the contrary, nobody expects me to be President . . .

Events subsequent to the senatorial contest of which the debates were the chief feature, conspired to turn a giant table: the man whom everybody expected to be president did not get there, and the man whom nobody expected, did. There were reasons for it, as inexorable as the tides and the seasons. But the greatest switch, because it was the deepest, took place within the rivalry itself. From Lincoln's uttermost adversary, Douglas became his staunchest champion. And that contains a moving story, of a kind not often encountered in the political life of any country. It was a richly and uniquely American twist.

If the only Douglas one were to meet was the character projected in the stenographic texts of the joint debates, the impression would be less than flattering by modern standards. We have one of the giants of our history saying, boldly and nakedly, "When it becomes necessary to acquire any portion of Canada or Mexico, we must take them as we find them, leaving the people free to have slavery or not, as they choose." It was not even whether, or if, but *when*. Even though the talk of the time was to buy Cuba for a price of one hundred million dollars, it is still startling to see in print, "Indeed, the time has now come, when our interests would be advanced by the acquisition of the Island of Cuba." And there were other, worse shockers to the people of his day. But this was not the A to Z of the man.

Formidable as was the Douglas of the debates, his true dimensions are to be realized only in the perspective of Before and After. His noble sacrifice of personal and party gain in his effort to stave off dismemberment of the Union, and his heroic support of Lincoln after his arch adversary became president, stamp him as a patriot of rare coinage.

But the debates were Lincoln's triumph, after all; and these comments are not meant to throw the weight of consideration to Douglas. They are simply intended to index the degree to which history has reversed the field. The Lincoln of 1858 was the relative unknown. For every book that has been written about Douglas, perhaps a hundred have been done on Lincoln. A century ago, before the debates, the odds could have been a hundred to one, the other way round.

Carl Sandburg refers to "the tangled weave of the awesome rivalry" between Lincoln and Douglas, and he is accurate as well as poetic in the use of his adjectives. Tangled is the word—the tangle was that of the whole nation, not just of two men or two parties. All national life was involved. As Lincoln said: ". . . All this difficulty in regard to the Negro . . . doesn't it render the churches asunder? Isn't it this same, mighty, deep-seated power that operates on the minds of men, exciting and stirring them up in every avenue of society—in politics, in religion, in literature, in morals, in all the manifold relations of life?"

The weave held in it a thousand thousand filaments, some of them bright, some funny, many somber, most of them tragic. One of the awesome things about the vast crowds that turned out to hear the debates is that so many of the men in the audience were doomed to be killed or maimed, and their families bereft, in the ultimate struggle over that same "deep-seated power." These same people who listened raptly, cheering or heckling while desperate issues churned and fermented before them, were to be swept into the maelstrom of the most terrible war ever fought between countrymen.

The following notes, fragments, legends, asides, and shards of fact and color, are part of the Tangled Weave of which Mr. Sandburg speaks. They are from many sources and represent an amalgam of the gifts of many hands.

To begin with, there was the challenge. Lincoln challenged Douglas with a two-sentence letter that read:

Hon. S. A. Douglas

My Dear Sir: Will it be agreeable to you to make an arrangement for you and myself to divide time, and address the same audiences the present canvass? Mr. Judd, who will hand you this, is authorized to receive your answer; and, if agreeable to you, to enter into the terms of such agreement.

Your obedient servant,
A. Lincoln

Douglas was prompt in his reply. On the same day he wrote Lincoln a long letter, first explaining that there were difficulties in the way of such an arrangement, that time was very tight; then dragging in the report that a third candidate for the Senate was being groomed to insure Douglas' defeat "by dividing the Democratic party for your benefit," and raising the question of whether such a person would claim the right to speak from the same stand as Lincoln and himself "so that he and you, in concert, might be able to take the opening and closing speech in every case." He then chided Lincoln for waiting so long to come forward with such a challenge, but finally came around to accepting it—on his terms:

I will, in order to accommodate you as far as it is in my power to do so, take the responsibility of making an arrangement with you for a discussion between us at one prominent point in each Congressional District in the State. I will indicate the following places as those most suitable . . . to wit: Freeport, Ottawa, Galesburg, Quincy, Alton, Jonesboro, and

Charleston. I will confer with you at the earliest convenient opportunity in regard to the mode of conducting the debate, the times of meeting at the several places, subject to the condition that where appointments have already been made by the Democratic State Central Committee at any of those places, I must insist upon you meeting me at the times specified.

Very respectfully, your most obedient servant,

S. A. Douglas

There were several outcroppings of petulance in the three letters that followed. Lincoln a few days later wrote, among various quibbling points:

As to your surprise that I did not sooner make the proposal to divide time with you, I can only say, I made it as soon as I resolved to make it. I did not know but that such proposal would come from you. I waited, respectfully, to see.

Douglas replied curtly:

Dear Sir: Your letter dated yesterday, accepting my proposition for a joint discussion of one prominent point in each Congressional District was received this morning.

He then designated the times and places, and added:

I agree to your suggestion that we shall alternately open and close the discussion. I will speak at Ottawa one hour, you can reply, occupying an hour and a half, and I will then follow for half an hour. At Freeport, you shall open the discussion and speak one hour; I will follow for an hour and a half, and you can then reply for half an hour. We will alternate in like manner in each successive place.

Lincoln accepted, but with a growl that was unworthy of him:

Dear Sir:
Yours of yesterday, naming places, times, and terms, for joint discussions between us, was received this morning. Although, by the terms, as you propose, you take *four* openings and closes, to my *three*, I accede, and thus close the arrangement. . . .

In any division of seven debates, somebody had to open and close four times against his opponent's three, and it was only natural that Douglas, consenting to meet Lincoln at all, should have picked the number to his advantage. Since each of the seven joint debates ran three hours, the total elapsed time was twenty-one hours. There were also earlier speeches, made unilaterally, but with the opponent either present or close by, and these are included in the over-all speechmaking for the campaign. Thus the total time would run almost thirty hours.

A set of questions was propounded by each candidate and submitted to the other. Douglas' strategy was to cut off Lincoln from a certain element of his following, by framing questions that would show Lincoln in agreement with abolitionists on various key policies held repugnant by moderates. Lincoln avoided the trap, and came up with five questions of his own, dealing with slavery policy. Douglas' answers to these had the effect of destroying his presidential prospects, although he seemed not to be preoccupied with this possibility. "Few leaders," writes Allan Nevins of Douglas, "were as careless of the 'long look ahead.'"

Readers of the full text of the debates will be amazed by the profusion of local names and issues, many of which have passed from all but the textbooks. Naturally, great emphasis was placed on the events which anticipated these contests— the Mississippi Compromise of 1820, the Wilmot Proviso of 1846, the Fugitive Slave Law of 1850, the Kansas–Nebraska Act of 1854, the Lecompton Constitution proposed for Kansas in 1857. Through all of these events, the broad outlines of the problems created by the "deep-seated power" remained the same.

The cast of characters in this drama was enormous. The speeches reverberate with topical allusions to Trumbull, Shields, Giddings, Chase, Fred Douglas, Major Harris, Charles Lanphier, etc. The split between Douglas and President Buchanan was not ignored; much was said concerning the

"Danites," or Buchanan Democrats; charges were made of conspiracy on the part of Douglas, the Supreme Court, and Buchanan, to make slavery perpetual and fashionable; Lincoln further charged that certain resolutions, referred to by Douglas as having been passed by a Republican Convention, were forged.

The rivals—and they were frequently alluded to as such in their time—were destined to test each other's powers almost from the beginning of their public life. At one time they were both interested in the same girl. Douglas is said to have "paid marked attention" to Mary Todd, who later married Lincoln. The legend is that it was Mary's ambition to marry a future president, and that as early as twenty years before the presidential contest between the two, she foresaw that Lincoln would attain the White House and Douglas would not.

It is fortunate for historians of the debates that its speeches were taken down by shorthand. But there was a great deal of bitterness about the accuracy, or lack of it, with which the speeches were reported, and each side accused the other of flagrant misrepresentation of the ideas expressed by its spokesman. There was malice afoot. "BLACK REPUBLICAN OUTRAGES" cried the Chicago *Times* in a headline. Ruffianism was charged against Lincoln's supporters:

> The Black Republicans evidently intend to be consistent in one thing—and for that one thing, unfortunately, they have fixed on ruffianism. When Douglas went upon the stand, some villain threw at the latter a melon, hitting him on the shoulder. Nor was that the only indecent act perpetrated by the enemies of the Democracy.

Douglas' supporters were referred to as "loafers and boys . . . hired puffers." Lincoln was attacked on the Mexican War issue, as being unable to "quibble out of the odium of his unpatriotic course . . . he was as serviceable an ally of Mexico as if he had met his countrymen upon Mexican soil with a

Mexican musket, to welcome them with bloody hands to hospitable graves."

According to a correspondent of the *Missouri Republican,* the Lincoln supporters in Galesburg "paraded dirty designs and beastly caricatures," while the Democrats were chaste and dignified. The correspondent concluded that, at the end of this debate, Lincoln's face "was a little longer than a horse's collar and the eyes looked woefully like weeping." The Chicago *Times* generally agreed with the *Missouri Republican* that Lincoln cut a dismal figure:

> Mr. Lincoln, when he mounted the stand, was nervous and trembling; whether from cold, or through fear of what was in store for him, we are unable to say; but before the close of the debate, he was the most abject picture of wretchedness we have ever witnessed. His knees knocked together, and the chattering of his teeth could be heard all over the stand. When Senator Douglas replied to his charge, he looked pitiful beyond expression, and curled himself up in a corner to avoid facing the bitter denunciation of the Senator and the scorn and derision with which he was treated by the crowd.

> When Senator Douglas concluded, the applause was perfectly furious and overwhelming; he was surrounded by an immense mass of people who accompanied him to his hotel, which, during the whole evening was thronged with people going and coming to congratulate him upon his great success; whilst Lincoln, entirely forgotten, was taken care of by a few friends, who wrapped him in flannels and tried to restore the circulation of blood in his almost inanimate body. Poor Lincoln! He was not even *visible* to the friends who came to weep with him.

Hard words, mean words, burned in print. "Niggerism" found its way into news columns more than once; cries of "foul" went up on all sides. The Galesburg *Democrat* screamed that the Chicago *Times* in its report of a single speech of Lincoln, had made 180 mutilations. "Rascality! . . . the whole aim has been to blunt the keen edge of Mr. Lincoln's wit, to mar the beauty of his most elegant passages, and make him talk like a booby, a half-witted numbskull. —We believe an action for libel would hold against these villains, and they richly deserve the prosecution." The *Times* retorted in kind; claimed that Douglas' speeches were marred and mangled, and added, characteristically, "poor Lincoln requires some such advantage, though it be mean."

The present image of Lincoln is so sainted that it is startling to find the Lincoln of the debates described as follows:

> Pleading his humility, and asking for forgiveness of Heaven for his enemies, he stood washing his hands with invisible soap in imperceptible water, until his friends, seeing that his mind was wandering, took him in charge, and bundled him off the ground. . . .

Douglas fared no better:

> In sound, manly argument, Lincoln is too much for him. While the former shakes his black locks vaingloriously and explodes in mere fustian of sound and smoke, the latter quietly, unassumingly, but effectually drives home argument after argument, heavy as cannon balls, and sharp as two-edged swords, until his adversary is so thoroughly riddled, cut up and "used up," that in the view of discriminating men, nothing remains of him but a ghostly appearance.

Douglas was called "a wild beast in looks and gesture, and a maniac in language and argument." A correspondent of the Peoria *Transcript* said he had "never looked upon a convention so livid with brutal passions." "Mr. Douglas," viewed the Quincy *Whig*, "is as much a blackguard as he is a demagogue, and scarcely has an equal in either respect." The same paper assured its readers that "Douglas actually foamed at the mouth during his speech."

From the start the debates attracted national attention, for the whole country realized that more than state issues were at stake. It took no discerning observer to realize that on the outcome of this contest rested the victory or defeat of the reigning administration, the fate of "squatter sovereignty," the presidential nominations at the next conventions, and the future of the Union itself. Eastern newspapers dispatched special correspondents to the battleground, and the pages of journalistic history are full of impressive reporting in the New York *Post,* New York *Tribune,* Boston *Daily Advertiser,* Cincinnati *Commercial,* Charleston *Mercury.* And while their comments were generally quieter, they were not sweetened by distance. The Boston *Courier,* for example, referred to Lincoln's speech as "inelegant, discursive, and laborious."

Even Douglas' fondness for liquor was not spared by the press: "Bad whiskey and the wear and tear of conscience have had their effects," said one reporter. Crowed the Chicago *Democrat:*

> Habits of temperance in all things, commend themselves nowhere so highly as in the ways of Lincoln and Douglas. Douglas is all worn out, while Lincoln is as fresh as the morning.

The Springfield (Massachusetts) *Republican* commented of Douglas: "Too near the dipper." The Chicago *Journal* added its comment to a quote from a provincial paper:

> The editor of the Stark County paper says Douglas frothed at the corner of his mouth at Charleston. Instead of being crazy, he must have the hydrophobia—dread of water!

A St. Louis paper, noting that Douglas was described as "whistling to keep his courage up," asked pointedly: "Does he not whet his whistle sometimes for the same purpose?"

The extravaganzas of the press were not the only colorful atmosphere to invest the debates. What political event before or since occasioned railroads to offer excursions at half fare to rooters wishing to attend in a distant city? When has a steamship line chartered a ship by the enchanting name of *White Cloud* to sail up a river carrying debate fans? Fare for round trip, one dollar.

What reader can find in what newspaper of today such a gem of annoyed description as:

> At this juncture a blockhead on the upper balcony commenced firing off rockets, and of course made a dozen horses crazy. Those attached to the carriage in which Mr. Douglas sat, plunged frantically in every direction. Several persons were bruised. One man had his leg broken in three places, and was borne fainting into a drug store. Mr. Douglas escaped indoors, and almost immediately reappeared on the north balcony.

The factions vied with each other not only in the press and on the speaking platform, but in the matter of arrangements. Each tried to outdo the other by the size of delegations, the number of banners, the numbers of pretty girls mounted on horses, representing states. The archives are full of colorful, homely, amusing details. The feature of one evening was the arrival of "The German Republican Club of the Seventh Ward with a band of music and their new banner." They were "vociferously greeted with the wildest kind of hurrahs."

In Bloomington, Douglas was greeted on arrival by a salute of thirty-two guns, courtesy of the Bloomington Guards. Douglas' own cannon, a brass sixpounder, which he carried with him on his special train, contributed its own sound effect too.

One night in Freeport, Lincoln was ready to begin his speech when he noticed that the shorthand reporter was not on the platform. Lincoln shouted, "Where's Hitt? Is Hitt present?" Hitt called back that he could not get through the crowd to the stand, whereupon he was lifted by the stronger members of the audience and passed along over the heads of the crowd to the platform.

Throughout the debates an imposing display was made out of those things that one paper called "the etceteras of a great campaign." The hotels of each town were crowded. The streets were hung with flags and banners; bands, sometimes competing, struck up the airs of the day. There were guns and music and shouts and applause. "All prairiedom has broken loose," proclaimed the New York *Evening Post.* "The streets are fairly black with people. . . . Douglas was greeted with a turnout of torches, a salvo of artillery, and a stunning illumination of the hotel. . . . Lincoln was received by a host of staunch friends who roared themselves hoarse on his appearance."

In the minutiae of the etceteras there was even some straw voting. On a train returning to Springfield from the debate in Alton, the passengers took a poll which came out: Lincoln, 167; Douglas, 137; and again, on the excursion train from Oquawka, the voting went: Lincoln, 252; Douglas, 116; Buchanan, 3. That Lincoln seems to have captured the ladies was indicated by the fact that out of 60 women on the train, 56 voted for him.

There were laughs, too. No president before Lincoln or since had so ready a sense of humor. Less well known, however, is the humor of his opponent, and the comical aspect, sometimes maliciously comical, of their contemporaries.

Douglas was capable of mingling charm with his humor, and there is an ingratiating story connected with his interview with the Empress Eugénie during a triumphal visit to France five years before the debates. During their meeting, the Empress commented caustically on the anxiety of the United States to acquire Cuba. "Were I Queen of Spain," she said, "I would spend my last coin and shed the last drop of Spanish blood before the United States should even have a foothold on that Island." Douglas bowed graciously and answered, "Madam, were you the Queen of Spain it would not be necessary either to spend money or shed blood, as love would keep all your subjects loyal." The Empress was delighted by the retort, and Douglas was pinned up somewhere near Franklin among American statesmen who had left a happy impression in that land.

The fun of the campaign was not all caustic. One newspaper correspondent, far enough from his home base in New York to have a sharp eye for local Illinois color, reported a procession in Charleston, wherein thirty-one young ladies dressed in white rode in a large, profusely decorated, canopied wagon. "Behind it was a young lady on horseback, bearing the banner 'Kansas—I will be free.' I may here remark, in passing, [it was] an unfortunate decoration for a young lady."

In the same procession was easily what must have been the worst pun of the campaign. It was emblazoned on one side of that same wagonload of young ladies, a banner reading:

Westward, the star of Empire takes its way,
The girls *link-on* to Lincoln, as their mothers did to Clay.

The italics are of 1858.

The currency of print was given to a story about Lincoln by the writer "Sauganash" in the New York *Tribune* of September 9, 1858. Its charm is set off by the sentence which follows the anecdote:

Being out in the woods hunting, Lincoln fell in with a most truculent looking hunter, who immediately took a sight on him with his rifle. "Halloo!" says Lincoln. "What are you going to do, stranger!" "See here, friend; the folks in my settlement told me if ever I saw a man uglier than I was, then I must shoot him; and I've found him at last." "Well," said Lincoln, after a good look at the man, "shoot away; for if I am really uglier than you are, I don't want to live any longer!"

But you will see him in Washington, and then you can form your own opinion as to his looks. We mean to send him there.

There was unconscious humor in the dispatch describing a group among Douglas' reception array, called The Scandinavians, as "A Swiss Company." One of the most amusing passages from either speaker occurred in one of the side-speeches that were interposed between the major, joint debates. It was Lincoln, speaking in Havana, Illinois:

I am informed that my distinguished friend yesterday became a little excited—nervous, perhaps—(laughter)—and he said something about *fighting*, as though referring to a pugilistic encounter between him and myself. Did anybody in this audience hear him use such language? (Cries of yes.) I am informed, further, that somebody in his audience, rather more excited or nervous than himself, took off his coat, and offered to take the job off Judge Douglas' hands, and fight Lincoln himself. Did anybody here witness that warlike proceeding? (Laughter, and cries of yes.) Well, I merely desire to say that I shall fight neither Judge Douglas nor his second. (Great laughter.) I shall not do this for two reasons, which I will now explain. In the first place, a fight would *prove* nothing which is an issue in this contest. It might establish that Judge Douglas is a more muscular man than myself, or it might demonstrate that I am a more muscular man than Judge Douglas. But this question is not referred to in the Cincinnati platform, nor in either of the Springfield platforms. (Great laughter.) Neither result would prove him right or me wrong. And so of the gentleman who volunteered to do his fighting for him. If my fighting Judge Douglas would not prove anything, it would certainly prove nothing for me to fight his bottle-holder. (Continued laughter.)

My second reason for not having a personal encounter with the Judge is, that I don't believe he wants it himself. (Laughter.) He and I are about the best friends in the world, and when we get together he would no more think of fighting me than of fighting his wife. Therefore, ladies and gentlemen, when the Judge talked about fighting, he was *not* giving vent to any ill-feeling of his own, but merely trying to excite—well, *enthusiasm* against me on the part of his audience. And as I find he was tolerably successful, we will call it quits." (Cheers and laughter.)

But it was not all scornful laughter and brickbats. Both candidates came in for praise that was as lavish as their dispraise was cyclonic. The correspondent of the Philadelphia *Press* pulled out all stops in his account of the opening debate:

Douglas came like some great deliverer, some mighty champion, who covered himself with imperishable laurels, and saved a

nation from ruin; he came as the immortal Washington, or the
patriotic Lafayette, with a nation ready to do him hom-
age. . . .

When Judge Douglas rose to reply, his countenance brightened
up with that peculiar intellectual and demolishing look that he
is so famous for when he is about to make a great point. . . .
He commenced to rend his antagonist to atoms . . . turning
around and facing Lincoln, who was beginning to get very
blue about his chops, he impaled him at once—then, clutching
him in his intellectual grasp, he held him up before the crowd
as it were, in imagination, till you could see him like a
captivated spider. . . .

Elsewhere Lincoln was called "high-toned, honorable, bold,
pungent, earnest, one of nature's noblemen." Especially after
the election he was praised in unstinting phrases, and his star
began to ascend as Douglas' began to wester.

Up to and including the senatorial contest with Lincoln,
Douglas never succumbed to a competitor. But he had a hard
time with this one. The figures on campaign expenditure alone
give some indication of how seriously Douglas took his opponent: Douglas spent $80,000; Lincoln, $1000.

The importance of the election was fully understood both
inside and outside of Illinois. The Burlington *Gazette,* in
neighboring Iowa, described the tension with which the country
awaited the outcome of the contest:

What a night next Tuesday will be all over the Union! The
whole Nation is watching with the greatest possible anxiety for
the result of that day. No State has ever fought so great a
battle as that which Illinois is to fight on that day. Its result
is big with the fate of our Government and the Union, and
the telegraph wires will be kept hot with it until the result is
known all over the land.

The triumph of Douglas, Pyrrhic though it was to be, and
won at such a heavy cost in funds and energy, was nevertheless
a smashing personal victory. For Douglas had rebelled against

the president, the head of his own party. He was excoriated
by high Democrats as a traitor; his friends were removed from
office; he went on to Illinois, and into the teeth of a campaign
in which he was opposed by the whole state machine and the
Republicans to boot. He fought off two Republican leaders of
extraordinary ability, Lincoln and Lyman Trumbull, a former
state Supreme Court judge and incumbent national senator,
who was perhaps Lincoln's most powerful supporter in the
campaign.

As far away from Springfield, Illinois, as Rochester, New
York, and Lowell, Massachusetts, Lincoln's emergence from
the election with high honors was observed. The Rochester
paper remarked that:

> Mr. Lincoln now has a reputation as a statesman and orator,
> which eclipses that of Douglas as the sun does the twinklers of
> the day.

And Lowell:

> No man of this generation has grown more rapidly before the
> country than Lincoln, in this canvass.

Perhaps worth noting is a minor literary coincidence relating
to the outcome of the election. It occurred on the same day in
the same city. The Chicago *Journal,* with a well-done-good-
and-faithful-servant flourish, quoted the lines:

> More true joy Marcellus exiled feels
> Than Caesar with the Senate at his heels.

The *Press and Tribune* of the same city commented:

> Mr. Lincoln, at Springfield at peace with himself because he
> has been true to his convictions, enjoying the confidence and
> unfeigned respect of his peers, is more to be envied than Mr.
> Douglas in the Senate.

The same article made a prophetic evaluation of Lincoln's speeches, in language worthy of the object of its praise:

> His speeches will become landmarks in our political history, and we are sure that when the public mind is more fully aroused to the themes which he has so admirably discussed, the popular verdict will place him a long way in advance of the more fortunate champion by whom he has been overthrown.

A fine prophecy, which looks better than ever, more than a hundred years after the ink dried on the editorial. That we are still untangling the weave is beside the point. There were many men who saw the pattern firsthand and spoke out. It is a stupendous record.

SHERRILL HALBERT

Lincoln Suspends
The Writ of Habeas Corpus

MONDAY, MARCH 4, 1861, was a turbulent day in the history
of the United States. The weather itself was in keeping with
the political crisis, and when the country lawyer from Springfield, Illinois, faced the chief justice of the United States to
take the presidential oath of office, it was raw, blustery, and
threatening. The chief justice, Roger B. Taney, administered
the oath prescribed by the Constitution:

"I do solemnly swear that I will faithfully execute the
Office of President of the United States, and will to the best
of my Ability, preserve, protect and defend the Constitution of
the United States."

As Abraham Lincoln assumed his obligations as our sixteenth president, he was brought face to face with the author of
the despised Dred Scott decision, with whom he was shortly
to be locked in a dramatic legal struggle, not to be settled
during the lifetime of either man. These two honorable and
dedicated men were to be the principal adversaries in a conflict
over the question whether the president or the Congress has
the power to suspend the privilege of the writ of habeas
corpus. They were both men of great intellectual and moral
strength, and their struggle was titanic in character.

In his inaugural address Lincoln said: "In your hands, my dissatisfied fellow countrymen, and not in mine, is the momentous
issue of civil war. The government will not assail you. You

can have no conflict, without being yourselves the aggressors. You have no oath registered in Heaven to destroy the government, while I shall have the most solemn one to 'preserve, protect, and defend it.' "

Even Lincoln, in all probability, had no idea how extensive was the dissatisfaction of his fellow countrymen. The gravity of the situation was accentuated by the fact that it was not confined to the southern half of the nation, but had spread to all sides of the District of Columbia, where he was then speaking. Virginia, on the south and west, was to secede from the Union on April 16, and Maryland, on the north and east, was teetering on the brink. If Maryland followed Virginia, then the capital of the nation would find itself in the midst of rebel territory—an intolerable situation, both from the standpoint of strategy and from the standpoint of morale.

Congress was not then in session, so one of the three principal branches of the government was at the moment not functioning. Travel and communications were slow, and travel was being further impeded by the insurgents in Maryland. As a result, though the president called a special session of the Thirty-seventh Congress to consider the unfortunate situation, this session did not convene until July 4, 1861. Some of Lincoln's critics insisted that he could have convened Congress sooner, if he had wished, but a careful analysis of the situation seems to leave them with nothing to support their position, other than the innate desire of one political group to criticize another. In any event, Lincoln was the president of the United States with secession, rebellion, intrigue, subversion, treason, and even armed conflict on his hands. Congress was not to convene until four months after he took the oath of office; a period during which he had no choice but to govern without the assistance of the legislature.

During the weeks immediately following his inauguration Lincoln discussed with his Cabinet the matter of the April 26 meeting of the Maryland legislature, and consideration was given to attempting to prevent the meeting entirely. At that time there was some cause to believe that the Maryland legislature would attempt some act of secession, and close the pincer on Washington. Lincoln, after seeking the advice of his Cabinet, concluded that it was unwise to take any steps against the legislature, since this body had a legal right to meet. He did, however, on April 25, issue an order to the commander of the nation's army, General Winfield Scott, which ended as follows:

> I therefore conclude that it is only left to the commanding General to watch, and await their action, which, if it shall be to arm their people against the United States, he is to adopt the most prompt, and efficient means to counteract, even, if necessary, to the bombardment of their cities—and in the extremest necessity, the suspension of the writ of habeas corpus.

Lincoln's astute handling of the situation bore fruit, for while Maryland was a seething caldron of secession, almost more violent at times than some of the states that did secede, it never left the Union, and the capital was never isolated. The course of events in Maryland did, however, ultimately provoke the suspension of the privilege of the writ of habeas corpus.

On April 19 the Sixth Massachusetts Militia arrived in Washington, after having literally fought their way through Baltimore. On April 20 the railroad communications with the North were severed by Marylanders, and thus Washington was practically isolated from the part of the nation of which it remained the capital. On April 25 the Seventh New York Militia finally reached Washington after struggling through Maryland. This was the situation with which Lincoln had to deal when he elected not to prevent the meeting of the Maryland legislature by force, and hesitated to suspend the privilege of the writ of habeas corpus. He looked upon the bombardment of the cities of Maryland as preferable to the suspension of the writ, having instructed General Scott that he might, in case of "necessity," bombard the cities, but only "in the extremest necessity" was he to suspend the writ of habeas corpus. A study of the records during the Lincoln administration indicates that the president never had any desire to suspend the privilege of the writ of habeas corpus; but ultimately he was driven to it, on April 27. Even then he did not issue a general order. His order to General Scott read:

> You are engaged in repressing an insurrection against the laws of the United States. If at any point on or in the vicinity of the military line, which is now, or which shall be used between the City of Philadelphia and the City of Washington, via Perryville, Annapolis City, and Annapolis Junction, you find resistance which renders it necessary to suspend the writ of Habeas Corpus for the public safety, you, personally or through the officer in command at the point where the resistance occurs, are authorized to suspend that writ.

In Maryland there was at this time a dissatisfied fellow countryman of the president by the name of John Merryman. Merryman's dissent from the course being charted by Lincoln was made evident both by word and by deed. He spoke out vigorously against the Union, and in favor of the South; followed this by recruiting a company of soldiers to serve in the Confederate Army; and became their lieutenant drillmaster. Thus, he not only disagreed with what the government was doing, but was engaged in raising an armed group to attack and attempt to destroy the government. This young man was to bring together in legal conflict the president and the chief justice. On May 25, 1861, Merryman was arrested by the military and lodged in Fort McHenry for "various acts of treason, and with being publicly associated with and holding a commission as lieutenant in a company having in their possession arms belonging to the United States, and avowing his purpose of armed hostility against the government."

Shortly after Merryman's arrest, his counsel sought a writ of habeas corpus from Chief Justice Taney, alleging that Merryman was being illegally held at Fort McHenry. Taney took jurisdiction in this case as a circuit judge, and on Sunday, May 26, 1861, issued a writ to General George Cadwalader, in command at the fort, directing him to produce Merryman before the court the next morning at 11 A.M. Cadwalader respectfully refused on the ground that President Lincoln had authorized the suspension of the writ of habeas corpus. To Taney this was blasphemy. He immediately issued an attachment for Cadwalader for contempt. The marshal could not enter the fort to serve the attachment, so the old gentleman, recognizing the impossibility of enforcing his order, settled back, and produced the now famous opinion in *Ex parte Merryman*. This is the best-known recorded opinion of a federal court on the subject of the suspension of the privilege of the writ of habeas corpus by the president, and the only one which touches upon the precise question of whether the Executive or the Congress has the right, under the Constitution, to suspend the writ.

Notwithstanding the fact that he was in his eighty-fifth year, the chief justice vigorously defended the right of Congress alone to suspend the privilege of the writ of habeas corpus. To him, the question had theretofore been "too plain and too well settled to be open to dispute," but he said that since "the president has exercised a power which he does not possess under the constitution, a proper respect for the high office he fills, requires me to state plainly and fully the grounds of my opinion." He then proceeded to attempt to demonstrate that his position was sound, and that that of Lincoln was unsound. In the opinion he discussed the matter from the standpoint of American historical precedent, English historical precedent, constitutional history, and constitutional law; but he either failed or refused to see the true situation which then existed. He spoke in terms of a great legal in-

justice which was being done to Merryman through a denial to
him of his civil rights, but nowhere did he recognize the fact
that a rebellion was in actual existence, and that the fate of
the nation was in fact hanging in a balance. He missed the
crucial point made in the draft of Lincoln's report on the
matter to Congress:

> The whole of the laws which I was sworn to [execute] were
> being resisted . . . in nearly one-third of the States. Must I
> have allowed them to finally fail of execution, even had it
> been perfectly clear that by the use of the means necessary
> to their execution some single law, made in such extreme
> tenderness of the citizen's liberty, that practically it relieves
> more of the guilty than the innocent, should, to a very limited
> extent, be violated? . . . Are all the laws but one to go
> unexecuted, and the Government itself go to pieces, lest that
> one be violated?

Ex parte Merryman has been pointed to as a scholarly and,
by some, a definitive discussion of the right of the Executive
to suspend the privilege of the writ of habeas corpus; but at
the time it did little more than to bring down upon both
Taney and Lincoln virulent and widespread criticism. The
old wounds created by the Dred Scott decision were re-
opened so far as Taney was concerned. As for Lincoln, he
was accused of many things, and called many names, of which
despot, tyrant, and dictator were some of the milder. Lincoln
chose to take no public notice of the Merryman decision,
although Taney directed the clerk of the court "to transmit a
copy [of the opinion], under seal, to the president of the
United States," and added:

> It will then remain for that high officer, in fulfillment of
> his constitutional obligation to "take care that the laws be
> faithfully executed," to determine what measures he will take
> to cause the civil powers of the United States to be respected
> and enforced.

Lincoln may have taken no public notice of *Ex parte Merryman,* but it is evident that he was very much aware of it, for in the original autograph draft of his first message to Congress, to which reference has already been made, he wrote:

I have been reminded from a high quarter that one who is sworn to 'take care that the laws be faithfully executed' should not himself be one to violate them. Of course I gave some consideration to the questions of power and propriety before I acted in this matter.

Later in this same draft he wrote:

In my opinion, I violated no law. The provision of the Constitution that 'The privilege of the writ of *habeas corpus* shall not be suspended unless when, in cases of rebellion or invasion, the public safety may require it', is equivalent to a provision—is a provision—that such privilege may be suspended when, in cases of rebellion or invasion, the public safety does require it. I decided that we have a case of rebellion, and that the public safety does require the qualified suspension of the privilege of the writ of *habeas corpus.*

This was his answer to Taney and those who supported Taney's views. Nothing more was done about Merryman at the time. Merryman was thereafter released from custody and disappeared into oblivion so far as history is concerned.

When the first and special session of the Thirty-seventh Congress met on July 4, Lincoln reported to them in detail what he had done in their absence, and ended this portion of his message by saying:

"Now it is insisted that Congress, and not the Executive, is vested with this power. But the Constitution itself, is silent as to which, or who, is to exercise the power; and as the provision was plainly made for a dangerous emergency, it cannot be believed the framers of the instrument intended, that in every case, the danger should run its course, until

Congress could be called together; the very assembling of which might be prevented, as was intended in this case, by the rebellion.

"No more extended argument is now offered; as an opinion, at some length, will probably be presented by the Attorney General. Whether there shall be any legislation upon the subject, and if any, what, is submitted entirely to the better judgment of Congress."

This statement should be sufficient to establish with certainty that Lincoln was not, and did not wish to be, a dictator.

Attorney General Bates delivered the anticipated opinion to President Lincoln on July 5. In it he reached the conclusion that the president had been both legally and morally right, and within his constitutional powers, when he suspended the privilege of the writ of habeas corpus, and had acted as the result of the rebellion, which was in actual existence. Congress took no action until March 3, 1863, at which time a bill was passed giving Lincoln more power than he sought. The pertinent portion of the bill provided: "That, during the present rebellion, the President of the United States, whenever, in his judgment, the public safety may require it, is authorized to suspend the privilege of the writ of habeas corpus in any case throughout the United States, or any part thereof."

Careless writers have brought about a belief in some quarters that President Lincoln suspended the privilege of the writ of habeas corpus promiscuously. Prior to the virtual carte blanche granted him by the Habeas Corpus Act of March 3, 1863, Lincoln did not issue any general authorization for the suspension of the privilege of the writ of habeas corpus outside the theater of the rebellion. Here is what the entire record shows:

April 25, 1861—General Scott's authorized suspension of the writ in Maryland.

April 27, 1861—Authorized suspension on the line between Philadelphia and Washington.

May 10, 1861—Authorized suspension on the Florida Coast.

June 20, 1861—Authorized suspension in the case of one Major Chase, alleged to be guilty of treason. (Chase had resigned from the United States Army and become a major general in the Confederate Army.)

July 2, 1861—Authorized suspension on the line between New York and Washington.

October 14, 1861—Authorized suspension on the line between Bangor, Maine, and Washington, and places in between.

December 2, 1861—Authorized suspension in the Military Department of Missouri "to secure the public safety and the authority of the United States."

Two important aspects of Lincoln's personal attitude toward the suspension of the writ are also clarified by the record. The first is that Lincoln honestly and sincerely believed that he had the right to do what he did; and there were many who agreed with him. The second is that he exercised the power, which he believed that he had, reluctantly and sparingly. In the original autograph draft of his message to the special session of Congress, in 1861, he wrote: "At my verbal request . . . this authority has been exercised but very sparingly." This was his inner soul speaking, for it was not for public consumption that he wrote.

Lincoln always looked to giving up rather than seeking power. As early as 1862 he issued an order through the War Department in which he noted that conditions had improved, and stated that he desired a return to normal procedures. At that time he directed that all political or state prisoners held by the military be released on their subscribing to a parole by which they agreed not to aid or comfort the enemy. Only spies and persons whose release would endanger the public safety were excepted. In line with this attitude was his order to General Henry W. Halleck authorizing the suspension of the writ in the Military Department of Missouri. In that order he expressly stated that the writ was to be suspended *only* when it was necessary "to secure the public safety and the authority of the United States." Here again we see him looking to the safety of the nation, and not to his own personal aggrandizement.

The obvious reluctance on the part of President Lincoln to suspend the privilege of the writ of habeas corpus gives rise to a logical question: "If he did not wish to suspend the writ, why then did he do it?" The answer is not simple. It is, in fact, very complex, and is based upon the state of affairs which existed throughout the nation at that particular time. No similar situation had ever existed before. As Lincoln himself viewed it, the United States of America were "engaged in a great civil war, testing whether that nation, or any nation so conceived, and so dedicated, can long endure." The nation was torn by conflict and strife, which was in the nature of a "family quarrel"; a type of quarrel characterized by bitterness and intensity found nowhere else. The armed enemy was a potent threat, but the problems thus created were in some respects less perplexing than those created by the intrigue, subversion, and outright treason which existed in certain of the so-called loyal states. Trying to wage a war, and hold off the subversion of the Confederate sympathizers in the North, was comparable to a man trying to fight with his hands tied behind his back. Although the president could ill afford to turn his attention from the armed enemy for a single moment, he was constantly called upon to take steps to prevent active support of the Confederacy in the North. Neither sabotage nor destruction of property was the real problem, however. The real problem was to be found in the group of people who, by word and conduct, sought to undermine the war effort and destroy the morale of the people. What could be done with these people? They could not be summarily executed; yet they could not be allowed to carry on their activities undeterred. These were the people who caused Lincoln to write in anguish:

Must I shoot a simple-minded soldier boy who deserts, while I must not touch a hair of a wily agitator who induces him to desert? . . . I think that in such a case, to silence the agitator, and save the boy, is not only constitutional, but, withal, a great mercy.

Summary judgment and execution he would not accept for the agitator, any more than he could accept a similar fate for the lonely soldier boy who listened to the agitator's siren song. Under these conditions there was no course but to put the agitator in a place which would silence him, and make his whereabouts known at all times. This was the basic reason for the suspension of the writ.

What of the courts? As has already been suggested, *Ex parte Merryman* was in reality the only case which touched upon the precise subject with which we are here concerned. Someone will say, "What about *Ex parte Vallandigham* and *Ex parte Milligan?*" They were both decided after the period which is now under consideration; but even if this were not so, these cases do not in reality touch upon our subject.

Ex parte Vallandigham involved the authority of military tribunals, and though this case went to the Supreme Court, the court avoided the real issue by holding that it was without jurisdiction since a military commission was not a court within the meaning of the provisions of the Judicial Act of 1789, from which Act, appellate jurisdiction was secured by the courts. The war was still in progress when this decision was handed down on February 15, 1864. By choosing the course that it did the Supreme Court found an easy avenue of escape from a troublesome problem. The Vallandigham case decided nothing so far as the suspension of the privilege of the writ of habeas corpus was concerned.

Ex parte Milligan was decided April 3, 1866. It, too, had to do with trial by a military commission, when the civil courts were open and functioning. A careful reading of the opinion in this case will show that the fact that the war was over had a marked and obvious bearing upon the attitude assumed by the court. The decision can be summed up in the court's own words thus:

> "Martial law cannot arise from a threatened invasion. The necessity must be actual and present; the invasion real, such as effectually closes the courts and deposes the civil administration. . . . Martial rule can never exist where the courts are open, and in the proper and unobstructed exercise of their jurisdiction. It is . . . confined to the locality of actual war."

There is ample reason to speculate as to what course the Milligan case would have taken if the war had still been in progress when the decision was handed down. But on the issue of whether the president or the Congress has the power to suspend the privilege of the writ of habeas corpus, there can be no speculation. There was no attempt on the part of the court to resolve this issue in that case.

Ex parte Merryman is the one decision which really considered the question directly. But it was the opinion of only one justice of the Supreme Court serving in the circuit court. It did not, therefore, have the dignity of a Supreme Court decision and, so far as is known, it had the blessing of no other member of the Supreme Court. It was an able opinion which requires respect, but it had frailties, and the reasoning behind it is by no means infallible.

Judge Taney referred to Chief Justice Marshall's opinion in *Ex parte Bollman and Swartout* as authority for his conclusion, but he did not point out that what he was quoting was no more than obiter dictum, and even then, all that Marshall had said was that at any time the public safety required the suspension of the powers vested by the Judiciary Act of 1789 (which gave the United States courts the authority to issue the writ of habeas corpus), it was for Congress and not for the courts to say so. Further, Taney went to some considerable length to point out that the clause of the Constitution authorizing the suspension of the privilege of the writ of habeas corpus is found in Article I, which is apparently devoted to the legislative rather than to the executive branch of the government. But what he did not point out was the fact that this clause, as originally drafted, provided that the privilege should not be "suspended by the Legislature, except upon the most urgent and pressing occasions, and for a limited time not exceeding —— months," and that later, while the powers of the judiciary were under consideration, Gouverneur Morris moved the clause practically as it now stands. It was the Committee on Style and Arrangement which grouped the habeas corpus clause with the other clauses concerning Congress. In contravention of the position taken by Judge Taney there have been suggestions from able sources that the selection of Morris' wording shows clearly that the Constitutional Convention consciously and deliberately rejected phraseology which would have attached the suspending function exclusively to the legislative branch of the government.

There were some other decisions bearing upon the suspension of the privilege of the writ of habeas corpus handed down by the federal courts during the period with which we are now concerned, but none of them is of the stature of *Ex parte Merryman*. All leave much to be desired so far as providing any real help with the problem we are attempting to explore. *Ex parte McQuillon,* decided by Judge Betts of the Southern District of New York on August 5, 1861, recognizes *Ex parte Merryman,* but would seem to damn it with faint praise, if not a bit of cynicism. Judge Betts stated that he was aware of the Merryman decision, and added that, "The questions raised in that case had never been solved." He then proceeds to add insult to injury by concluding that of the Merryman opinion he "would express no opinion whatever, as it would be indecorous on his part to oppose the chief justice." Two other cases are *Ex parte Benedict,* decided by Judge Hall in the Northern District of New York, September 30, 1862, and *Ex parte Field,* decided by Judge Smalley of the District of Vermont, on October 7, 1862. Each of these cases recognizes

Ex parte Merryman, but they appear to be in conflict, and therefore are of no real help in connection with the problem.

What of Congress? President Lincoln called a session of Congress as soon as the conflict was a reality. This was a special, and the first, session of the thirty-seventh Congress. To it he made the report which has already been alluded to in some detail. This was his very first message to the Congress, and it was read to both Houses on July 5, 1862. Bills were immediately introduced dealing with, among other things, what the president had done in connection with the suspension of the privilege of the writ of habeas corpus. Congress liked to talk, and their opinions frequently were flavored, if not actually created, by the policy of the political party to which they belonged. Their partisan quarrels over whether the president did or did not have the authority to suspend the privilege of the writ of habeas corpus dragged on until the session was at an end, and no real action was taken by either House. There was some claim that a very general bill did ratify and confirm all of the acts of the president. There is, however, slight basis for this claim. The most significant thing about the situation which existed is the fact that the first and ideal time for Congress to assert its exclusive right to suspend the privilege of the writ of habeas corpus, if it had such right, had come and gone; and gone in the face of a claim by the president that he had acted lawfully, and in his own right, in suspending the writ.

The second session of the Thirty-seventh Congress convened on December 2, 1861. The session was extended, and the debates were wordy, but the work of the Congress on the subject of the suspension of the privilege of the writ of habeas corpus can be summed up in two words: "More inaction." On December 1, 1862, the Thirty-seventh Congress met for its third session. By this time some members of Congress were beginning to feel that it was too late for Congress to assert exclusive jurisdiction in the matter. On December 22 Senator Lane of Indiana expressed the view held by many:

"Gentleman speak of the President's usurpation of authority. The Constitution authorizes the suspension of the privilege of the writ of *habeas corpus,* without saying in express terms who shall exercise that authority. The President has done it. It is an accomplished fact and cannot be undone. Suppose we now say that, in our opinion, the authority is given to Congress, can we change his convictions of duty or control his actions? Such a course will only bring about a conflict of authority between Congress and the President, and weaken the power of both."

A similar thought was expressed by Senator Collamer of Vermont, on January 9, 1863, when he said:

"The Executive is just as much clothed with authority, and bound in duty when called on, to give construction to the Constitution in the execution of it as we are, and his decision is just as binding as ours. . . . It is not common courtesy for one department of this Government to say to another, 'We say the Constitution means so and so, and we are infallible.' The judiciary, when the question arises before them in the proper form, decide the Constitution in the particular suit, and that is all there is to their decision."

These were Republicans who were willing to concede the authority of the president. The Democrats were quite unwilling to make any such concession, and sought to make political capital of the situation, although they offered no legislative program of their own. On March 3, 1863, what is now known as the Habeas Corpus Act was passed. It was thereafter signed by the president, and became the law of the land.

The Habeas Corpus Act, as it was passed, was so loosely drawn that one side contended that it recognized the right of the president to suspend the privilege of the writ of habeas corpus, and the other side, with equal vigor, contended that it did no such thing: that it only put the stamp of legality on what had already been done. The existence of this dispute, even among the supporters of the Act, makes it evident that nothing that Congress did gives us any assistance in solving the riddle of whether President Lincoln acted within or without legal authority.

In adopting the Habeas Corpus Act, Congress put the dispute at rest for the moment. The Constitution provides that "The Privilege of the Writ of Habeas Corpus shall not be suspended, unless in Cases of Rebellion or Invasion the public Safety may require it." This certainly implies that someone has the right of suspension. But the question is, "Who?"

President Lincoln claimed the right for the Executive. That he honestly believed that he had the right, and was sincere in his claim, is beyond any reasonable doubt. Congress, in the face of this claim, chose to do nothing. When Congress did act, it made no positive claim to an exclusive right, and in fact tendered to Lincoln more power than he had ever indicated he wished. Chief Justice Taney was the only man to dispute openly the right claimed by Lincoln for the Executive.

Taney was an honorable man, and believed what he wrote in his opinion in the Merryman case with a fervor of no less intensity than that of Lincoln for his views. It is, however, inescapable that the old gentleman, in his zeal to protect the apparent legal right of an individual citizen, lost sight of the precarious position in which the whole nation found itself. Taney focused the light of justice upon the individual liberty Americans so thoroughly cherish, but Lincoln saved the nation, without which all, including our liberty as individuals, would have been lost.

DAVID MILLER

Lincoln and the Sioux Outbreak

ℰ

ABRAHAM LINCOLN is most often remembered for his humanity. During his years as a wartime president, Lincoln time and again displayed his patience with human foibles and his love for his fellow man. This was never better demonstrated than in the dreadful second year of the Civil War when, against the grim panorama of a divided and battle-torn nation, a wave of carnage and horror swept the prairies and forests of Minnesota.

The summer of 1862 was at best an exasperating era in Lincoln's career. While the Union was winning in the West, it was definitely losing in the East. The capture of Memphis and Corinth, the fall of New Orleans, and other Union successes were all but nullified by McClellan's expensive failures in the Peninsular Campaign and Robert E. Lee's emergence as a formidable military genius for the Confederacy.

On August 15, far from the White House, a gaunt Indian, who physically resembled Lincoln, entered Myrick's trading post at Redwood agency in Minnesota. The Indian was Little Crow, chief of the Mdewakanton band of Santee Sioux. Little Crow had come repeatedly to Redwood agency on behalf of the Santees to ask for rations of flour and beef promised by the white men in the Mendota Treaty of 1851. Now, eleven years later, beef shipments were sold to whites while traders like Myrick pawned off spoiled pork and flour on the starving Santees, and charged them exorbitant prices.

For years white settlers had been making inroads into the

sacred land of the Santees until the Indians held only a narrowing strip of their once vast territory. Their best hunting grounds had long since been plowed into wheat fields by white farmers. Now the traders, sparked by Myrick, were abruptly cutting off the Indians' last source of food. Signs appeared in all the trading posts: NO CREDIT FOR INDIANS. With hard cash lacking, it was a sentence of death for the Santees.

In Washington the president was not unaware of the problem. Impending starvation among the Indians had reached such a point in July that Lincoln had sent his personal secretary, John G. Nicolay, out to Minnesota to investigate.

As yet, however, no overt acts of violence among the tribes had occurred. Minnesota's Governor Alexander Ramsey continued his wartime policy of stripping forts of their garrisons to provide additional regiments for the Union Army, which so sorely needed troop replacements.

The Sunday following his visit to the trading post Little Crow attended regular morning services at the local Redwood Episcopal Church. Outwardly unruffled, tall and majestic in spite of the castoff though neat white man's garb, Little Crow exhibited much the same mixture of dignity and quiet humor that was so characteristic of Lincoln. Aside from beaded moccasins and the gleaming black braids that framed his gaunt copper features, the Santee chief might have been a rector, or even a politician. His oratory, though in Sioux rather than English, was well-known to all those present who had long considered him a steadfast friend of the white man. At forty-two, Little Crow was a respected man. His presence caused only passing comment among the stolid German and English farmers and agency employees who made up the congregation. After the service the chief shook hands with fellow members of the church, mounted his horse, and rode away.

Minutes later, some forty miles to the north at Acton post office, four young Wahpeton Sioux, Santees married to women of Little Crow's Mdewakanton band, entered the homestead cabin of Robinson Jones. An eating place for wayfarers as well as a post office, the Jones home was known as a "public house." Neighbors frequently gathered there and Indians would often drop by to sample the cheap whisky Jones sold them by the drink.

The four young Wahpetons were already rowdy and boisterous. One of them, anxious to prove that he was not afraid of a white man, boasted that he would shoot the postmaster. Although he understood little Sioux, Jones sensed danger. Herding the womenfolk and children into the house, he turned to face the Indians and was shot dead by rifle fire. Two other homesteaders, Jones's son-in-law, Howard Baker, and Viranus Webster, were also shot down. Jones's wife was killed when she opened the door. The Joneses' adopted daughter, Clara, was murdered as the Indians raced away. In as many minutes five whites lay dead. Word spread quickly to other Santee villages. One by one, the lesser chiefs faced a stubborn reality. While few of them professed any love for the whites, they were young and their authority limited to their own bands. None was powerful enough to lead a war. Only one leader among the Santees had the prestige and stature that was needed: Little Crow.

The chief of the Mdewakanton was hesitant, however, when the other chiefs appealed to him to lead them. Little Crow's mind must have raced with misgivings. For a long time he had advocated farming. He lived like a white man in a frame house. He was assisting agency employees to build him a new brick building. He was a civilized Indian and white men called him friend. Moreover, he was two years past the age when Indians usually gave up fighting.

Yet he was a man impelled, like Lincoln, by a sense of destiny. His people were starving and needed his leadership. It was a time when Gargantuan forces were clashing, as one race attempted to conquer and dislodge another. So Little Crow, against his better judgment, cast his lot with those who

looked to him for leadership. With his Mdewakantons as a
nucleus, he rallied the other Santee or Isanyati tribes: Wahpetons, Wahpekutes, and Sissetons. Seeking to unite all seven
"council fires" of the Sioux Nation, Little Crow sent the pipe
to his western kinsmen, the Yankton, Yanktonai, and Teton
Sioux, in an invitation to join him in war. Overnight the
frontier was ablaze as Little Crow led the bloodiest Indian
uprising in history.

On Monday, August 18, at daybreak, traders and agency
employees at Redwood agency were awakened by warwhoops
and gunfire. Rushing from their homes, they were shot down
in their doorways by Santee warriors fully accoutered for
war. Although early reports indicated that "the whites had
not the slightest suspicion of the coming storm," Little Crow
had given warning to at least two old friends at the agency:
Philander Prescott, the government interpreter; and the
Reverend S. D. Hinman, the Episcopal rector and missionary. Apparently satisfied that their safe departure fulfilled
any obligations he owed the whites, the Mdewakanton chief,
bedecked in buckskin and feathers and with a savage yell
rising in his throat, joined his fighting men in a grisly carnage.
"Once he had supped full with horrors, he outdid all the
rival chiefs in zeal and bloodshed."

One trader, Francis La Bathe, was slain on his store
counter. Another, who "had been accustomed to laying his
hand on the scale when weighing out groceries to the Indians," was caught and several warriors "cut off his hand and
put it on the scale to see how much he had cheated them."

Ferryman Hubert Miller, unsung hero of the hour, carried
load after load of terror-stricken refugees to the far shore of
the Minnesota River. Returning for a final boatload, he was
killed in mid-river. With the Santees in hot pursuit, those
who had already made the crossing were far from safe. During a harrowing fifteen-mile race downriver to Fort Ridgely,
seven more whites were brought down by Indians.

Later in the day Little Crow led his raiders in a wide

sweep through settlements surrounding the agency. Farms were sacked and burned, farmers and their sons were slaughtered, young women were hauled away as captives. Children were spared or butchered according to the whim of individual warriors. As the Sioux struck one settlement after another, entire counties were drenched in blood. In the first twenty-four hours of the outbreak over two hundred whites were killed. Hundreds more, mostly women, were taken captive.

Next morning Lean Bear, a war chief under Little Crow, led a war party against the unprotected settlements that ringed Lake Shetek in southwestern Minnesota, wiping out half the whites in that area. Terrified settlers began streaming into Fort Ridgely, nearest military outpost.

The fort, undermanned and jammed with refugees, was Little Crow's next target. While white women at the outpost begged the soldiers to shoot them lest they fall into the hands of the Sioux, the Santee chief marshaled his warriors for a full-scale assault. More refugees poured into the fort. Little Crow let them through, for their wholesale destruction there would save his warriors pursuing the whites all over the countryside. During the confusion two small detachments of troops made it through from Fort Snelling. As ready as they would ever be, the reinforced garrison waited for the dreaded attack. All through the long day and night of August 19 not an Indian was seen.

Then on the morning of the 20th, Little Crow rode alone and unarmed within hailing distance of the fort's west gate and demanded a parley. Settlers blinked in wonder. They could scarcely believe that the bronze rider, whose handsome face and half-naked body glistened with fresh war paint, was their former friend.

The garrison gathered along the west parapet to watch for signs of Indian trickery. Sharp firing from the fort's east side announced Little Crow's real purpose, to divert the whites while his warriors stormed the unguarded east wall. So successful was the ruse that howling Santee warriors burst through the second line of defense, invading barracks buildings within the fort.

Only the last-minute firing of rusty old cannon at point-blank range by the fort's gun crew saved the day for the whites. Little Crow and his fighting men were appalled at the roar and discharge of the "wagon guns." Slightly wounded, the Santee chief rallied his warriors for another charge. At that moment a fresh blast of cannister and grape thundered from the cannon, scattering the Indians in disorder. Despite Little Crow's exhortations, the warriors fled in panic.

Next morning the Santee chief managed to stir up his fighting men for another mass assault. But when the cannon blazed again, the warriors lost their zest for battle and demanded that Little Crow lead them against less formidable objectives.

Little Crow had staked everything on his attack on Fort Ridgely. Now his hopes of driving the white men east of the Mississippi were fading. He must win a sharp victory or his fighting men would fall away from him.

His fury mounting, Little Crow led his warriors toward New Ulm, a few miles downriver from Fort Ridgely. Flooded with refugees, the little German settlement seemed completely defenseless. Little Crow knew that here the whites had no wagon guns to frighten off his warriors. Early Saturday, August 23, the Sioux struck.

Brandishing war clubs, bows, and spears, Little Crow's fighting force swept like a grass fire toward New Ulm. Green volunteer troops fell back in dismay at the frightening spectacle. The west side of town was abandoned to the Indians, who quickly used the deserted houses as cover. The militia held the houses to the east in spite of increasing Sioux pressure.

After setting fire to several buildings Little Crow massed his warriors for a charge through town. As flames licked the sky, the entire west part of New Ulm went up in smoke. Using the smoke as a screen, the Indians charged, but were repulsed by a withering volley of gunfire. A vigorous counter-charge by the whites caught Little Crow off guard and drove his warriors beyond the town limits.

The militia did the unexpected by burning most of what was left of New Ulm. One of the town's brick houses was hurriedly converted into a fortress and the rest of the day and through the night the volunteers and refugees dug entrenchments around the improvised redoubt. By morning they were ready for the worst. But the expected renewal of the attack never came. Little Crow had again lowered his sights and turned to more vulnerable targets.

Although he had been twice repulsed by the whites, the Santee chief still regarded the uprising as a success for the Sioux. They had won back much of their best hunting territory, had captured many prisoners and much plunder. Best of all, the Indians were no longer starving. Food stores taken from the whites were distributed among the Santee lodges, and Little Crow was a great chief in the minds of his people.

Most of Minnesota now lay open to Sioux war parties, which raided east into Wisconsin, southwest into Iowa, northeast into the deep forests around Lake Superior. One group of warriors again struck at Spirit Lake on the Iowa–Minnesota line, where a bloody trail had been blazed only five years earlier by Little Crow's kinsman Inkpaduta, Scarlet Top. Far to the north, for the first time in many years, the Sioux penetrated the country of their old enemies, the Chippewas.

The Chippewas were themselves on the verge of outbreak. Several whites had been murdered at Breckinridge, presumably by Indians. The northern part of Minnesota was rife with rumors that Hole-in-the-Day, head chief of the Chippewas, was about to join forces with Little Crow.

Immediately east of the Santee country the Winnebago tribe was also restless. Chief Little Priest had sympathized openly with Little Crow. After the defense of Fort Ridgely and New Ulm by the whites, however, the Winnebagos were undecided. Taking no chances, white settlers in Mankato conspired to murder Little Priest, whose head was cut off and paraded around Mankato's streets.

On August 26 Governor Ramsey telegraphed President Lincoln advising him that "half the population of the State are fugitives." The following day John Nicolay wired the chief executive from St. Paul to say that "we are in the midst of a terrible and exciting Indian war. Thus far the massacre of innocent white settlers has been fearful. A wild panic prevails in nearly one-half the State. All are rushing to the frontier to defend settlers."

Lincoln wired back to Ramsey, "Attend to the Indians." The president may well have been deeply disturbed at news from Minnesota, coming as it did when Pope's position in northern Virginia was growing increasingly tenuous, and the campaign to be known as Second Bull Run was already under way.

Both Lincoln and Secretary of War Stanton were receptive to Ramsey's suggestion that "a well-drilled force . . . resist the overwhelming force of Indians now attacking our frontier settlements," and authorized the release of paroled Union prisoners from Benton Barracks at St. Louis for the purpose. Insubordination and mutiny among parolees at other camps added to the replacement of frontier garrisons by "galvanized Yankees," but no reference to the actual service of paroled regiments in Minnesota has been found except for a portion of the Third Minnesota Volunteers first requested by Governor Ramsey.

On the heels of news of the Union disaster at Second Bull Run on August 29 and 30, word reached Washington from Ramsey that "he had swallowed his pride" and called on his old political enemy, Colonel Henry H. Sibley, to take command of all troops in Minnesota. Sibley was not only a fine tactician, but had a profound knowledge of Indians, particularly the Sioux, even speaking their language. Fourteen hundred whites answered his call for volunteers. Reaching Fort Ridgely on August 28, Sibley whipped his untrained force into fighting shape while he assigned burial details to the task of interring settlers killed by Indians in outlying areas.

Such a burial detail was Major J. R. Brown's company of two hundred men dispatched to Birch Coulee the night of September 1. The Sioux had been watching Brown's every move. Another opportunity for a decisive strike seemed to have presented itself to Little Crow. As dawn broke on the 2nd, Little Crow and his warriors lashed out at the bivouacked soldiers.

In a short, terrible battle almost every horse of Brown's command was killed and the company faced with annihilation. Sibley rushed out with reinforcements, arriving just in time to rescue Brown and fall back to Fort Ridgely. The Santees withdrew after inflicting heavy casualties.

Sibley realized that his recruits were not yet ready for a full-scale clash with Little Crow's warriors. Moreover, knowing Indians, he feared that white prisoners captive in the Sioux camps might be slaughtered if his next move failed.

Not only did Sibley have the fate of the prisoners to worry him; he was also plagued by the chance that Little Crow and his warriors might slip through his fingers and escape unscathed west to Dakota Territory. As he dawdled, Sibley became the center of a storm of abuse and criticism from restive newspapers throughout the state. One dubbed him "a snail who falls back on his authority and assumed dignity and refuses to march." Another referred to him as "the state undertaker with his company of grave diggers," alluding to his burial of hundreds of dead settlers.

Jeered at most of all for his moderation in dealing with Little Crow, Sibley at last took action. On September 18 he marched against the Santee chief's main encampment on Yellow Medicine River. He had with him 1450 troops and two pieces of artillery, but only ten days' provisions, all that was available. He had "but twenty-seven horses, all of the others having been killed at Birch Coulee. His troops were badly clothed and had no blankets." Three hundred of the men were members of the Third Minnesota Volunteers, a paroled regiment. Altogether it hardly seemed a formidable fighting force to pit against several thousand Indians.

Surprise was out of the question. Santee scouts watched every foot of Sibley's advance. Sibley had learned that the Sioux would not attack until his column had passed Yellow Medicine River. He did not find out until later that Little Crow was up most of the night arguing with the other chiefs; Little Crow wanted to attack Sibley that night. But he was overruled by the council and "agreed to wait until Sibley's force was strung out and indefensible the next morning."

Near Wood Lake the road to Yellow Medicine passed through rugged terrain. Beyond the lake it entered a heavily-timbered canyon, an ideal spot for an ambush. Little Crow divided his warriors into three large bands, one hidden on either side of the road, the third ready to seal off retreat after the column had entered the canyon.

The elaborate ambush was foiled by a small party of white hunters who unwittingly approached the canyon from the opposite direction and drew the fire of overanxious warriors. Halting the column before it had entered the canyon, Sibley sent a patrol in force to investigate the gunfire. The patrol arrived in time to extricate the hunters from the Indians' crossfire, which "cut the leaves from the trees overhead so that they fell in showers." After an hour of intense fighting the patrol fell back to Sibley's now well-established battle lines.

Little Crow signaled charge after charge against the troops. Hordes of Sioux horsemen hurled themselves and their mounts into the fray. As the battle raged, the furious onslaught began to take toll of the soldiers. Sibley realized his position was becoming untenable. He had to act quickly or attempt a costly retreat.

Knowing the demoralizing effect artillery often had on Indians, he ordered up his two antiquated cannon and had them readied for firing. Corroded with rust, the old field-pieces barely held together as they thundered into the on-coming warriors. As at Fort Ridgely, the roar of the guns struck terror into the otherwise fearless Sioux. From a hilltop Little Crow watched the wagon guns pound his dream of victory into rubble.

The Santees wavered, then broke. Sibley ordered a charge and a battalion of troops left the line, driving the bewildered Indians before them. Desultory firing kept up briefly, but there was no more Sioux charges. After two hours of fighting the Indians withdrew.

"Scatter over the plains like wolves!" Little Crow shouted to his tribesmen. It was a needless last command. Broken, the warriors were scattering in all directions. The Battle of Wood Lake was done, a clear-cut victory for the whites. Nine soldiers had been killed and over forty wounded. But thirty Sioux were killed. Sixteen dead Indians were left on the bat-tlefield. Sibley refused to allow Little Crow to take the bodies.

Marching through Santee territory in the days that fol-lowed, Sibley rescued hundreds of white hostages held cap-tive among the dispersed bands and rounded up more than fifteen hundred Sioux. The Indians were herded into an im-provised village called Camp Release. Sibley at once de-manded the release of all whites still in Sioux hands.

On September 26, friendly Indians who had taken no part in the uprising led nearly three hundred white refugees into Fort Ridgely. For their pains the friendlies were taken pris-oner and forced to join the Indians already quartered at Camp Release, now a concentration camp for all Indians in southern Minnesota, regardless of tribe or affiliation to Little Crow. Seizures and surrenders swelled the total there to about two thousand.

Sibley sought to accomplish two things: to seize such In-dians as were handy; and to "hang the villains." Before he had decided upon a legal process whereby he could deal with those accused of guilt in the uprising, he ordered the arrest of more than four hundred adult Indian males, who were clapped in irons and thrown into log jails. Then he wrote General John Pope, in charge of fighting Indians in the Military Department of the Northwest since his defeat at Second Bull Run: "They will be forthwith executed. Perhaps it will be a stretch of my authority. If so, necessity must be my justification."

General Pope was of like mind. "It is my purpose utterly to exterminate the Sioux," he answered, instructing the colonel that "they are to be treated as maniacs or wild beasts."

Late in September, following his promotion to brigadier general, Sibley issued a special order creating a judicial device "to try summarily the Indians and mixed bloods engaged in raids and massacres." He called his device a military commission. Writing to President Lincoln, Governor Ramsey called it a military court. Others called it a court-martial. All seemed to overlook the fact that Indians were not members of the armed forces, hence technically not subject to military law.

From the first the procedure denied the defendants the right of counsel. Acting as interpreters and chaplains, several missionaries were in effect defense attorneys. But their position was primarily that of translating testimony rather than giving advice to the prisoners. The Sioux were at an added disadvantage in that it was tribal custom to recite one's individual exploits in battle or in raids as a means of attracting deserved recognition. A warlike act, however bloody or one-sided the contest, was deemed honorable if performed against an enemy. The responsibility of determining who was friend or foe rested with chiefs or lesser leaders. Moreover, an Indian made no distinction as to man, woman, or child when it came to an enemy. All were fair game during a war. So the defendants were "given to boasting of their crimes, and very few of them were inclined to deny their guilt when charged."

With few exceptions the prisoners at Camp Release were

arraigned on charges based on the testimony of women and children who had been held captive by the Sioux. They would blurt out, "He killed my husband!" or "He killed my parents!" Others were convicted on the say-so of a Negro named Godfrey, who was married to a squaw, and who was finally let off with ten years imprisonment for turning state's evidence.

The trials continued through October and into November. After members of the commission became familiar with details of the different battles, as many as forty-two Indians were sometimes tried in a day. Five minutes often would dispose of a case. By November 5 the commission had tried three hundred and ninety-two prisoners and had sentenced three hundred and six to be hanged.

On November 7 the convicted Sioux were chained, placed in wagons, and hauled to Camp Lincoln, just outside Mankato. The wagon train of soldiers and Indians stretched along the road for two miles. At New Ulm the convicts were attacked by a mob made up largely of women whose relatives had been killed in the outbreak. A number of Indians were badly injured.

As a matter of form, the names of the condemned men were telegraphed to President Lincoln. The telegram cost over four hundred dollars to transmit and excited much criticism across the country. Even the New York *Times* was moved to suggest that the cost of the telegram be deducted from the salary of the military commander responsible.

Governor Ramsey was informed that "the Sioux prisoners will be executed, unless the President forbids it." Hardly anyone in Minnesota expected that the chief executive would interfere.

On November 10, however, Lincoln requested "the full and complete record of the convictions; if the record does not fully indicate the more guilty and influential of the culprits, please have a careful statement made on these points and forward to me." Aware of the criticism brewing over the telegram, the president added, "Send by mail."

When the president received records of the trial, he observed they were far from complete. He assigned clerks George Whiting and Francis Ruggles to the task of trying to distinguish between those "guilty of crime and those guilty only of participation in battles." Such a distinction was vitally important to Lincoln. He "did not propose to give the Confederates reason to declare to the world that he had agreed to the execution of three hundred prisoners of war."

Lincoln's approach to the matter of the Sioux outbreak is all the more remarkable in light of his own pioneer heritage. A product of the frontier, he might well have been expected to throw the weight of his office on the side of the Minnesota settlers, and to deal harshly with all the Indians concerned. His family history included deadly conflicts with Indians, his grandfather having been killed by a Shawnee warrior at Green River in Kentucky in 1784.

But Lincoln's own past indicated the trend of his thinking. During the Black Hawk War of 1832 young Abraham Lincoln, newly elected captain of a volunteer militia company, had protested when fellow volunteers had dragged an old Indian into camp and were about to hang him from the nearest tree. "Men, this must not be done," Lincoln had told them. An upstart in the company had called Lincoln a coward, whereupon the lanky captain called his bluff and told him, "Choose your weapons." The old Indian turned out to be a friendly. Lincoln had saved his life. Moreover, he had saved his comrades from committing a murder.

It was the same sense of justice, tempered with charity, that prompted Lincoln to intervene in the mass executions in Minnesota. On December 6, by order of the president, the names of thirty-nine Indians finally chosen to die were submitted to Sibley. Lincoln instructed Sibley, now a brigadier general, to hold the other two hundred and sixty-four condemned prisoners "subject to further orders, taking care that they neither escape, nor are subjected to any unlawful violence."

The president's action enraged the whites of Minnesota. Residents of Mankato, New Ulm, and other communities involved in the uprising formed a vigilance committee and set out one night early in December to remove the three hundred and three imprisoned Indians. If the government would not punish the Sioux, the committee would take matters into its own hands.

Approaching the prison at Camp Lincoln on the outskirts of Mankato, the mob found it surrounded by soldiers. Confronted by fixed bayonets, the vigilantes lamely explained that they were merely admiring the prison by moonlight. Its ardor dampened, the mob dispersed.

First set for December 19, the hanging was postponed one week due to the shortage of rope in Mankato. The stoic composure of the thirty-nine Sioux prisoners under sentence of death broke for the first time on December 24. Imprisoned in a stone jail, the condemned were allowed to bid final farewells to relatives and friends from Camp Release. As they sent their last messages, those who had wives and children were moved to tears. Many advised their children to become Christians and to lead a life of good will toward the white man. On Christmas Day all seemed resigned to death. Some sat motionless on the floor of their cell, staring resolutely into space, as lifeless as statues. A few sang mournfully:

> "Our women pass to and fro
> As they gather up their dead.
> The voice of weeping comes back to us."

During their final days in prison the condemned Indians were consoled by the Reverend T. S. Williamson, a Protestant missionary and doctor, and Father Ravaux, a Catholic priest. On Christmas night all but two of the Sioux prisoners were baptized into the Christian faith. Onlookers, including members of the press and prison guards, were much impressed by the "sincere feeling" showed by the Indians during the services.

At midnight a last-minute pardon from President Lincoln arrived for Round Wind, one of the condemned Sioux. Dr. Williamson had collected evidence which proved this Indian had actually helped whites to escape during the massacres.

At seven-thirty in the morning of December 26 the chains and leg irons were removed from the prisoners and their arms were tied. The Indians, apparently relieved because the ordeal was nearly over, smiled and seemed cheerful as they chatted with each other and shook hands with the soldiers to bid them good-by.

At nine o'clock they were arranged in a row around the cell. The three half-breeds and several of the full bloods were dressed like white men. But most of the Indians donned brilliant war paint and tribal decorations. Nearly all displayed religious emblems which they wore in a prominent place. The chaplains read prayers and spoke comfortingly to the Indians. Every trace of Sioux bravado seemed gone. Tears appeared in the prisoners' eyes as they listened.

Outside, crowds of people had been gathering since daybreak to stare at a newly built structure which stood on the bank of the Minnesota River across from the stone jail. Built of stout white oak timbers, it was a twenty-four-foot-square gallows. Forty hangman's ropes, ten on each side of the square, swung from the scaffolding. Beneath the ropes a raised platform ran all the way around the gallows. The platform could be dropped by cutting a single rope at the foot of the scaffold.

By nine-thirty, troops under the command of Colonel Stephen Miller, military head of the army post at Mankato, formed solid ranks around the gallows. Between five and six thousand civilians thronged behind the soldiers, on housetops and at windows, and along the river banks.

At the foot of the gallows stood Captain John Duly, nervously fingering the blade of an ax. John Duly had asked for the job of executioner. Three of his children had been killed by Indians and his wife and two other children were still supposedly captives of Little Crow. Now he had just been offered five dollars by David J. Davis to let him cut the rope, but Duly had turned him down.

Every eye was turned toward the jail. Between two lines of soldiers, thirty-eight Indians quickly filed from the building. Seeing the gallows for the first time, the Sioux prisoners broke into a wild, weird chant. They mounted the scaffold without assistance and took their places beneath the dangling nooses. None faltered, not even an old man.

"White men, we will show you how to die!" one of the condemned men shouted.

The doomed Indians sang and shouted as the soldiers pulled muslin caps over their eyes and adjusted the ropes around their necks. Some even helped adjust the nooses. Feet shuffled and bodies swayed to an insistent rhythm. Over and over the Sioux sang:

"Wahiyedo! I am here!"

This was not a cry of defiance, but an improvised chant in which each singer assured the others they would die together. The wail of voices was occasionally interrupted by a piercing scream, far more unsettling to the watching whites than to the condemned Indians. Few spectators in the crowd were ever to forget the weird swaying of the hooded figures, the wild singing, and the last pitiful attempts of the Indians to hold hands.

At ten-sixteen the signal officer, Major Brown, gave three distinct taps on his drum. Captain John Duly poised his ax and swung. He missed. Still nervous, he again hefted the ax. This time his aim was true. The platform dropped with a crash, abruptly cutting off the doleful chant. The crowd stood stunned.

Then a young soldier whose family had been slain by one

of the executed Indians pointed at the convulsing body and cheered. His shout swelled into a deafening roar as the huge throng joined in the cheering.

Most of the Indians died quietly. Two held hands in death. Several kicked savagely. One man, heavier than the others, snapped his rope and fell down the river bank. Soldiers hurriedly ran his body up on one of the spare ropes. Death by hanging was a severe fate for a Sioux, for he believed that the spirit of a man hanged could never leave his body through his mouth to reach the Happy Hunting Ground. A choking rope might permanently imprison the soul.

Within twenty minutes all of the Indians were pronounced dead. Four teams of horses were driven up to the scaffold and the bodies were cut down and hauled to a long trench on the river bank for burial.

The end of 1862 found the Sioux entirely driven out of their old territory in Minnesota. Except for some fifteen hundred prisoners transferred from Camp Release to Fort Snelling near Minneapolis, there was not a Sioux Indian in the state. On February 21, 1863, Congress formally abrogated all existing treaties with the Sioux.

Little Crow and four thousand followers were still at large, making winter headquarters at Devil's Lake near the northeastern corner of Dakota Territory and not far from British America. Through the winter and spring of 1863 nearly thirty thousand Indians of various tribes—Yankton, Yanktonai, and Teton Sioux, Cheyennes, Arikaras, and even Chippewas—gathered, mostly out of curiosity, to hear Little Crow's frequent exhortations. The Santee chief proclaimed the whites as swindlers, liars, and cowards, but admitted that they had become numerous and that keeping them away was a job for all the tribes. "United action was the only way the Plains country could be saved for the Indians." Little Crow's "famed eloquence won attention and sympathy, but did not achieve unity." Few grievances that he recited applied, thus far, to any but the Santees. White emigration was a vague threat to most of his listeners. Each tribe had separate interests and problems, and lacked a common cause with other Indians that would impel its members to accept Little Crow's authority in a unified force. All but a few held back when Little Crow led small-scale raids during the spring of 1863.

Meanwhile, as Doane Robinson relates in "The South Dakota Historical Collections": ". . . General Pope, acting upon the belief that Little Crow had assembled a large army of hostiles in the neighborhood of Devil's Lake, fixed upon a plan of campaign by which he hoped to crush at one blow the hostility of the [Sioux]. . . . Pope's plan contemplated sending two columns of troops into the Indian country, one under Sibley to cross Dakota Territory by way of Devil's Lake, and the other to go up the Missouri under Sully, and the two columns to catch and crush the hostiles between them, as they came to a junction upon the upper Missouri."

Sibley rendezvoused his troops on the upper Minnesota at a new outpost called Camp Pope. He left the outpost at a leisurely pace, on June 16, 1863, with two hundred and twenty-five wagons to cart his supplies. By the end of July, having moved at an average of fifteen miles a day, Sibley's cumbersome column reached a point forty miles from Devil's Lake and established a permanent camp called Atchison, from which he sent out scouting parties to try to locate the Indians. One such party picked up an exhausted sixteen-year-old Indian boy, who claimed he was a chief and demanded to be taken to the commander of the troops who had captured him. Before Sibley he made a statement of which the following is a part:

"I am the son of Little Crow; my name is Wowinapa. . . . Father hid after the soldiers beat us last fall. He told me he could not fight against the white men, but would . . . steal horses from them . . . and then he would go away off. Father . . . wanted me to go with him to carry his bundles. . . . There were no horses . . . we were hungry. . . . Father and I were picking red berries near Scattered Lake. . . .

It was near night. He was hit the first time in the side, just above the hip. . . . He was shot the second time . . . in the side, near the shoulder. This was the shot that killed him. He told me he was killed and asked me for water. He died immediately after. . . ."

Sibley concluded that the boy was telling the truth when he learned that on July 3, 1863, a farmer named Nathan Lamson and his son Chauncey, deer hunting in the Big Woods about six miles north of Hutchinson in McLeod County, Minnesota, had surprised two Indians picking berries. Since no Sioux was considered friendly, the elder Lampson fired, wounding one of the Indians. Chauncey Lampson shot him dead. The other Indian got away.

Although the 1863 campaign against the Sioux was ended, Little Crow's crusade against the settlers was taken up by other leaders: Sitting Bull, Red Cloud, and Crazy Horse, who waged sporadic warfare against the whites for nearly thirty years in Dakota and Wyoming.

Thanks to President Lincoln's continuing intercession and interest in the captive Sioux remaining in Minnesota, the prisoners at Fort Snelling were removed by river steamer to Davenport, Iowa. Little Crow's son was tried by one of General Sibley's military commissions and sentenced to death by hanging for having helped his father try to steal horses near Hutchinson. When the army's Judge Advocate General disapproved of the proceedings, Wowinapa was sent to Davenport to join the others. Their sentences were revoked three years later. Renouncing agency life, the Indians took claims in Dakota Territory and followed the white man's road. Upon his release from prison Wowinapa changed his name to Thomas Wakeman and became an active church member and a deacon.

The white settlers could draw a deep breath at last. Peace had come to stay in Minnesota.

JUSTIN TURNER

Lincoln and the Hampton Roads Peace Conference

℘

THROUGHOUT the Civil War there were many discussions and proposals by prominent men relating to a reconciliation of the differences between the North and the South. The general opinion in the North was that the war would be over in a short time and the seceded states would return to the Union. As the war dragged, the populace became war-weary and the opposition press clamored for the administration to terminate hostilities. As pressure mounted for peace, several eminent statesmen and editors were parties to meetings held for the purpose of arranging a peace.

The only official conference in this connection, and the only one in which President Lincoln participated, was the meeting at Hampton Roads on February 3, 1865. This meeting is reminiscent of the abortive conference during the Revolutionary War between Benjamin Franklin, John Adams, and Edward Rutledge, representing the Continental Congress, and General Sir William Howe and Earl Richard Howe of England, which was held at Staten Island in September 1776 for the purpose of effecting a reconciliation.

On July 4, 1863, while the Battle of Gettysburg was being concluded, Alexander H. Stephens, Vice-President of the Confederacy, was attempting to reach Washington as a commissioner of the Confederate government for the purpose of holding a conference with President Lincoln. While Lincoln was opposed to having Stephens meet with him in Washington, he considered sending someone to meet with Stephens at Fort Monroe. Lincoln's Cabinet, however, objected to such a meeting, and as a result Stephens was halted before he reached Washington and was obliged to return to Richmond.

A secret peace mission originated with Reverend Colonel James Frazier Jaquess, a Methodist clergyman from Illinois who raised the Illinois Seventh Regiment Volunteers. He was permitted to cross the lines in company with James R. Gilmore, author and lecturer. An interview with Jefferson Davis on July 17, 1864, was unproductive, and both emissaries left Richmond on July 21.

Horace Greeley, the influential editor of the New York *Tribune,* had importuned Lincoln to meet with Confederate ambassadors in Canada to discuss peace terms. Greeley had been highly critical of the President's policy, but Lincoln could not very well disregard Greeley's desire to meet with the Confederate representatives in an endeavor to reach an agreement. On July 18, 1864, Lincoln sent his secretary, John Hay, to meet Greeley with the following message:

To Whom it May Concern:

Any proposition which embraces the restoration of peace, the integrity of the whole Union, and the abandonment of slavery, and which comes by and with an authority that can control the armies now at war against the United States, will be received and considered by the executive government of the United States, and will be met by liberal terms on other substantial and collateral points, and the bearer or bearers thereof shall have safe conduct both ways.

Greeley had planned to bring the commissioners to Washington without mentioning terms at all, and to involve them deeply in negotiations before revealing any terms or conditions. Lincoln's message resulted in checkmating Greeley's intentions. Greeley delivered the President's message to the Confederate agents at Niagara Falls in Canada and returned to New York disappointed and chagrined, the butt of editorials in Bennett's *Herald* and Raymond's *Times*.

As early as December 16, 1864, a Mr. Turner of North Carolina introduced a resolution in the Confederate House of Representatives requesting President Davis, with consent of the Senate, to appoint a commission "to tender to the Government of the United States a Conference for negotiating an honorable peace." On the same day a Mr. McMullin also introduced a resolution upon the subject of peace . . . "whilst it is not expedient and would be incompatible with the dignity of the Confederate States to send Commissioners to Washington City for the purpose of securing a cessation of hostilities, yet it would be . . . proper that the house . . . should dispatch . . . to some convenient point, a body of Commissioners . . . to meet and confer" with the U.S. peace commissioners. Other resolutions were also adopted within the next few days pertaining to negotiating a peace. These resolutions were the first serious indication on the part of Southern officials that they would favor resolving the differences that then existed if a reasonable peace could be obtained.

Grant was applying the final pressure upon Lee before Richmond when on January 29, 1865, three Confederate commissioners presented themselves at his headquarters near City Point, asking for a safe conduct to proceed to Washington for a conference with President Lincoln. All three commissioners were prominent and distinguished statesmen who, prior to Fort Sumter, had adopted a moderate position as opposed to that of the Southern firebrand radicals.

Robert Mercer Taliaferro Hunter had been a member of Congress and served as speaker of the House of Representatives. He also had served as senator, was chairman of the powerful finance committee, and was one of the first to advocate a Civil Service reform. He had been offered, but had declined, the position of Secretary of State in President Fillmore's Cabinet. At the National Democratic Convention in

1860 at Charleston, Hunter, as Virginia's favorite son for President, was defeated by Douglas. He favored Breckinridge as a presidential candidate. Hunter did not regard Lincoln's election as sufficient cause for secession. He served for a term as Secretary of State in the Confederacy. Thereafter, as a member of the Senate, he was a caustic critic of Davis' administration.

Associate Supreme Court Justice John Archibald Campbell of Alabama had concurred in the Dred Scott decision. Upon his appointment to the Supreme Court he had emancipated his slaves and thereafter employed as servants only free persons of color. He resigned from the Supreme Court in 1861. As a moderate, Campbell exerted his influence to prevent war, and, although he believed secession was justifiable, he opposed it.

Alexander Hamilton Stephens of Georgia served as a member of the House of Representatives from 1839. In 1859 he anticipated war and resigned from Congress saying, "I saw there was bound to be a smash-up on the road and resolved to jump off at the first station." Shortly after the conclusion of the Hampton Roads conference, Stephens, being at odds with President Davis, left Richmond and returned home. Stephens had preferred Douglas to Breckinridge, the professed exponent of states rights during the 1860 Democratic campaign, holding that the territorial views of Douglas were his lifelong principles. Stephens was opposed to secession. As Vice-President of the Confederacy, he was highly critical of and opposed to Davis' policies during almost the entire period of his administration.

Lincoln and Stephens had both represented the Whig party in the Thirtieth Congress. Both had opposed President Polk and his administration in waging the war against Mexico. Lincoln was the sole Whig congressman from Illinois. Lincoln's correspondence indicates his deep affection for Stephens. In a letter to Herndon from Washington, February 2, 1848, he wrote: "Dear William—I just take up my pen to say that Mr. Stephens of Georgia, a little slim pale-faced consumptive man, with a voice like Logan's, has just concluded the very best speech of an hour's length I ever heard. My old withered dry eyes are full of tears, yet, if he writes it out anything like he delivered it, our people shall see a good many copies of it. Yours truly, Abraham Lincoln."

That Lincoln was deeply impressed is evidenced by the fact that this is the sole subject matter of this letter to his law partner. Lincoln's reference in this letter was to Stephen's vigorous denunciation of the Mexican War as a resort by force to compel the people of Mexico to sell their country to the United States.

Although differing with the President as to the justice or even propriety of a war with Mexico, Lincoln voted with the majority of his party for the funds and supplies necessary to conduct the war. He did this reluctantly, protesting all the while that the war was unnecessarily and unconstitutionally begun by President Polk. Lincoln attained unpopularity in the Middle West with his "Spot Resolutions," in which he demanded that the exact spot where the first American blood was shed be identified as being in American territory. This unpopular position during a time of war was one of the factors which induced Lincoln not to be a candidate for re-election to Congress.

On November 14, 1860, shortly after Lincoln had been elected, he wrote Stephens: "I have read in the newspaper your speech recently delivered for the Georgia Legislature or its assembled members. If you have revised it, as is probable, I shall be much obliged if you will send me a copy." Stephens replied that the speech had not been revised and that the report was substantially correct.

Thereafter, on December 22, 1860, Lincoln again wrote Stephens thanking him for his note. "I fully appreciate the present period the country is in and the weight of responsibility on me. Do the people of the South really entertain fears that a Republican administration would directly or indirectly interfere with the slaves, or with them about the slaves? If they do, I wish to assure you as once a friend, and still I hope not an enemy, there is no cause for such fears. The South would be in no more danger in this respect than it was in the days of Washington. I suppose, however, that this does not meet the case. You think slavery is right and ought to be extended, while we think it is wrong and ought to be restricted. That, I suppose is the rule. It certainly is the only substantial difference between us."

In a speech in which he opposed secession by Georgia, Stephens stated that if Lincoln should *first* violate the Constitution that it would *then* be time enough for Georgia to take action. Stephens pleaded that the South should remain in the Union and that he did not anticipate that Lincoln would violate the Constitution. He pointed out that the Democratic gains in the recent election gave that party a majority of thirty in the House of Representatives; that with a majority of four against him in the Senate, Lincoln would be powerless to act; and that he could *not* appoint an officer or form a Cabinet without the consent of the Senate.

Stephens' position was that the legislature was not the proper body to sever relations with the federal government and that this question should be referred directly to the people. The legislature had no power to act. Throughout his talk he referred to "our common country." He did his utmost to attempt to prevent war by resorting to conciliation.

In an address delivered after Lincoln's death, Stephens stated, "Lincoln and I had been in Congress together. We had both opposed the policy of the Mexican War, and we both cordially co-operated together in the nomination and election of General Taylor to the Presidency in 1848 as the surest means of arresting a consummation of their policy. We succeeded in the election but not in the object. Neither Mr. Hunter, nor Mr. Campbell, knew much of Mr. Lincoln except from his public acts after his elevation to the Presidency. Personally, I knew him well and esteemed him highly, and to them

I mentioned this correspondence while enroute to Hampton Roads as evidence of our kind relations individually anterior to the war."

In mid-December of 1864 the politically prominent Francis P. Blair visited Lincoln with a proposal to go to Richmond with a view of obtaining peace. Blair had been the intimate adviser of Andrew Jackson, and had acted as counselor to Lincoln. In December 1864 he received a long letter from Horace Greeley which awakened a motive that had been dormant in Blair for some time. Greeley stated that it was time to open peace negotiations with the Confederacy and that the South should at least be placed in the position of refusing peace. He suggested that Blair, an able publicist, "the counsellor and trusted advisor of men high in authority," consider the suggestion of moving toward peace. Blair replied that months before he had written to President Lincoln suggesting that Greeley's peace negotiations at Niagara should be transferred to Richmond; that he had a scheme "benevolent as well as radical," which he would hint to President Lincoln.

Lincoln refused to listen to Blair's proposals, but promised to give him a hearing after Savannah had fallen. Three days after this occurred, Lincoln wrote one sentence on a card, "Allow the bearer, F. P. Blair, Sr., to pass our lines, go South, and return."

Blair and Jefferson Davis had been schoolboys together in Lexington, Kentucky. Blair sent two notes to Davis, one as a blind which stated that he sought some title papers which "may have been taken by some persons who had access to my house when General Early's army were in possession of my place." (After the Battle of Monocacy in July 1864, en route to Washington, Early's men had destroyed Blair's home at Silver Springs, Maryland.) The second and longer note stated that he wished to "confidentially unbosom my heart frankly and without reserve." The first note would serve to answer any inquiries as to why Blair was in Richmond.

Blair went to Richmond under a flag of truce, dined with Davis, and fraternized with old cronies of yesteryear. He noticed with surprise the great number of able-bodied men who were walking the streets, men he would have expected to be in Lee's army. Blair read a memorandum to Davis containing his proposal, the gist of which was that the Civil War cease; that inasmuch as Emperor Louis Napoleon of France had violated the Monroe Doctrine by placing Maximilian on the throne in Mexico, thereby converting a republic into a monarchy, both sides should combine to overthrow Maximilian; that Matías Romero, the Mexican minister at Washington, favored the plan and believed that the fugitive Mexican President, Juárez, would be agreeable to have Davis act as dictator; that if this was accomplished, Davis' name would be linked to those of Washington and Jackson; that Mexico could, in time, be adapted to the Union, and a new Southern constellation would round off our possession at the Isthmus, thus completing the work of expansion begun by Jefferson.

Davis suggested that he was willing to send representatives to a conference and gave Blair a letter dated January 12, 1865, to this effect, in the hope that peace might be restored.

When Blair returned to Washington, he now made known to Lincoln, for the first time, the nature of his peace proposal. According to Nicolay and Hay, Lincoln "had not the slightest interest in it, and considered more seriously the low morale of the Confederate leaders. . . ." In his report to Lincoln, Blair stated that Davis thought the American adventure might be the solution of the pending problems; that a divided country at war usually resulted in monarchy; that Europe hoped to see the two sections destroy each other; that no circumstances would sooner restore better feelings than the two sections united in a war on a foreign power.

This was not the first reference to a peace plan involving the Mexican adventure. General Nathaniel Banks, who had succeeded General Benjamin Butler in New Orleans in December of 1862, conceived himself to be a peacemaker. Lincoln's chiropodist, Isachar Zacharie, had been helpful to Banks in New Orleans. The General had been, for some time, anxious to learn whether Confederate leaders were open to some proposition that might terminate the war. He approved of Zacharie as a peacemaker and, on July 2, 1863, Banks wrote a letter of introduction to Secretary of State Seward for Zacharie to deliver in person, and sent him off to the North. Thereafter, Zacharie consulted with Seward and with President Lincoln, who authorized Zacharie to meet with Confederate officials.

Zacharie met with Judah P. Benjamin, Secretary of State; Stephen R. Mallory, Secretary of the Navy; James A. Seddon, Secretary of War; and Brigadier General John H. Winder, provost marshal and commander of Northern prisoners at Richmond. After several days' consultation Zacharie returned North and reported that the conferences were of a most friendly nature; that the South was receptive to peace and recommended that General Banks be recalled to Washington for the express purpose of continuing the consultations with Richmond.

Lincoln had acted against the advice of his Cabinet in permitting Zacharie to discuss a possible peace with leaders of the Confederacy. Chase, as well as other Cabinet members, was utterly opposed to any negotiations with the rebels. Seward was angry that Lincoln had overruled him.

Sometime later the New York *Herald* caught wind of this episode and reported a fantastic version of the Zacharie peace plan in an editorial in its issue of October 31, 1862. Davis, the rebel Cabinet, and the rebel armies were to go to Mexico. Our government was to furnish them with transportation to that favored land and with rations en route. Jefferson Davis planned to land in Mexico with one hundred and fifty thousand veteran fire-eaters, "each of whom can devour a Frenchman at a meal." With this force he would drive away Napoleon's hordes and proclaim himself President of the new Mexican republic. Simultaneously, the seceded Southern states would return to the Union. This would end the war satisfactorily to all concerned.

Apparently, any venture associated with Zacharie brought the press's sense of humor and satire into play. It is unlikely that such a plan as the *Herald* reported would have received Lincoln's serious consideration, or the Confederate statesmen's either.

On January 5, 1865, Lincoln had authorized General James W. Singleton, a Democratic congressman from Illinois, "to go south with any southern products and to go to any of our trading posts." Singleton, like Blair, had gone to Richmond as a self-appointed agent to ascertain the prospects for peace. Although his mission was supposed to have been a secret, it provoked much comment in the Northern press. One Washington correspondent reported, "The President has given a pass to the notorious Copperhead of Illinois, General J. W. Singleton, to go to Richmond to have a talk with Jeff Davis."

On February 1 Singleton returned to the White House and reported to Lincoln that the South was anxious for peace under the following conditions: that the North would reconstruct by offering liberal terms, which the Confederacy would consider and act upon during a sixty-day armistice; that each state would have the right to determine for itself all questions of local and domestic government, slavery included. To this they added that the only goal to which slavery would be surrendered was the goal of Southern independence, *unless* the surrender of both goals would receive fair compensation together with liberal terms of reconstruction secured by constitutional amendments. The *unless* clause was important since it meant there was a possibility of an early peace with reunion and with abolition of slavery, which were Lincoln's minimum terms, provided Lincoln could assure the Southerners that they would be compensated for the loss of their slaves.

When Grant telegraphed that the Southern commissioners had arrived and requested instructions, Lincoln decided to send Major Thomas T. Eckert as his personal emissary to meet the Confederates and sound them out before granting their request. His selection of Eckert was the natural manifestation of Lincoln's "high esteem" and even affection for Tom Eckert, as evidenced by the following letter, being a reply to Eckert's request to Robert T. Lincoln for a memento of his father:

Executive Mansion
Washington, May 21/65

Major:

Major Hay told me this morning that you were desirous of some relic of my Father, and I take pleasure in complying, for I know how high you stood in his esteem.

Nearly all of our effects have already been sent away, but I have found the pair of dividers, which he was accustomed to use, and with which you have doubtless often seen him trace distances on maps.

With great regards, I am

Very truly yours,
R. T. Lincoln

Lincoln and Eckert had spent many hours together in the telegraph headquarters of the War Department. The President had stoutly defended Eckert on one occasion when Secretary Stanton, acting on erroneous information, wanted to dismiss him. Robert Lincoln, in a letter dated June 22, 1907, referring to the Hampton Roads Conference, stated:

I remember my father telling me one evening all that occurred in the matter, and his indicating to me that he was not feeling quite comfortable as to the way in which the matter was being handled at army headquarters at City Point [referring to preliminary telegrams]; and that, therefore, he had that day sent Tom Eckert, as he affectionately called him, with written instructions, to handle the whole matter of the application of these visitors from Mr. Davis to get into our lines. He said that he had selected Tom Eckert for this business because, to use his language as nearly as I can remember it, 'he never failed to do completely what was given him to do, and to do it in the most complete, tactful manner, and to refrain from doing anything outside which would hurt his mission.' He was so emphatic in expressing this reason for sending Eckert that it made a deep impression upon me, and I never see General Eckert without thinking of it.

Another reason for Lincoln's choice was that he knew that Eckert and Stephens were old friends. Stephens had saved Eckert's life at the hands of a mob in Atlanta in July of 1861, when Eckert was making his way North from his residence in North Carolina, where he had been engaged in operating a gold mine controlled by a group of Baltimore capitalists. Also, Eckert's cousin, George Eckert, had been a roommate of Stephens some years before when Stephens was a member of Congress in Washington.

Lincoln had requested that Eckert accompany him to the Ford Theatre on the night of the assassination, but Stanton discouraged Eckert as he had also discouraged Grant from attending. Major Eckert was at Lincoln's bedside at his death.

Lincoln had given a one-page letter to Blair on January 18, in which he stated: "You may say this to him [Davis] that I have constantly been, am now, and shall continue ready to receive any agent whom he, or any other influential person now resisting the National authority, may informally send to me, with the view of securing peace to the people of our common country."

For the first time since the Confederate capital had been moved to Richmond, Davis requested Vice-President Stephens to meet with him in conference. After conferring with his Cabinet, Davis on January 28, 1865, appointed the three peace commissioners and in his letter of instruction stated: "In conformity with the letter of Mr. Lincoln, you are requested to proceed to Washington City for informal conference with him upon the issues involved in the existing war, and for the purpose of securing peace to the two countries."

The last two words in these respective letters of instruction from the great antagonists must be noted. In the one case, *common country;* in the other, *two countries.* They were, as Lincoln said on another occasion, "the rock on which we split." We may be sure that when Lincoln talked with Eckert and sent him on his mission, he stressed these two words and that Eckert listened attentively. In essence, as Nicolay and Hay put it, ". . . [Jefferson Davis'] instructions to the commissioners . . . carried a palpable contradiction on its face."

Major Eckert started immediately for Grant's headquarters on January 30. Before he arrived, however, the Confederate commissioners addressed a new note to Grant, deviating from their own instructions from Davis. They now asked "permission to proceed to Washington to hold a conference with President Lincoln upon the subject of the existing war, and with a view of ascertaining upon what terms it may be terminated, in pursuance of the course indicated by him in his letter to Mr. Blair of January 18."

It is not known what prompted them to modify their request. Perhaps they realized the impasse presented by the conflicting nature of their own orders and the conditions outlined by Lincoln, and desired to work out a *rapprochement* on their own initiative. If only they could talk with Lincoln, a way might be found. Stephens, especially, was a reasonable man, and evidently he was determined, at this desperate stage of the conflict, to stretch a point in order to have the all-desired personal talk with the President.

Grant telegraphed this apparent change of front to Lincoln, and since it seemed to be a compliance with the terms

of the Blair letter, Lincoln decided to send Secretary of
State Seward to meet the Southern commissioners. In his instructions to Seward, Lincoln again specifically referred to the
conditions of the letter and stated that the prerequisites to
peace were: "restoration of national authority throughout
all the states; no receding by the exercise of the United
States on the slavery question from the position assumed
thereon in the late annual message to Congress and in the
preceding documents; no cessation of hostilities short of an
end of the war, and the disbanding of all forces hostile to
the government." All propositions of theirs not inconsistent
with these points would be considered in a spirit of sincere
liberality. He was to hear all they might choose to say but
definitely was not to consummate anything. Seward left
Washington for City Point on the morning of February 1.

In the meantime Major Eckert arrived at Grant's camp
and met the commissioners. General Grant was desirous of
attending the conference, but Eckert refused to permit him to
do so. "You are the commanding general of the army. If you
make a failure or say anything that would be subject to
criticism, it would be very bad. If I make a mistake, I am
nothing but a common business man and it will go for naught.
I am going to take the responsibility, and I advise you not to
go to the conference." Grant was vexed and for years thereafter was angry with Eckert. It took courage for a mere
major to question Grant's authority in the presence of the
representatives of the government whose army he was fighting.

Lincoln was determined that this conference and its negotiations were not to interfere with the impending military
activities. On February 1 he telegraphed Grant: "Let nothing
which is transpiring hinder or delay the military movements
or plans."

Eckert followed to the letter the instructions given him by
President Lincoln:

Executive Mansion
Washington, Jan. 30, 1865

Major T. T. Eckert

Sir:

You will proceed with the documents placed in your hands; and on reaching Gen. Ord, will deliver him the letter addressed to him by the Secretary of War; then by Gen. Ord's assistance, procure an interview with Messrs. Stephens, Hunter and Campbell, or any of them, deliver to him or them the paper on which your own letter is written, note on the copy which you retain, the time of delivery, and to whom delivered, receive their answer in writing, waiting a reasonable time for it, and which, if it contain their decision to come through, without further condition, will be your warrant to ask Gen. Ord to pass them through as directed in the letter of the Secretary of War to him. If, by their answer, they decline to come, or propose other terms, do not have them passed through. And this being your whole duty, return and report to me.

Yours truly,

A. Lincoln

On the afternoon of February 1, therefore, he presented to Stephens, Hunter, and Campbell, his letter of instructions from Lincoln, repeating the entire text of the January 18 letter to Blair. He asked for a reply in writing and received the following:

City Point, Va.
February 1st, 1865

Thomas T. Eckert
Major & A.D.C.

Major:

Your note delivered by yourself this day has been considered. In reply we have to say that we were furnished with a copy of the letter of President Lincoln to Francis P. Blair, Esq. of the 18th of Jan'y ult, another copy of which is appended your note.

Our instructions are contained in a letter of which the following is a copy:

"Richmond Jan'y 28th, 1865

In conformity with the letter of Mr. Lincoln of which the foregoing is a copy, you are requested to proceed to Washington City for informal conference with him upon the issues involved in the existing war and for the purpose of securing peace to the two countries.

With great respect,

Your obt serv't

Jefferson Davis."

Confronted with this definitive demand, the commissioners could not do otherwise than present their own exact instructions from Davis. Thus they reversed their own unofficial statements to Grant of January 30. On Eckert's specific insistence and reference to Lincoln's treating of questions affecting "our common country," they perforce had to counter with Davis' proposal of securing peace "to the two countries." With the issue squarely joined, they could not repudiate their own orders. Whatever they said to Grant in informal conversation had to be discarded.

Eckert was quick to note the essential refusal to meet Lincoln's terms, and told them that no further negotiation was possible. He dutifully noted that he had presented Lincoln's letter, and that it had been, in turn, read by each of the commissioners. At ten o'clock that night (February 1), he telegraphed Lincoln that he had delivered his communication, had received a reply that was "not satisfactory," and that he had notified them that they "could not proceed further unless they complied with the terms expressed in my letter." In soldierly fashion he concluded with: "Having complied with my instructions I will return to Washington tomorrow unless otherwise directed."

Thus, for all practical purposes the conference was at an end, and the peace venture was a failure. It all hinged on the "two words." But those two words expressed the entire issue of the Civil War. They contained the determination of Lincoln that the Union was one and inseparable, as opposed to the doctrine of secession.

Early the next morning, February 2, the President went to the War Department and was handed simultaneously the reports from Eckert and from Seward. He was about to recall them both when he received a telegram from Grant to Stanton, stating that he was convinced, upon conversation with the commissioners, that their intentions were good and their desires sincere to restore peace and union.

In a letter to Eckert, February 2, 1865, the commissioners stated their desire to accept Lincoln's terms. Accordingly, they were conveyed from Grant's headquarters at City Point to Fort Monroe. Major Eckert then made the necessary arrangements for Lincoln to meet with the three commissioners on board the *River Queen,* lying at anchor near the fort. In the salon of the steamer on February 3, 1865, a conference of four hours' duration took place. Only Lincoln, Seward, and the three Confederate commissioners participated. The meeting was not unpleasant; small talk was indulged in, reminiscences were exchanged, and it was evident that the war had not destroyed old friendships. The only other person admitted to the conference was a colored servant who waited upon the conferees and served cigars, water, and refreshments.

According to Professor James Randall, the parley was badly muddled from the beginning by the self-inspired visit to Richmond of Blair, who conferred with Jefferson Davis and proposed entering into war against the French Imperial forces in Mexico. Randall further points out that the failure of the Hampton Roads Conference was due to a complete disagreement as to its purpose. Jefferson Davis anticipated that an armistice could be arranged, suspending hostilities, and that the war might be ended with permanent independence for the Confederacy.

Lincoln, on the contrary, made it clear that there could be no suspension of the fighting until the South laid down its arms and rejoined the Union. He insisted that restoration of the national authority was indispensable. Thus the conference broke up in a deadlock for which each government blamed the other.

No notes or records were made at the meeting. The only sources for what took place at this conference are the recollections of the Confederate commissioners, with the exception of the summary reports made in Washington and in Richmond.

For many of the details regarding the conference, reliance must be placed upon the memory and veracity of the account made by Alexander Stephens in Volume II of his *Constitutional View of the War*. Stephens pursued Blair's Mexican project, but Lincoln explained that this had not been revealed to him in advance and had never received the least authority from him. Stephens attempted to argue that, after the Armistice and the vindication of the Monroe Doctrine, reunion was bound to follow regardless of whether there was an advance commitment regarding it.

"A settlement of the Mexican question in this way," it seemed to Stephens, "would necessarily lead to a peaceful settlement of our own." Lincoln repeated that he could make no treaty or agreement of any kind with Confederate states, jointly or separately, until the question of reunion had been satisfactorily disposed of. Seward clinched the point by reading the relevant passages of the President's last Message to Congress, concluding: "In stating a single condition of peace, I mean simply to say that the war will cease on the part of the Government whenever it shall have ceased on the part of those who began it."

Seward then advised the commissioners that Congress had passed the proposal for a constitutional amendment abolishing slavery as a war measure. He implied that, if the Confederate states would quit the war, they could defeat the amendment by voting it down as members of the Union, since the Thirteenth Amendment did not pass into law until after its adoption by the states. Lincoln himself did not suggest that they could defeat the amendment, but he did suggest that they could postpone its adoption. Lincoln also stated that there was a possibility that slaveowners might be compensated, although he could not guarantee compensation.

The meeting is a significant demonstration of some of Lincoln's attitudes. Lincoln indicated at Hampton Roads that once the war was ended and the Union preserved with the acceptance of emancipation, he would be generous in other matters. He would favor compensation to slave holders, and would act with the utmost liberality as to the seizure of Southern properties. Lincoln hewed to the line that "there was but one way for peace, and that was for those who were resisting the laws of the Union to cease the resistance." There was no way of reconciling "the last two words."

JAY MONAGHAN

Books and Libraries
in Lincoln's Time

THE YOUTHFUL LINCOLN, reading before a log-cabin hearth, is a familiar image in art and literature. We can rest assured that young Abe did not borrow his book from the nearest public library, for in the early nineteenth century there were no free, tax-supported libraries in all the United States. Noah Webster had declared in 1800, nine years before Lincoln's birth, "There are not more than three or four tolerable libraries in America and these are extremely imperfect." One of these early reading rooms was maintained by the Library Company of Philadelphia, which had been established by Benjamin Franklin and his friends in 1731. It set a pattern for numerous other "social libraries" but all charged a fee for membership or the use of books. It would be a mistake, however, to assume from this an absence of reading matter on the frontier of Lincoln's youth.

Some of Lincoln's biographers have taken for granted, without investigating, that Lincoln's early reading was limited to a few classics like *Aesop's Fables,* Bunyan's *Pilgrim's Progress,* and the Bible. These writers have even concluded that Lincoln's mastery of the English language came from a study of such basic books. They have overlooked the fact that, though lacking free public libraries, boys in Lincoln's day, even on the frontier, had access to a great quantity of publications, with as big a percentage of trash as confronts boys a hundred and fifty years later. True, a book bound in boards cost $1.50, so poor people could not afford to purchase many of them. However, during Lincoln's short attendance at school at least two books on literature and composition were being used in Kentucky's smallest schools. One of them was Murray's *English Reader,* highly praised by Lincoln in later life. It contained extracts from Dr. Johnson, Milton, Addison, Goldsmith, Cowper, Pope, Gray, Gouverneur Morris, John Adams, Hamlet's soliloquy, and Cardinal Wolsey's lament. Other books used in Lincoln's school were the *Kentucky Preceptor,* Lowe's *Columbian Class Book,* Scott's *Lessons in Elocution,* Dupuy's *Song Book,* Bailey's *Etymological Dictionary,* and William Grimshaw's *History of the United States,* which ran to more than twenty-five editions during the pioneering days before free public libraries.

When Lincoln had become one of Illinois' leading lawyers and had married into a prominent social and political family, he said, after being nominated for the presidency of the United States, "there was absolutely nothing to excite ambition for education" in his early environment. However, we must remember that the backwoods of Indiana, to which his father brought him from Kentucky, was not far from two highly intellectual settlements: the Owenite colony of New Harmony, and the English Settlement in Illinois, both within horseback distances. The big river towns like Zanesville and Natchez supported good subscription libraries, but a boy in young Abe's circumstances could hardly take advantage of them.

Without nearby libraries many eighteenth-century books, some of them pure trash, circulated widely on the frontier. Among those which we know Lincoln read was M. L. Weems's *Life of Washington,* which in the fifth edition added the big lie about a little cherry tree in order to influence the rising generation to tell the truth. Parson Weems wrote several other books and many tracts, such as *God's Revenge against Gambling* and the *Drunkard's Looking Glass.* The *Bad Wife's Looking Glass* appeared while the Lincolns were living in

Indiana. Weems was an itinerant book agent, a literary Johnny Appleseed, who believed he could best serve the Lord by planting printed matter in cabins and plantation homes. Besides vending his own compositions he carried the standard works of Goldsmith, William Guthrie, Edward Montagu, Henry Hunter, and others. Another American writer of popular history with whom Lincoln was familiar was David Ramsay, who had written at least ten worthless volumes before Lincoln was seven years old. William Cullen Bryant, at the age of fourteen, saw his first work go to two editions the same year Lincoln was born. "Thanatopsis" was written in 1811, and "To a Waterfowl" in 1815. Thomas Moore's *Lalla Rookh* was so well known on the frontier that some communities forbade the holding of masked balls which gave willful girls an opportunity to impersonate the Oriental beauty.

Lincoln's first law book contained the statutes of Indiana, the Declaration of Independence, the Constitution, and the Northwest Ordinance with its prohibition of slavery. Before being qualified to practice law in 1836, Lincoln also studied Blackstone's commentaries on English common law, certainly no rare book. Lincoln must also have read Justice Joseph Story's work on equity and perhaps Story's well-known legal articles in the original *Encyclopedia Americana*, which he later owned.

It is important to note that Lincoln, in the primitive backwoods settlement of New Salem, began his lifelong acquaintance with Burns, Shakespeare, Paine, Volney, Voltaire, and Gibbon. He could say later, "The books, and your capacity for understanding them, are just the same in all places."

While Lincoln lived at New Salem, Dorothy Dix became known as a popular writer for women and she published seven volumes during the 1820s. James Fenimore Cooper also came to the height of his fame, turning out books almost yearly. His Leatherstocking series had many imitators long since forgotten. Most of them tried to immortalize the Indians as Cooper did. Pages were devoted to the red man's eloquent descriptions of the beauties of nature and the sins of white men, until a contemporary realist complained, "The 'abrogynes' are not in the habit of making interminable speeches, they leave that to white members of Congress."

Writers of this type exaggerated frontier characters, in the droll lingo which Lincoln sometimes imitated. Most outstanding of these heroic figures was Mike Fink. (Paul Bunyan appeared in literature almost a century later.) Mike was a keelboatman who could do everything any other man could do and then whip the other man. His rollicking exclamations became part of the Western language. "I'll be fly-blowed before sundown to a dead moral certingty," he would say, or, "I'm a Salt River roarer, I'm a ring-tailed squealer! I'm a regular screamer from the ol' Mississip'."

Another character quoted and imitated in the Lincoln country in the 1820s stepped out of a poem by Samuel Woodworth, author of the "Old Oaken Bucket." His play *The Forest Rose,* produced in 1825, enjoyed the longest run of any American drama before the Civil War. His poem *The Hunters of Kentucky,* a ballad of Jackson's victory at New Orleans, became immensely popular on the frontier. Perhaps its best stanza is:

> And if a daring foe annoys,
>   No matter what his force is,
> We'll show him that Kentucky boys
>   Are alligator-horses.

This rhyme, set to music, was sung by the actor Noah Ludlow dressed in hunting shirt and squirrel rifle at the old French Theatre in New Orleans. The pit was filled with flatboat boys "havin' 'em a time" and Ol' Noahy was greeted with "a prolonged whoop, or howl, such as Indians give when they are specially pleased."

Young Lincoln, a stripling when he visited New Orleans, has been reported to have improved his time in the Crescent

City by shaking his fist at a slave market. This was reported
years later when it was fashionable to remember dramatic
antislavery incidents in Lincoln's youth. Moreover, the only
reporter of this incident happened to be a man who was not
present. What young Lincoln really did in New Orleans will
never be known. Other boys of his age reveled in theatrical
performances and tramped back up the Natchez Trace to their
cabins on the Ohio, whiling away weary hours chanting as
much as they could remember of the song:

> That every man was half a horse
> And half an alligator.

Somehow the tune stuck in the minds of young men in
Western clearings. They wanted to dress and act like "Noahy"
Ludlow. Politicians echoed the theme song and when Henry
Clay, Lincoln's favorite, failed once more to reach the presi-
dency, cartoonists pictured him astride the alligator-horse
(the Western vote) trying to ride it to the White House.

"Ol' Noahy" was a well-known figure in the log-cabin West
before he opened in New Orleans. For eleven years following
1815 he had been playing barns, taverns, tobacco sheds, mills
and woodyards along the Ohio, through Kentucky, down the
Mississippi. By 1835 he had become wealthy and he spent
the next eighteeen years managing theaters in New Orleans,
Mobile, St. Louis, and Cincinnati, the latter two in Lincoln's
country.

Another player in the 1820s was Edwin Forrest, who began
his stage career trooping Ohio River towns when Lincoln was
growing up in Kentucky and Indiana. Still another, Joe Jefferson, beloved as Rip Van Winkle and veteran of seventy-one
years on the stage, spent the first twenty-three of them barn-
storming log towns from pioneer Chicago to Nashville, Tennessee, and beyond. He requested a permit to play Springfield,
Illinois, in 1839. Young lawyer Lincoln pleaded his case and
no doubt swapped a few stories.

Among all the trouping players who disseminated "culture" before the day of the public library, the black-faced comedians, or Sable Harmonists, must not be overlooked. America's minstrel show originated in the Lincoln midlands and played the back-country without props, scenery, or elaborate costumes. Certainly they did their part to build in the Northern mind a sympathy for the Negro, and an appreciation for his humor and music. And it should be noted that the lyrics sung by these players were written by Midwestern Northerners. Stephen Foster, knowing practically nothing of the Deep South, wrote "Swanee River," "Uncle Ned," "Old Folks at Home," "Massa's in de Cold, Cold Ground," "My Old Kentucky Home," "Oh! Susanna," "Nellie Was a Lady," and "Old Dog Tray." Thus the songs of the Civil War and of the California gold seekers originated in Lincoln's backwoods. Even "Dixie" was a minstrel tune, written by an Ohioan, Daniel Decatur Emmett, who as a boy had run away from home with a circus.

The appreciation of more serious literature in the West of the 1830s is difficult to measure, but the publishing business in America was beginning a period of tremendous expansion when the twenty-one-year-old Lincoln floated down the Sangamon to enter a new life as store clerk and postmaster in New Salem, Illinois. Back East in commercial and industrial cities a new kind of library was coming into existence. Not free or public, these new subscription libraries were designed for clerks and workingmen. Some received support from wealthy humanitarians. This effort to educate workers in the 1830s seems especially noteworthy when one remembers that at this time it was against the law to teach a slave in the South to read.

The spate of newly published books of this era catered to the low level of the new readers. Backwoods dialect stories continued to be popular. Davy Crockett, a backwoods politician, sat in Congress when Lincoln became old enough to cast his first vote, and four books, allegedly by him but probably ghost-written, appeared while Abe was at New Salem. As a

Whig, Lincoln must have known them. Crockett immortalized the parliamentary rejoinder "The honorable gentleman is barking up the wrong tree." Correct spelling he pronounced "contrary to nature." Backwoods Davy became the showpiece for Whig conservatism. His life and language were capitalized politically in the "log-cabin campaign" of 1840, which elected a Whig president. The same technique, to attract the labor vote, was used by ex-Whig Lincoln in the Rail Splitter campaign twenty years later.

The increase in book publication while Lincoln resided in New Salem corresponded with an increase in literary magazines, even in small Illinois towns. Vandalia, with only a thousand inhabitants in 1830, boasted the *Illinois Monthly Magazine,* and many other towns copied the venture, until the editor could say, "This is the golden age of periodicals." Three years earlier, when Lincoln was still in the Indiana backwoods, the New York *Mirror* had announced, "The mania for periodicals has extended itself to children," referring, of course, to the five standard juveniles open to subscription, among them the *Youth's Companion* established in 1827.

The *Knickerbocker,* probably the best adult magazine in the middle period, appeared in 1833. In the more than forty years of its existence, its pages carried stories by most of America's distinguished authors from Hawthorne to Bayard Taylor. And it is noticeable that many Western writers also contributed to it. In this magazine Parkman's *Oregon Trail* first appeared as a serial, and another article, "Mocha Dick, or the White Whale" by J. N. Reynolds, was published twelve years before Herman Melville printed his famous volume with almost identical title.

Women were beginning to assert their rights, and magazines for them abounded. Schools were offering females "a college education" and Lincoln's much-disputed Ann Rutledge planned to attend the academy at Jacksonville. However, she died in the summer of 1835, before classes opened. The best-known of the new women's magazines was *Godey's Lady's*

Book, which made a million for its publisher. Probably few publications have succeeded so well in feminine appeal. It seemed to have just what was wanted by ladies, and women endeavoring to be ladies. Its sentimental poems were memorized, its stories read, reread, and cried over, its fashions copied. Its charming colored illustrations were framed in luxurious boudoirs and pinned to the log walls of cabins on the prairies. Each issue, besides being useful for dressmakers, carried a personal message. Correspondence was encouraged. "We have received a note from some fair lady," wrote the editor on one occasion, "requesting us to give another description of Love than that found in the February number. This shall be done, and another fair lady has it now in charge."

Much of the magazine's success was due to its able editor, Mrs. Sarah Josepha Hale, author of "Mary Had a Little Lamb," whose persistence in the Civil War years induced Lincoln to declare Thanksgiving Day.

By 1837, when Lincoln moved from the village of New Salem to establish his home in the rapidly growing Springfield, a new movement which paved the way to public libraries had become popular. As early as 1834 there were two thousand lyceum associations encouraging debates and lectures. Many of these maintained collections of books for circulation among members. Lincoln had participated in the activities of such a club in New Salem before he left there, and within a year after his arrival in Springfield he delivered a speech before the local lyceum.

In the 1840s, with Lincoln permanently settled in the Illinois state capital, the surge of publications reached a new high. Whereas the number of books coming from the presses had increased sixty per cent from 1830 to 1840, it increased one hundred per cent from 1840 to 1850. Blood-and-thunder fiction prospered enormously. In the South the novels of Sir Walter Scott were read so widely that Mark Twain declared their picture of chivalry one of the causes of the Civil War.

It should be noted, too, that Twain's ante-bellum river ragamuffins, Tom Sawyer and Huckleberry Finn, who apparently were never inside a public library, read widely enough to pretend on occasion that they were knights in armor, heroes of Bulfinch's *Age of Chivalry,* quite as often as of Scott's *Ivanhoe.* Tom Sawyer, also in imagination, enacted the part of the Black Avenger of the Spanish Main from Ned Buntline's shilling shocker.

On a higher level literary magazines continued to multiply in hundreds of communities. Charles Ray, later editor of the Chicago *Tribune,* published a temperance paper in Springfield in 1846. Many of the best literary men contributed to such serials. Lawyer Lincoln even felt the literary urge and followed the romantic fashion by writing "My Childhood Home I See Again" and the humorous "Bear Hunt." Local newspapers, and they were legion, adopted a literary flavor. It was in one of these that Lincoln read the unsigned poem, "Oh, Why Should the Spirit of Mortal Be Proud?" He memorized it, but twenty years elapsed before he learned from a Civil War officer that the author's name was William Knox.

In 1842 James K. Paulding, as associate of Washington Irving in the *Salmagundi* essays, planned to visit Springfield. Irving was at the top of his literary fame, and Paulding too had a reputation which ranked him as one of the great realists, though his fame soon perished. Muddy roads delayed him at Rochester, Illinois, and young Mr. Lincoln rode out to meet the celebrity. In the tavern they told each other stories for most of the night and after sunup traveled into the capital together.

Late that same year the Illinois State Library was established in the brand-new Illinois state capitol, which had been started in 1837 but was not open for occupancy until 1840. The library's registry of books withdrawn has been preserved in the Illinois State Archives and the first signature in Volume I of the register is that of Stephen T. Logan, written by the hand of Abraham Lincoln, his junior law partner. Both Lincoln and Logan were then members of the legislature.

These were the years in which Lincoln spent much of his time following the court around the Eighth Judicial Circuit. At night he read books by candlelight in hotel rooms, sometimes with a snoring bedfellow nearby. Talcott Williams long afterward repeated his father's assertion that, staying at a hotel in Bloomington, Illinois, he found Lincoln there reading a translation of the *Iliad*.

In the autumn of 1847 Lincoln left Springfield to enter Congress. During his term he borrowed books from the United States Supreme Court library. On one such occasion, Elihu B. Washburne tells us, "Getting together all the books he [Lincoln] wanted, he placed them in a pile on a table. Taking a large bandanna handkerchief from his pocket, he tied them up, and putting a stick which he had brought with him through the knot he made in the handkerchief, adjusting the package of books to his stick he shouldered it, and marched off from the library to his room. In a few days he returned the books in the same way."

On this trip to Washington, Lincoln visited his wife's father in Lexington. The Todds were people of culture. The best as well as the latest books were likely to be there. Mary Todd Lincoln, before her marriage, had studied under French tutors and been drilled in the classics.

The 1840s was the decade of the so-called "Gift Editions." In one year over fifty authors embellished their works in embossed leather with brass latches. Such *objets d'art* became fixtures on the marble tops of drawing-room tables, but Lincoln never treasured these curiosities, nor did he care about books as permanent possessions.

In 1850, when Lincoln had returned to Springfield after serving his term in Congress, the United States was experiencing a huge population growth. It had increased about 103 per cent in twenty-five years. Along with this unprecedented growth in the 1850s the government census noted

15,615 libraries in the United States. Among these, 1217 were called "public," with 33 of them in Lincoln's Illinois. The leading libraries of the nation could be listed in the following order: Harvard College, the Library Company of Philadelphia, Yale, the Library of Congress, and the Boston Anthenaeum. Total library holdings amounted to 4,636,411 volumes.

Much more noteworthy is the fact that during the period prior to 1850, in which the population more than doubled, the number of periodicals multiplied six times. And what is more important, the circulation of these magazines reached amazing proportions. Bonner's *New York Ledger,* a literary miscellany designed for the mentality of nursemaids, stable boys, and bored housewives, claimed weekly sales of 400,000. Tucker's *Country Gentleman* boasted 250,000, *Leslie's* 164,-000, *Godey's* 150,000, with *Harper's* and *Mercury* in close competition. In all, thirteen periodicals claimed over 110,000 circulation.

In 1853 the idea of a free public library received its initial fillip in Boston, Massachusetts. Two great Harvard scholars, George Ticknor and Edward Everett, the former a professor, the latter an ex-president of Harvard, had studied together in Germany. They may have been shocked to learn that the University at Göttingen, where they studied, contained 360,-000 volumes when Harvard shelved only 84,200. In any event both became interested in establishing a tax-supported, free, public library in Boston. However, like so many scholars, they differed in their definition of the library's purpose, and argued about it. Should the books include volumes of a popular nature? If so, how popular? Should they be loaned freely, or should they be kept always for consultation within the building?

The academic dispute had not reached its height when Lincoln returned to Illinois from Washington. He traveled by way of Boston, but there is no evidence to indicate that he even heard about it. He left Congress determined to give up politics and devote his life to the practice of law. The West to which he returned seemed to be developing private rather than public libraries. Church and Sunday-school collections were growing. Chicago's Young Men's Association now possessed the largest number of books in the city.

Lincoln's determination to give up politics changed in 1854 when the Kansas–Nebraska Act opened to slavery heretofore free soil in the West. He began speaking against this extension of slavery, and one opposition paper reported him to be "mousing about the libraries of the State House" hunting citations on the question. His son, Robert Todd Lincoln, a student attending the college preparatory department of the Illinois State University in Springfield, also "moused about the libraries," withdrawing several dozen books from the newly-founded State Library, among them copies of Hugo and Dickens. But there was a demand for a wider range of reading material, and in 1857 Springfield incorporated a Library Association. William H. Herndon, Lincoln's partner since 1844, became its secretary. Shareholders paid five dollars as voting members, plus twenty-five cents monthly dues for the privilege of borrowing books. The volumes were kept in the office of the United States district court. Those who did not wish to borrow books might pay one dollar to participate in the exercises of the association. What did they get for their money? Well, for instance, on February 22, 1859, members of the association heard Abraham Lincoln deliver an address on discoveries and inventions.

By 1860 libraries of various kinds dotted the entire nation from the Eastern cities to the remote frontier. Most of the Western libraries were small, but the census of 1860 listed more than 10,000 public ones with a total of nearly 8,000,000 volumes. The military and naval academies at West Point and Annapolis both contained the latest and best fiction in their libraries, and we can readily unearth the reading preferences of young men soon to become famous in the Civil War.

Lincoln, early in 1860, spent many days in the Illinois State

Library preparing the Cooper Union Address, which did so much to further his nomination for the presidency in May. The Cooper Institute in New York was a new educational organization which maintained a lecture hall, a library, and an employment agency for workmen.

In the fall of 1860, on November 13, just a week after being elected president of the United States, Lincoln withdrew *The Statesman's Manual* from the State Library. It contained the inaugural addresses of the presidents from Washington to Polk. On the same day a New York *Evening Post* reporter saw him studying Jackson's nullification proclamation in Volume II. Like most speakers, Lincoln wanted to examine other presidents' remarks before preparing his own. He returned this volume on December 29, 1860.

Before leaving for his inauguration Lincoln gave away his personal library, indicating that he prized books for their contents though not for themselves. In the White House he continued his general reading. Unconfirmed reports say that he, as well as Secretary of State Seward, enjoyed the dime novels which were so popular with soldiers. Records show that his office borrowed from the Library of Congress some 125 volumes on diverse subjects, including works on the Constitution, military tactics, guns, and also one book on fishing. These may have been withdrawn by his secretaries, Nicolay and Hay, but Lincoln himself throughout his presidency enjoyed the comic books by Artemus Ward, and Petroleum Vesuvius Nasby. Mrs. Lincoln, when she refurbished the White House library, purchased copies of Hood, Goldsmith, Elizabeth Barrett Browning, Lydia Sigourney, Scott, Cooper, the poetic works of Edmund Spenser, and other recognized writers. Personal contact with, and constant sampling of, such a wide assortment of English writings, both in and out of public libraries, gave Lincoln a knowledge of English composition which led to his own immortal style.

MORT LEWIS

Lincoln's Humor

℘

On February 26, 1841, Lincoln, at that time a member of the Illinois state legislature, took it upon himself to silence a troublesome confrere with an arrow from his quiver of wit. His fellow legislator, Wickliff Kitchell, of Montgomery County, had been finding microscopic points with which to question either the constitutionality or desirability of practically every bill brought up on the floor during the session.

Kitchell's attack on a bond issue Lincoln was championing reminded Lincoln of a story about an old friend of his, a grizzled frontiersman, with bushy eyebrows and spectacles, which by a curious coincidence Kitchell also had. One day the old man imagined he saw a lively squirrel on a tree near his house, and, grabbing his gun, fired at the animal, which apparently paid no attention and kept frisking. After firing a dozen times he threw down his weapon in disgust, muttering there was something wrong with the rifle. His son, who had been watching him said, "Rifle's all right, but where's your squirrel?" The old man said, "Can't you see him hanging from that tree?" "No, I don't," said the boy. Then looking at his father, he cried, "You've been firing at a *louse* on your eyebrow!"

This is the classic Lincoln story, classic because it's pithy, pointed, and paints a picture; it's brief, earthy, drawn from a background with which Lincoln was personally familiar; it's easily understood; and it had a moral. The big object you think you're aiming at may turn out just to be a louse on your own eyebrow.

Only a fraction of those stories supposedly told by Lincoln actually were. The "louse on the eyebrow" story appears in a slightly different form in the Sangamon *Journal* of March 5, 1841, summarizing the legislative discussion. According to Lincoln's friend, Reporter Noah Brooks of the Sacramento *Daily Union,* Lincoln indicated that perhaps a sixth of the jokes credited to him were legal tender in his treasury of stories. Since Lincoln's death, the number of stories he is supposed to have told has snowballed. Had he actually told them all, he would have had little time for his legal career and practically none in which to run a war.

There is a possibility that among the five-sixths of the stories he did not tell, is the famous one about Grant and his whisky, even though during his presidency it was relished as an authentic example of Lincolnian wit. The protest having been made by a delegation of congressmen that Grant drank too much, Lincoln is credited with the retort that he'd like to discover the brand so he could send some to his other generals. John Eaton, a former Union chaplain, in his book *Grant, Lincoln, and the Freedmen,* published in 1907, reports the entire incident as being related to him by Lincoln himself. David Homer Bates, in his book, *Lincoln in the Telegraph Office,* also published in 1907, makes a point of recording Lincoln's denial of the Grant whisky quip. Bates says that the president "disclaimed this story in my hearing, stating that King George III [*sic*] of England was said to have remarked, when told that General Wolfe, then in command of the English army in Canada, was mad, that he wished Wolfe would bite some of his other generals."

The Wolfe story to which Bates claimed Lincoln referred appears in the 1845 edition of *Joe Miller's Complete Jest Book.* Lincoln was familiar with *Joe Miller,* indeed one or another of the many editions of this famous old jest book was a primary source for jokes he told. The Grant whisky story is what comedy writers call a "switch" of the Wolfe jape. The whisky anecdote was the result of a switch by somebody, but it may not have been Lincoln.

Lincoln did have a talent for turning stories; that is, he could make what appeared to be a brand-new story out of an old one by taking the nucleus of a joke he had read or heard and changing its externals. Clothing an elderly jest in fresh raiment, he gave it the appearance of youth.

There are many apocryphal Lincoln comic anecdotes which have been widely accepted as genuine. In February 1959, during the Lincoln Sesquicentennial, a national magazine acted as accessory to the perpetuation as fact, of some fictional witty Lincoln repartee. According to this publication, during one of the Lincoln–Douglas debates Douglas stated that when he first knew Lincoln his opponent was a grocery keeper and sold whisky, cigars, and such. Lincoln's riposte was, "What Mr. Douglas has said is true enough. I did keep a grocery and I did sell cotton, candles and cigars and sometimes whiskey; but I remember in those days that Mr. Douglas was one of my best customers! Many a time have I stood on one side of the counter and sold whiskey to Douglas on the other side, but the difference between us now is this; I have left my side of the counter, but Mr. Douglas still sticks to his tenaciously as ever."

This is such a delightful counterthrust it's too bad it was never delivered. Neither the Little Giant's nor Honest Abe's remarks, as reported in this national magazine, are recorded in contemporary texts of the Lincoln–Douglas debates. Nor do they appear in any authentic version. There was certainly no reason for deleting them. Nor did journalists reporting color for the Chicago *Press and Tribune,* or the Chicago *Times,* covering practically every meeting the two candidates held, make any mention of this verbal interchange. And Lincoln's salty response is just the kind of thing reporters traveling with the two men would have picked up.

A quip of Lincoln's, in the same vein, was recently printed

in another magazine of considerable repute, and is equally fictitious. In the course of a debate Lincoln refers to a Douglas claim that he, Douglas, had been apprenticed by his father, a cooper, to learn the cabinetmaking business. Lincoln remarks that he had not known his opponent's father had been a cooper. Nevertheless, he must have been a very good one, for (bowing slightly toward Douglas, no stranger to John Barleycorn) "he had made one of the best whiskey casks I have ever seen." However, not only does it not appear in any contemporary text of the debates, but Douglas' father died when Stephen was an infant. Only through a spirit medium could Father Douglas have apprenticed his son to any trade whatever.

The reason for pinning down the complete implausibility of these incidents is that they are believed by so many people, including sincere Lincoln students and writers, to be authentic Lincoln lore. These are but two of the many examples of Lincoln humorous apocrypha which have gained credence. How did these and other such fabrications originate? Deliberate invention? In some cases, undoubtedly. While Lincoln was president, publishers printed many books of Lincoln jokes. Most of these were never related by the president. The majority were so unfunny that Lincoln on a bad day, suffering simultaneously from hypochondria and an onslaught of George Brinton McClellan, would not have told them. But the publishers wanted the reading public to think he had. Lincoln had a reputation as a wit; if it were he who had related the story, and you liked Honest Abe, then the joke was half sold as comic before you even read it . . . and so was the book.

Writing reminiscences of Lincoln in the magazine *Success,* in 1906, Thomas H. Tibbles, a respected Populist Party leader, recalled Lincoln's quip about Douglas being one of his liquor customers at New Salem. (Lincoln, correcting a proof sheet of W. D. Howells' *Life and Speeches of Abraham Lincoln,* wrote in the margin that he had never seen Douglas in New Salem.) According to Tibbles the repartee occurred during the Lincoln—Douglas debate at Galesburg in *1857,* at which Tibbles had been an auditor. The Galesburg debate was held in 1858. Furthermore, there is no mention in the texts of that debate of Douglas and his penchant for drinking. It is true that during the *Ottawa* debate, Douglas remarked that Lincoln had been a "grocery keeper," which in those days meant he kept liquor as part of the stock-in-trade, an allegation Lincoln denied. But he did not make the humorous rejoinder Tibbles so distinctly recalled. Either Tibbles' memory was at fault, or during a long passage of time he had sincerely identified an apocryphal story he had read or heard with his own experience.

Deliberate invention for commercial purposes; faulty recollection; a wish by some who had personal interviews with Lincoln to inflate their egos in reporting yarns told them personally by the country's most famous storyteller, whether he had or not; jokes heard second or third hand, and so embroidered that they bore little if any resemblance to the originals; these are some of the reasons for the existence of apocryphal Lincoln humor lore.

Under the circumstances it is a mammoth task for any researcher to separate the genuine wit from the spurious chaff. However, there is enough bona fide Lincoln humorous material, some of it in his speeches and in his letters, some of it reported by reliable witnesses, to prove not only that he could be a very funny man when he wanted to, but that he also had a creative sense of humor.

In the days when Lincoln was one of the shining legal lights of the Eighth Circuit, his law associate in Danville, Ward Hill Lamon, tore the seat of his breeches during some horseplay in front of the courthouse. A petition was passed around among the lawyers, requesting contributions for the repair of the damaged trousers, whereupon Lincoln wrote, "I can contribute nothing to the end in view."

There is his dry endorsement on a letter dated February 17, 1863, written to Mrs. Lincoln by an Edgar Harriott of

New York City. Requesting that the president's wife use her influence in securing him a position as acting assistant paymaster in the Navy, Harriott boasted that he was "a direct descendant of John Randolph of Roanoke." Since John Randolph was impotent, this would have been something in the nature of a biological miracle. Lincoln indicated this, when he wrote across the letter, *"A direct descendant of one who was never a father."*

Apropos of other office seekers, by whom he was besieged, the president, coming down with varioloid, an illness resembling smallpox, quipped, "Now, at last, I have something I can give everyone."

In a letter dated June 12, 1863, and written to Erastus Corning of Albany, New York, Lincoln replied to resolutions censuring his conduct in suspending the writ of habeas corpus and making military arrests of civilians. In defending his course the president referred to his fear of a jury's freeing the subversives, no matter how guilty, remarking, "A jury too frequently have [*sic*] at least one member, more ready to hang the panel than to hang the traitor."

That Lincoln's original wit could demolish an opponent in the courtroom is shown in an incident in which Lincoln's opposite number in a particular case was Stephen T. Logan, a grave and earnest lawyer, but careless in his dress. Lincoln had discovered that Logan, in donning a new pleated bosom shirt, was wearing it with the bosom in back. He saved this tidbit until it was his turn to address the jury. After paying tribute to Logan's usual effectiveness as an attorney, he went on to say, "Still he is sometimes wrong. Since the trial has begun, I have discovered that with all his caution and fastidiousness, he hasn't knowledge enough to put his shirt on right!" Lincoln won the case.

He was a past master of the ad lib, his quick wit could and did spark original spontaneous quips, triggered by an immediate situation. But he was not above drawing from his tenacious memory witticisms he had read or heard. He probably originated few of the stories or funny anecdotes he told, as distinguished from his comic remarks. According to Noah Brooks, "Lincoln very seldom invented a story. Once he said to me, 'You speak of Lincoln stories. I don't think that is a correct phrase. I don't make the stories mine by telling them. I am only a retail dealer.'"

Chauncey M. Depew wrote that Lincoln told him he had created only two stories. On the other hand, Henry Clay Whitney, who knew Lincoln on the Illinois Eighth Circuit, pays tribute to Lincoln's talent for story improvisation when he says, "In our walks about the little towns where courts were held, he saw ludicrous elements in everything and could either narrate some story from his store-house of jokes, else he could improvise one."

There seems to be considerable area of disagreement as to just how many of his stories Lincoln originated. Experience has shown that, where an individual has a strongly creative humorous talent, he will create in the direction of his natural bent. And Lincoln's natural bent was toward storytelling, particularly illustrative anecdote, in his case a concentrated short story which included background description and character development and most important, made a point. It had to make a point! That is why it is probable that at least a few of the stories Lincoln told grew out of the rich loam of his own mind, fertilized by his particular experiences.

Lincoln's sense of humor was an important fraction of the man's integral character. It was the saving counterbalance to his profound sensitivity to tragedy. Without it he might have gone mad, a victim of the deep melancholy from which he so often suffered. Bowed down as he was by the oppressive weight of Civil War, laughter was more than just relief to Lincoln; it was the elixir necessary to his very survival. He recognized its therapeutic qualities, and sometimes called it an "emollient."

At a particularly disastrous period during the national holocaust he referred to his propensity for telling jokes, when he said to Congressman James M. Ashley of Ohio, "Ashley, were it not for this occasional vent, I should die." An Illinois cavalry colonel, John F. Farnsworth, reported that Lincoln told him that a funny story, if it had the element of genuine wit, put new life into him: it had the same effect "as I suppose a good square drink has on an old toper."

There was nothing sham or restrained about Lincoln's laughter. F. B. Carpenter, the artist who had an unusual opportunity to study Lincoln at close range, during the months he worked at the White House preparing his Emancipation Proclamation painting, wrote, "Mr. Lincoln's 'laugh' stood by itself. The 'neigh' of a wild horse on his native prairie is not more undisguised and hearty." Carpenter is the authority for many Lincoln stories which are accepted as genuine.

Congressman George Washington Julian of Indiana, a member of the watchdog Committee on the Conduct of the War, gives a picturesque description of Lincoln splitting his sides at the conclusion of one of his own stories. He tells of Lincoln throwing his left foot across his right knee, clenching his foot with both hands and bending forward convulsed with laughter. Lincoln, the audience, appreciated Lincoln, the storyteller.

His close friend and sometimes bodyguard, lawyer Ward Hill Lamon, describes the president's storytelling as being "a labor-saving contrivance." It has also been called a "multiple-purpose tool." Attorney Lincoln found it a most effective one. A story sometimes served as a homely way of making a situation more easily understood by a jury. In an assault-and-battery case he was defending, Lincoln was able to prove the plaintiff was the aggressor, but the opposing attorney argued that the defendant should have protected himself without injuring his assailant. Lincoln refuted this by describing the defendant as being in the situation of a man who, in going along the highway carrying a pitchfork, had been attacked by a fierce dog that ran out at him from a farmer's dooryard. In warding off the dog with the pitchfork, he had killed the dog. The indignant farmer asked, "What made you kill my dog?" "What made him bite me?" was the answer. "But why didn't you go after him with the other end of the pitchfork?" And the answer, "Why didn't he come at me with his other end?" This simple example of what is legally known as *son assault demesne,* or justifiable self-defense, helped win Lincoln's case for him.

For Lincoln, the need to be understood was imperative. He early discovered, even before becoming a lawyer, that by telling a story which was a simile or a parable, a situation could be explained, made clear, be more easily digested. This was the Aesop-fable technique; Lincoln read, referred to Aesop's fables. He also studied the Bible thoroughly, and it is possible that he was influenced in the direction of story-telling as a simple means of explanation by the fact that biblical parables perform a similar function.

Lincoln would sometimes use a yarn to turn down a request he did not want to, or could not grant, without giving offense. Congressman Julian tried to get a command for General Frémont, who was, at the time, without one. Lincoln, in saying that he did not know where to place Frémont, said it reminded him of the old man who advised his son to take a wife, to which the young man replied, "Whose wife shall I take?" —the point being that the only way to find a command for Frémont was to take it away from some other general.

He would sometimes use humor as a lubricant to forestall friction. David Homer Bates, the telegrapher, tells how, when Secretary of the Treasury Chase was trying to raise money with which to carry on the war, some New York financial bigwigs came to the telegraph office for an interview with Lincoln. The spokesman apologized by saying that he did not like to find fault with the president, but . . . Lincoln smoothed the way by saying, "Never mind, go ahead with your story. You remind me of a grandson who threatened to whip his grandfather. The old man said, 'Come on, I waive the grandfather.' Gentlemen, go ahead with your plan. I waive the presidency." He could and did use a humorous picturesque turn of speech to controvert an argument and drive his own point home. During the 1864 campaign David R. Locke, a favorite Lincoln humorist, whose pen name was Petroleum V. Nasby, begged him to step into the middle of a brawl between two prominent Republicans that was contributing to party disunity. Lincoln replied, "I learned a great many years ago that in a fight between a husband and wife, a third party should never get between the woman's skillet and the man's axe helve."

Robert Lincoln told a story about a Todd relative who asked Mr. Lincoln if, now that the family had attained national prominence, Mary Todd Lincoln's relatives shouldn't embellish the name Todd by adding a final "e." After a moment's thought Lincoln replied, "I don't think it's necessary. God seems to get along all right."

Lincoln would sometimes lighten his own gloom with a story to relieve the almost unbearable tension under which he was laboring. Otherwise he might have snapped like a too taut violin string. After Governor Andrew Curtin of Pennsylvania had described to him the "butchery" at Fredericksburg, Lincoln, according to Curtin, "soon reached a state of nervous excitement bordering on insanity." The Pennsylvania governor then said he would give all he owned to rescue the president from "this terrible war." This statement struck a chord in Lincoln and his saving grace of humor came to his aid. He proceeded to tell Curtin a yarn about an old Illinois farmer who had a prize hog, of which he was very proud. One of the farmer's two sons let the hog out of his pen, and the porker drove one boy up a tree. The other boy tried to save himself by holding on to the animal's tail. After the hog had circled the tree numerous times, the lad shouted to his brother perched on a branch, "I say, John, come down and help me let this hog go." Lincoln added to Curtin, "Now, Governor, that is exactly my case. I wish someone would come down and help me let this hog go."

At a time when the Radical Republicans were bringing

almost irresistible pressure on Lincoln to emancipate the slaves before he was ready to do so, he told Senator John B. Henderson of Missouri that three party leaders, in particular, simply haunted him. They seemed to trail him wherever he went, with demands for immediate emancipation. Senators Charles Sumner and Henry Wilson of Massachusetts, and Congressman Thaddeus Stevens of Pennsylvania made up the persistent trio. Looking out of the White House window on to Pennsylvania Avenue, Lincoln suddenly smiled and told Henderson a story about the school he had attended as a boy. One day the lesson was from the Scriptures and the pupils stood up in a long line and read in turn. This particular assignment concerned the Israelites who escaped incineration in the fiery furnance through Divine intervention. One little fellow, who was the first in class to have to read the names of the three Israelites, "stumbled on Shadrach, floundered on Meshach and went all to pieces on Abed-nego." The schoolmaster cuffed him and left him blubbering. The boy quieted down as others took up the lesson. But as the first boy's turn to read approached again, he suddenly emitted a banshee wail. "Look there, marster: there comes them same damn fellers again!"

The president, smiling broadly, beckoned Henderson to the window and pointed to three men who were crossing Pennsylvania Avenue, toward the White House. They were Sumner, Wilson, and Stevens! This was typical of Lincoln's ability to call from the recesses of his memory an appropriate yarn and, with the soothing balm of humor, relieve his irritation.

The modern reader, perusing Lincoln's jokes or droll remarks, will find many of them unfunny. But they were meant to be told, not read. They depended for their effect not only on the story, but on the delivery. Lincoln was a master in the art of telling a joke. He had a gift for mimicry, a mobile face which could assume comic expression, and what any first-rate storyteller has: a split-second sense of timing, the knowledge of exactly how and when to deliver the punch line.

As is true of any master of the art of storytelling, he was well aware of the importance of joke construction. General John H. Littlefield, who had been a student in the Lincoln and Herndon law office, wrote that Lincoln was always grateful for the opportunity of hearing a good and new story. Whenever law student Littlefield came across a "howler," he would repeat it to his employer. One day Lincoln said, "John, that's a good story, but you don't tell it right. Your arrangement is slipshod. Why, you should be as careful to have your story precise and logical as if you were making a geometrical demonstration."

Lincoln's own stories were always precise, logical, geometric.

It is said that when Lincoln told a story he had heard from someone else, he made it peculiarly his own. He changed it somewhat, he added to it. Most people do that; but a master storyteller improves the original. A. J. Conant, a government official in Washington during the Civil War, told Lincoln a story which the president enjoyed and retold, giving due credit to Conant. The story concerned a man who hoped to become a county judge and who hired a horse and buggy to drive to the nominating convention, held in a town some sixteen miles away. He asked a neighboring livery-stable keeper to give him the best and fastest horse he had, explaining that (this is Lincoln's addition) *he was anxious to get there early and do a little logrolling—campaigning—before the meeting opened.* His neighbor, *being of opposing politics* (again Lincoln's addition), had other views and furnished him with a beast which, starting out very well, broke down completely. Long before he reached his destination the convention had adjourned, and he had lost the nomination. Late the following afternoon he pulled up in front of the stable, remarking, "Jones, I see you are training this horse for the New York market. I know you expect to sell him for a good price to an undertaker for a hearse-horse." The owner protested. "Don't deny it," said the would-be judge. "I know by his gait

how much time you have spent training him to go before a
hearse. But it is all labor lost, my friend. He is altogether too
slow. Why, this horse couldn't get a corpse to the cemetery in
time for the resurrection!" The few words that Lincoln added
to this story, the fact that the candidate explained *he was
anxious to get there early and do a little logrolling before the
meeting opened,* and that the livery-stable keeper was *of
opposing politics,* described the motives of the two men and
therefore made the story considerably funnier. Only a master
storyteller would have the comic insight to do that.

The fact that a man has a fund of stories, that he has a
prodigious memory for them or writes them down as an
aide-mémoire—Lincoln had the memory and sometimes also
wrote them down—does not make him a master storyteller.
The fact that a man has a rich sense of humor, an appreciation of the comic so sensitive that he becomes convulsed with
laughter when his funny bone is even delicately struck—this
does not make him a master storyteller. His is a talent that
must be painstakingly developed. Appreciation of a good story
and the ability to tell one is the difference between the artist's
audience and the artist.

Implicit in one's being this kind of artist is the possession of
a keen sense of humor. And one is either born with a sense
of humor, or not. It is not often an acquired characteristic.
The very earliest writings we have of Lincoln's, two of the
first three verses of his in Volume I of *The Collected Works
of Abraham Lincoln* (Rutgers University Press), are semi-
humorous. He wrote them in his sum book when he was
fifteen or sixteen years old:

> Abraham Lincoln,
> his hand and pen
> he will be good but
> God knows when.

And:

Abraham Lincoln is my name
And with my pen I wrote the same
I wrote in both haste and speed
And left it here for fools to read.

It is possible that either one or both these specimens of doggerel were traditional in Lincoln's family. The first is inscribed in the copy of Bailey's *Etymological Dictionary* that belonged to Abraham's Uncle Mordecai. The inscription differs only in that Mordecai appears instead of Abraham, and "you" instead of "God." But these efforts indicate a humorous bent at an early age. Lincoln did, a few years later, write some satirical verses, they were more in the nature of heavy-handed burlesque, called *The Chronicles of Reuben.* They were not very good, but they showed his feeling for the ludicrous and the highly exaggerated that are hallmarks of typically American humor.

Lincoln's wit, during his earlier years, smacked of the club or broadsword. Later it generally had the homeliness and often the sharpness of an old-fashioned straight-edged razor. Although he often used his quips and stories, original or otherwise, as "a labor-saving contrivance," he sometimes told jokes for the sheer enjoyment of telling them. Somebody would relate a funny yarn; Lincoln would match it. His fund of stories seemed endless. Actually, he said his store was limited to a few hundred. If Lincoln originated some of his stories himself, where did he acquire the ones he did not create?

In his early life he lived in or near villages and small towns, places like Gentryville, Indiana, and New Salem, Illinois. The people had to entertain themselves. There were foot races, "rasslin'" matches, logrollings, turkey shoots, corn-huskin' bees, infares, and other simple social functions; and then, there was the courthouse. But the storyteller was the prime source of entertainment; if he was really good, he was quite likely to be the most popular man in the place.

Lincoln had such examples in his own family; his Uncle Mordecai and his father, Thomas, both prime storytellers, were well liked in their communities. Lincoln would sometimes introduce a homely witticism by saying, "As my old father used to say," whether he actually had said it or not. One of Lincoln's early campaign biographies states: "From his father came that knack of story telling which has made him so delightful among acquaintances and so irresistible in his stump and forensic drolleries." When Lincoln corrected this biography he let that statement stand.

He acquired many of his stories, of course, from other wags. When Lincoln was traveling the Eighth Circuit in Illinois, there were many evenings when the circuit judge, David Davis, would gather the favored few in his hotel room where storytelling contests would be held. Lincoln as the champion storyteller would be there . . . when he was not at a magic-lantern or minstrel show. He matched yarns with such masters of the art as Ned Hannegan, John Pettit, Dan Mace, and Usher F. Linder; being human, he must have cribbed some of their best stories, as they did his.

A number of his stories were either the result of personal observation and experience, or of actual occurrences which had been brought to his attention. When he was in the White House, a visitor brought up the name of Thompson Campbell, a man with a dry sense of humor, an old Springfield friend of the president's. Lincoln then told of a stranger who came to see Campbell, during the time the latter was secretary of state for Illinois. It was during the legislative vacation and he sought Campbell's permission to use the assembly chamber in which to deliver a course of lectures on "The Second Coming of Our Lord." Campbell replied, "If you'll take my advice, you won't waste your time in this city. It is my private opinion that if the Lord has been in Springfield once, he won't come the second time." This incident Lincoln had banked in his story account for future withdrawal.

He did the same with an amusing story which concerned

President Millard Fillmore and Edward, the White House doorkeeper, an anecdote he related to William O. Stoddard, one of the Lincoln secretaries. After observing that there was a great deal of fun in Edward, Lincoln told how Fillmore, after succeeding to the presidency upon the death of Zachary Taylor, decided to purchase a carriage. In Lincoln's words, "Some gentleman here was breaking up housekeeping and had one for sale, and Fillmore took Edward with him when he went to look at it. It seemed to be a pretty good turnout, but Fillmore looked it carefully over and then asked Edward, 'How do you think it will do for the President of the United States to ride in a second-hand carriage?' 'Sure, your Excellency,' replied Edward, 'you're only a second-hand President, you know.'" Lincoln not only relished the story, but the fact that Fillmore told it on himself. Lincoln related many self-deprecatory anecdotes and he appreciated others doing the same.

Some stories and humorous sayings he mined from books he read. Besides *Joe Miller's Jest-Book,* Lincoln was amused by *Quin's Jests; The Flush Times of Alabama and Mississippi,* by Joseph Glover Baldwin; *Artemus Ward, His Book,* by Charles Farrar Browne; *The Nasby Letters,* by David Ross Locke; *The Life and Adventures of Private Miles O'Reilly,* by Charles G. Halpine; *The Orpheus C. Kerr Papers,* by Robert H. Newell; *Phoenixiana,* by George H. Derby, the California humorist; and the comic writings of the Englishman, Thomas Hood. He was also familiar with George D. Prentice's quips and humorous paragraphs, which appeared in the weekly issues of the Louisville *Journal.* As postmaster at New Salem, he had access to copies of this weekly paper, and Prentice's writing undoubtedly contributed to his treasury of humor.

Baldwin's *Flush Times of Alabama and Mississippi* was the source of Lincoln's story of the judge who was such a strict legalist it was said of him "that he would hang a man for blowing his nose in the street, but that he would quash the indictment if it failed to specify which hand he blew it with!"

Robert H. Newell (Orpheus C. Kerr), of the editorial staff of the New York *Sunday Mercury,* furnished Lincoln a fable with overtones of bitter humor which he used to give Ulysses S. Grant sage advice. Grant wrote that after receiving his commission as lieutenant general, Lincoln had spoken to him privately. Following a brief reference to the military situation, the president said he thought he could illustrate what he wanted to say by a story. Lincoln then proceeded to relate a fable in which, during a great war among the animals, one side had difficulty in discovering a commander with sufficient self-confidence. Finally a monkey named Jocko was found, who expressed willingness to command the army if his tail could be made a little longer. The simian soldier continued his request for more and more tail before attacking the foe, until finally, the very weight of his own tail caused Jocko to collapse. Grant, noting that he saw the point, replied, "Mr. President, I will not call for more assistance unless I find it impossible to do with what I already have." Lincoln, in this parable, could have been referring to no one but General McClellan, his former commander of the Army of the Potomac, twice removed. McClellan's excessive caution and almost constant demand for more and more reinforcements and supplies, before he would move against the enemy, had brought about his downfall. Lincoln found his allegory in "A Fable for Strategists," verse written by Newell, in which the rhymster had satirized McClellan even more than had Lincoln.

Orpheus C. Kerr also provided Lincoln with a yarn to poke fun at a Cabinet officer; for Lincoln found humor a catharsis for his intermittent irritation with members of his official family. The story ran that a dying sailor in one of the Washington hospitals said he was ready to go if he could see his old grandmother before he died. Upon the hospital attendant's asking Navy Secretary Gideon Welles if he would impersonate the old lady, Welles replied that he would do it with pleasure, except that he was too busy examining a model of Noah's Ark with a view of introducing it into the United States Navy.

Henry Clay Whitney, in his book, *Life on the Circuit with Lincoln*, says that Lincoln's "favorite story was known by us as 'The Earthquake Story' and he used to read it out loud in our room from *The Flush Times of Alabama*." The so-called Earthquake Story is a boisterous tale of a rowdy trial in which a bailiff, mistakenly thinking that a series of ludicrous happenings had been caused by earth tremors, shouts "earthquake" and precipitates a courtroom riot. It was typical of the kind of exaggerated story Lincoln hugely enjoyed reading, if not always telling.

Of the two joke books Lincoln particularly relished, one of them during his boyhood and the other in his maturer years, much less is known about *Quin's Jests* than *Joe Miller.* Copies of *Quin's Jests* are extremely hard to locate. Nathaniel Grigsby, one of Lincoln's boyhood companions, is authority for Lincoln's reading to his friends a book of humor which Grigsby remembered as being called *The King's Jester,* but which experts have since identified as actually being *Quin's Jests. Quin's Jests, Or The Facetious Man's Pocket Companion* contains what was reputed to be the wit, quips, and repartee of James Quin, the Irish actor, and was published in 1766, the year of Quin's death. A goodly portion of the one hundred and four pages of *Quin's Jests* consists of earthy anecdotes and lends credence to the belief that Lincoln, who came from the backwoods, at times had no delicacy about getting into the backhouse.

In a comic piece Lincoln wrote out and gave to Arnold Robinson, he used the elementary device of transposing the first letters of various words, and partly of transposing words themselves: "He said he was riding bass-ackwards on a jass-ack, through a patton-cotch, on a pair of baddle-sags, stuffed full of binger-gred, when the animal steered at a scump, and the lirrup-steather broke, and throwed him in the forner of the kence, and broke his pishing-fole. He said he would not have minded it much, but he fell right into a great tow-curd; in fact, he said it give him a right smart sick of fitness . . . He said about bray-dake he came to himself, ran home, seized up a stick of wood and split the axe to make a light, rushed into the house, and found the door sick abed, and his wife standing open. But thank goodness, she is getting right hat and farty again."

Lincoln would extract wit from wherever he found it, from the manure pile or the Bible. To him, the gem of wit was important, not its setting.

Comparison of the contents in *Quin* with the individual known stories Lincoln told, the yarns most authorities agree as being authentic, shows that he drew upon it very little, if at all, as a joke source. There are a couple of anecdotes in *Quin* that Lincoln might have used as a basis for stories he told, but if so, he switched them drastically.

On the other hand, there can be no doubt that Joe Miller provided him with a fund of anecdotes. This book, published originally in 1739 under the title of *Joe Miller's Jests, Or The Wit's Vade-Mecum,* ran through many editions. Whitney states that Judge Samuel Treat told him he had once lent Lincoln a copy of *Joe Miller* and that Lincoln had narrated the stories it contained around the circuit. This was probably a much later edition than the first.

The "Dog Story" ("Why didn't he come at me with his other end?"), which Lincoln used to win his law case, is found in *Joe Miller's Complete Jest-Book,* published in 1845. The original of another story Lincoln told, in which the governor, visiting a state prison, pardons the one prisoner who frankly admits his crime because, "I can't have you here corrupting all these good men," is in the 1845 edition of *Joe Miller.* The *Miller* version has the Duke d'Ossuna, Viceroy of Naples, pardoning the one galley slave who refuses to plead innocence to the crime for which he was convicted. Says the Duke, "Here, take away this rascal, lest he should corrupt all these honest men." Lincoln brought the story up to date.

Lincoln liked to share both the serious and humorous reading he enjoyed with an appreciative audience. Senator Orville H. Browning tells in his diary of how he went to see Lincoln one evening at the White House. The president was alone and complained of a headache. Their conversation turned upon poetry and Lincoln read aloud a favorite poem of his, Thomas Hood's *The Haunted House,* a gloomy work which had a characteristically morbid fascination for Lincoln. "He then," wrote Browning, "sent for another volume of the same work and read me the *lost heir* [*sic*], and then the *Spoilt Child,* the humor of which he greatly enjoyed."

John Hay writes in his diary about a highly amused Lincoln coming into his and Nicolay's office after midnight with a volume of Hood's works in his hands, to share with his secretaries the humor of a cartoon he had found particularly funny. The cartoon was captioned, "An Unfortunate Bee-ing" —and showed a man who had accidentally upset a beehive, fleeing from a swarm of the enraged insects. This was an era when punning was one of the most popular forms of wit. Puns were a kind of verbal acrobatics for which Lincoln was not only a delighted audience, but in which at times he was a performer. He was making a word play on the name of the Swedish Minister to the United States, Edward, Count Piper, when he told John Hay that Captain James M. Cutts, accused of peering over a transom at a disrobing lady, should be elevated to the peerage "with the title of Count Peeper."

Shortly before the fall of Vicksburg, Senator Ben Wade came to see the president. Dissatisfied because of what he considered Grant's tardiness in moving against the Confederate outer works, Wade urged his dismissal. Lincoln, according to his friend Lamon, to whom he related the incident, said, "That reminds me of a story." Wade blew up as if he had been mined. He exploded with, "Yes, yes! It is with you, sir, all story, story. You are the father of every military blunder that has been made during the war. You are on your road to hell, sir, with this government, by your obstinacy; and you are not a mile off this minute." Lincoln replied, good humoredly, "Senator, that is just about the distance from here to the Capitol, is it not?" The senator picked up his hat and stormed out. The president told Lamon he was afraid he had made an enemy for life. This was one time his humor had back-fired. But it had undoubtedly relieved his feelings.

Once, after confessing to politician Chauncey M. Depew that his telling funny stories might irritate some individuals, the president made an observation on their value to him. He had discovered that common people were more easily influenced and informed by means of a broad illustration. He did not give a tinker's dam about what the hypercritical few might think.

The afternoon of April 14, 1865, Lincoln's last conscious day on earth, he read aloud to friends some excerpts from the humorous writings of Petroleum V. Nasby. That night, he was shot at Ford's Theatre, while watching a comedy played on the stage.

During so much of his life Lincoln used laughter as a poultice for the pain of sorrow. It seems symbolic that these two opposite poles of human emotion, laughter and sorrow, were commingled at the end.

MARIANNE MOORE

Lincoln and the Art of the Word

❦

"I DISLIKE an oath which requires a man to swear he *has* not done wrong. It rejects the Christian principle of forgiveness on terms of repentance. I think it is enough if the man does no wrong hereafter." It was Abraham Lincoln who said this—his controlled impetuosity exemplifying excellences both of the technician and of the poet.

The malcontent attacks greatness by disparaging it, by libels on efficiency, interpreting needful silence as lack of initiative, by distortion, by ridicule. "As a general rule," Lincoln said, "I abstain from reading attacks upon myself, wishing not to be provoked by that to which I cannot properly offer an answer." Expert in rebuttal, however, as in strategy, he often won juries and disinterested observers alike, by anecdote or humorous implication making argument unnecessary. His use of words became a perfected instrument, acquired by an education largely self-attained—" 'picked up,' " he said, "under pressure of necessity." That the books read became part of him is apparent in phrases influenced by the Bible, Shakespeare, *The Pilgrim's Progress, Robinson Crusoe,* Burns, Blackstone's commentaries; and not least, by the Six Books of Euclid—read and "nearly mastered," as he says, after he had become a member of Congress. The largeness of the life entered into the writing, as with a passion he strove to persuade his hearers of what he believed, his adroit, ingenious mentality framing an art which, if it is not to be designated poetry, we may call a "grasp of eternal grace"— in both senses, figurative and literal. Nor was he unaware of having effected what mattered, as we realize by his determined effort when a first attempt failed, to obtain from the Chicago *Press and Tribune* "a set of the late debates (if they may be so called)" he wrote, "between Douglas and myself . . . two copies of each number . . . in order to lay one away in the raw and to put the other in a scrapbook." One notes that he did not neglect to say, "if any debate is on *both* sides of one sheet, it will take two sets to make one scrapbook."

Of persuasive expedients, those most constant with Lincoln are antithesis, reiteration, satire, metaphor; above all *the meaning,* lucid and neat. A determination "to express his ideas in simple terms became his ruling passion," his every word natural, impelled by ardor. In his address at the Wisconsin Agricultural Fair, he said regarding competitive awards about to be made, "Exultations and mortifications . . . are but temporary; the victor shall soon be vanquished, if he relax in his exertion; and . . . the vanquished this year may be the victor next, in spite of all competition." At the Baltimore Sanitary Fair of 1864, in an address conspicuously combining antithesis with reiteration, he said, "The world has never had a good definition of liberty. . . . We all declare for liberty; but in using the same *word* we do not all mean the same *thing*. With some the word may mean for each man to do as he pleases with himself, and the product of his labor; while with others the same word may mean for some men to do as they please with other men, and the product of other men's labor. Here are two, not only different, but incompatible things, called by the same name—liberty. . . . The shepherd drives the wolf from the sheep's throat, for which the sheep thanks the shepherd as a *liberator,* while the wolf denounces him for the same act as the destroyer of liberty, especially as the sheep was a black one." In Lincoln's use of italics, one perceives that he is not substituting emphasis for precision but is impersonating speech. In declining an invitation to the Jefferson birthday dinner of 1859, he wrote, "The principles of Jefferson are the axioms of a free society. One dashingly calls them 'glittering generalities'; another bluntly calls them 'self-evident lies.'" And in combating repeal of the Missouri Compromise (which would have extended slavery), he said, "Repeal the Missouri Compromise—repeal all compromises—repeal the Declaration of Independence—repeal all history—you cannot repeal human nature."

Crystalline logic indeed was to be his passion. He wrote to James Conkling, "You desire peace; and you blame me that we do not have it. But how can we attain it? There are but three conceivable ways. First, force of arms. . . . Are you for it? . . . A second way is to give up the Union. Are you for it? If you are, you should say so plainly. If not for force, not yet for dissolution, Compromise. I am against that. I do not believe any compromise is now possible." And to General Schurz, he said, "You think I could do better; therefore you blame me. I think I could not do better, therefore I blame you for blaming me."

Unsurpassed in satire, Lincoln said that Judge Douglas in his interpretation of the Declaration of Independence, offered "the arguments that kings have made for enslaving the people in all ages of the world. They always bestrode the necks of the people, not that they wanted to do it, but that the people were better off for being ridden." Of slavery as an institution he said, "Slavery is strikingly peculiar in this, that it is the only good thing which no man seeks the good of for *himself.*"

Metaphor is a force, indeed magnet, among Lincoln's arts of the word. Urgent that the new government of Louisiana be affirmed, he said, "If we reject it, we in effect say, 'you are worthless. We will neither help nor be helped by you.' To the blacks we say, 'This cup of liberty which these, your old masters, hold to your lips, we will dash from you, . . . discouraging and paralysing both white and black. . . . If on the contrary, we recognize and sustain the new government, we are supporting its efforts to this end—to make it, to us, in your language, a Union of hearts and hands as well as of states.'" Passionate that the Union be saved, he uses a metaphor yet stronger than the cup of liberty. He says, "By general law, life *and* limb must be protected; yet often a limb must be amputated to save a life; but a life is never wisely given to save a limb. . . . I could not feel that, . . . to save slavery, . . . I should permit the wreck of government, country, and constitution altogether."

Diligence underlay these verbal expedients—one can scarcely call them devices—so rapt Lincoln was in what he cared about. He had a genius for words but it was through diligence that he became a master of them—affording hope to the most awkward of us. To Isham Reavis he wrote, "If you are resolutely determined to make a lawyer of yourself, the thing is half done already. It is a small matter whether you read *with* anybody or not. . . . It is of no consequence to be in a large town. . . . I read at New Salem, which never had three hundred people living in it. The *books* and your *capacity* for understanding them, are just the same in all places."

Diligence was basic. Upon hearing that George Latham, his son Robert's classmate at the Phillips Exeter Academy, had failed entrance examinations to Harvard, Lincoln wrote, "Having made the attempt you *must* succeed in it. '*Must*' is the word . . . you *can* not fail if you resolutely determine that you *will* not." This intensity we have heightened in Lincoln's torment of anxiety during the war, that the struggle be ended. "The subject is on my mind day and night," he said. During August 1862, in a letter to Colonel Haupt on the 29th, he begged, "What news from the direction of Manassas?" On that same day to General McClellan he wrote, "What news from the direction of Manassas Junction?" On August 30, to General Banks, "Please tell me what news?" and again "What news?" on August 30 to Colonel Haupt. The result was a man wearing down under continuous desperation when General Meade, unable to conclude the war at Gettysburg, allowed the Confederate forces to retreat south.

In speeches and in letters Lincoln made articulate an indomitable ideal—that what the framers of the Constitution embodied in it, be preserved—"and that something is the principle of 'Liberty for all,' that clears the *path* for all—gives *hope* to all—and by consequence *enterprise* and *industry* to all." Inflexible when sure he was right, as in his reply to Isaac Schermerhorn, who was dissatisfied with the management of the war, he said, "This is not a question of sentiment or taste but one of physical force which may be measured and estimated as horse-power and Steam-power are measured and estimated. . . . Throw it away and the Union goes with it."

There is much to learn from Lincoln's respect for words taken separately, as when he said: "It seems to me very important that the statute laws should be made as plain and intelligible as possible, and be reduced to as small compass as may consist with the fullness and precision of the will of the legislature and the perspicuity of its language." He was "determined to be so clear," he said, "that no honest man can misunderstand me, and no dishonest one can successfully misrepresent me." Exasperated to have been misquoted, he protested "a specious and fantastic arrangement of words, by which a man can prove a horse-chestnut to be a chestnut horse." Consulted regarding a more perfect edition of his Cooper Institute speech, he said, "Of course I would not object, but would be pleased rather . . . but I do not wish the sense changed or modified, to a hair's breadth. Striking out 'upon' leaves the sense too general and incomplete. . . . The words 'quite,' 'as,' and 'or,' on the same page, I wish retained." Of Stephen Douglas he said, "Cannot the Judge perceive the difference between a purpose and an expectation? I have often expressed an expectation to die but I have never expressed a *wish* to die." The Declaration of Independence he made stronger by saying, "I think the authors of that notable instrument intended to include *all* men but they did

not intend to declare all men were equal *in all respects.*"
And to quibblers, after the surrender of the South, he replied,
"Whether the seceded states, so-called, are in the Union or
out of it, the question is bad . . . a pernicious abstraction!"
Indelible even upon a feeble memory—we recall the phrase,
"with malice toward none and charity for all," and in the
second inaugural address, "Let us strive on to finish the work
we are in." We are *in.* Lincoln understood in the use of
emphasis that one must be *natural.* Instead of using the word
confidential in a letter to A. H. Stephens, he wrote in italics
at the head of the page, *"For your eye only."* The result of
this intensified particularity was such that in his so-called
Lost Speech of 1856, which unified the Republican Party,
"newspaper men forgot paper and pad . . . to sit enraptured,"
and instead of taking down his eulogy of Henry Clay, "dropped
their pens and sat as under enchantment from near the
beginning, to quite the end."

Lincoln attained not force only, but cadence, the melodic
propriety of poetry in fact, as in the Farewell Address from
Springfield, he refers to "the weight of responsibility on George
Washington"; then says of "that Divine being without which
I cannot succeed, with that assistance, I cannot fail." Consider
also the stateliness of the three cannots in the Gettysburg
Address: "we cannot dedicate—we cannot consecrate—we
cannot hallow—this ground. The brave men, living and dead,
who struggled here, have consecrated it far above our poor
power to add or detract. The world will little note nor long
remember what we may say here, but it can never forget what
they did here." Editors attempting to improve Lincoln's punc-
tuation by replacing dashes with commas, should refrain—
the dash, as well known, signifying indigenous prudence.

With consummate reverence for God, with insight that
illumined his every procedure as a lawyer, that was alive in
his every decision as a president with civilian command of an
army at bay, Lincoln was notable in his manner of proffering
consolation; studiously avoiding insult when relieving an officer

of his command; instantaneous with praise. To General Grant —made commander of the Union army after his brilliant flanking maneuver at Vicksburg—he said, "As the country trusts you, so, under God, it will sustain you." To Grant "alone" he ascribed credit for terminating the war. Constrained almost to ferocity by the sense of fairness, he begs recognition for "black men who can remember that with silent tongues, and clenched teeth, and steady eye and well-poised bayonet, they have helped mankind to this consummation" (preserving the Union). He managed to take time to retrieve the property of a barber, a Negro, who had not recorded the deed to land he owned. Emphasizing by vivid addendum his request for promotion of a "brave drummer-boy" who "had accompanied his division under heavy fire," Lincoln said, "He should have his chance." For "a poor widow whose son was serving a long sentence without pay"—recommending the son for re-enlistment with pay—he wrote, "She says she cannot get it acted on. Please do it." In constant disfavor with officers in charge of penalties, he said, "Must I shoot a simple soldier boy who deserts while I must not touch a hair of the wily agitator who induces him to desert? To silence the agitator and save the boy is not only constitutional but withal a great mercy." Of Captain McKnabb, dismissed on the charge of being a disunionist, Lincoln wrote, "He wishes to show that the charge is false. Fair play is a jewel. Give him a chance if you can." Afflicted by self-obsessed factions in Missouri, where private grievances should have been settled locally, he summarized the matter: "I have exhausted my wits and nearly my patience in efforts to convince both [sides] that the evils they charged on the others are inherent. I am well satisfied that the preventing of the remedial raid into Missouri was the only safe way to avoid an indiscriminate massacre, including probably more innocent than guilty. Instead of condemning, I therefore approve what I understand General Schofield did in that respect. . . . Few things have been so grateful to my anxious feeling as when . . . the local force in Missouri aided General

Schofield to so promptly send a large force to the relief of
General Grant then investing Vicksburg and menaced by
General Johnston. . . . My feeling obliges nobody to follow
me and I trust obliges me to follow nobody."

With regard to presidential appointments, it was in 1849
during Zachary Taylor's administration, that Lincoln said, "I
take the responsibility. In that phrase were the 'Samson's
locks' of General Jackson, and we dare not disregard the
lessons of experience"—lessons underlying the principle
which he put into practice when appointing Governor Chase
Secretary of the Treasury. Pressed, in fact persecuted, to
appoint General Cameron, he said: "It seems to me not only
highly proper but a *necessity,* that Governor Chase shall take
that place. His ability, firmness, and purity of character produce the propriety." Purity of character—the phrase is an
epitome of Lincoln. To a young man considering law as a
career, he said, "There is a vague popular belief that lawyers
are necessarily dishonest. If you cannot be an honest lawyer,
resolve to be honest without being a lawyer." Deploring bom-
bast, yet tactful, he opposed investigating the Bank of Illinois:
"No, Sir, it is the *politician* who is first to sound the alarm,
(which, by the way, is a false one). It is he, who, by these
unholy means, is endeavoring to blow up a storm that he may
ride upon and direct it. . . . I say this with the greater
freedom, because, being a politician, none can regard it as
personal." Firm in resisting pressure, he was equally strong
in exerting it, as when he wrote to "Secretary Seward &
Secretary Chase" jointly: "You have respectively tendered
me your resignations . . . but, after most anxious consideration, my deliberate judgment is, that the public interest does
not admit of it. I therefore have to request that you will
resume the duties of your departments respectively. Your
Obt. Servt."

In faithfulness to a trust, in saving our constituted freedom
and opportunity for all, declaring that "no grievance is a fit
object of redress by mob violence," made disconsolate by

what he termed "a conspiracy" to "nationalize slavery," Lincoln—dogged by chronic fatigue—was a monumental contradiction of that conspiracy. An architect of justice, determined and destined to win his "case," he did not cease until he had demonstrated the mightiness of his "proposition." It is a Euclid of the heart.

ANDREW ROLLE

A Biographical Lincoln

THE SHOCK of Lincoln's tragic assassination, just as the Civil War was barely won, started a torrent of biographical writing about him that has hardly run its course. Lincoln's humble origins, his self-taught, roughhewn past, his kindness, humor, and sadness, as well as the mercy he showed even his enemies, were personal traits that attracted writers to ferret out the ingredients of his life story. To discern the inner workings of this captivating figure who placed so much faith in the people was, understandably, a major literary goal.

No single essay could possibly grapple with the hundreds of attempts to deal with the personality, life, and impact of Abraham Lincoln. As of 1939, Jay Monaghan's standard *Lincoln Bibliography* listed some four thousand separate titles (not including articles) concerning Lincoln. By now five thousand or more such works exist about the sixteenth president. Dozens of new volumes appear each year. These Lincoln items run from good to hopeless.

Out of the confusing welter of Lincolniana one can, however, discern a pattern by which earnest and honest writers— not those bent on canonizing and enshrining Lincoln—have fashioned an increasingly reliable portrait of the man and his times. Especially representative works, above the level of superficial treatments and campaign biographies, merit our attention.

Quite naturally, the earliest of Lincoln's biographies were among the weakest. Foremost of these, and yet important, was that published in 1889 by his law partner, William H. Herndon, in collaboration with Jesse W. Weik. They entitled their effort *Herndon's Lincoln: The True Story of a Great Life,* a book which almost immediately aroused controversy. Not only was Herndon's taste, in revealing personal facets of Lincoln's life, questioned by readers but so was his factual accuracy. Herndon originated what some modern historians consider to be a major myth: the story of Lincoln's alleged early romance with Ann Rutledge. This and a tale about Lincoln almost leaving his prospective bride waiting at the altar on their wedding day not only offended Mrs. Lincoln but opened to question the whole matter of Lincoln's domestic felicity. The colorful and provocative Herndon also filled his book with references to Lincoln's rough background, alleged that his mother was illegitimate, and that he was a crude, ungainly sort, subject to moodiness, periods of depression, and furthermore a man whose Christian faith and moral values were vague and unorthodox. Despite its faults, the book gives us a sense of immediacy and realism. Herndon knew Lincoln well and he realistically, if unreliably, presented the associate he wanted posterity to know. In his appraisal of the early Lincoln, Herndon remains fundamental but he must be read carefully, with corrections made for his demonstrably imperfect memory. One must particularly discount some of Herndon's more emotional and subjective judgments about Lincoln's personal idiosyncracies and take into account Herndon's inability fully to understand the later Lincoln who became one of the greatest American presidents. "To take Herndon at face value is no longer permissible," wrote J. G. Randall, a later biographer.

The year after the Herndon–Weik book appeared, a more ambitious work was brought out by Lincoln's two young secretaries, John G. Nicolay and John Hay. Entitled *Abraham Lincoln: A History,* this book was the result of more than twenty years of note-taking by men who had been given the opportunity to observe Lincoln intimately in his role as president, a role with which Herndon was unfamiliar. Furthermore, Lincoln had co-operated with his secretaries in gathering together manuscript materials. Although Nicolay and Hay had every possible opportunity to present a biography of the "inner Lincoln," particularly in times of great national stress, they fashioned instead a ten-volume history of the United States from Lincoln's birth until the end of the Civil War, serialized first for *Century Magazine*. In its pages he emerged primarily as the central figure of a "life-and-times" approach. The book encompasses the major facets of Lincoln's career, but it does so in a conventional way, reprinting documents and letters to which Nicolay and Hay alone had access—until these manuscripts were much later made available to scholars. Immersed as they were in the political atmosphere of post-Civil War Republicanism, a conservative and highly proper Lincoln, quite different from Herndon's image, emerges from the pages of this work. Nevertheless, Nicolay and Hay's exceedingly detailed volumes are indispensable to the serious Lincoln scholar. His two secretaries were dedicated and loyal men whose exhaustive writings mirror their close personal association with their chief. Their work, authorized by Lincoln's son, Robert Todd Lincoln, possessed both the merits and defects of an official biography. Though exhaustive, its argument was marred by party bias and was lacking in fundamental interpretive skill.

Another contemporary of Lincoln's who sought to capture the magic of his life was Carl Schurz, the intellectual German immigrant, Union general, senator, and influential editor. His *Abraham Lincoln: An Essay* (1891) attempts in 117 pages to appraise a man with whom Schurz had repeated personal meetings. As was customary during his generation, Schurz first published his essay in magazine form in the *Atlantic Monthly*. He did not intend his reprinted version to be a comprehensive biography. Yet it is an especially penetrating essay. He understood both Lincoln's strengths and weaknesses. He did not merely eulogize, he depicted Lincoln as wholly human, without sentimentalizing. Despite a closing sentence containing 256 words, Schurz's style was generally quite clear and possessed a certain muscular beauty, a style altogether appropriate to a description of Lincoln's life and work. He outdid Herndon in his re-creation of a believable human being whose faults he refused either to conceal or to exaggerate. He brought the interpretation of Lincoln a step closer to realistic proportions, and his book earned the admiration of Theodore Roosevelt, who wrote him: "I think your sketch of Lincoln is by far the best thing that has ever been published about him."

At the turn of the century Ida Tarbell, an open-minded author who had published widely in numerous reform journals, turned her attention to the Lincoln theme. The result was a two-volume *Life of Abraham Lincoln* (1900). She brought a new breath of feminine vitality into the stuffy air of Lincoln lore and legend, unraveling skillfully numerous folk beliefs, and challenging some of Herndon's intuitive assertions concerning Lincoln's personal mannerisms and philosophy of life. Miss Tarbell's book reached a wide audience because, like the work of Nicolay and Hay and of Carl Schurz, her appraisal was first serialized in a popular monthly, *McClure's Magazine*. The basis of this new work was a series of interviews with persons, both obscure and notable, who had known Lincoln. Its author emerged with a much more believable and life-sized image. Based upon the personal reminiscences she gathered, Miss Tarbell was able to bring the factual reliability of eyewitnesses to her biography. She used the cross-examination methods of the young and intellectually virile muckrakers of the Progressive era, of which she was one. By imaginative reporting she engaged in historical reconstruction similar to that of the modern researcher. Although hastily written, her book added a fresh dimension to Lincoln studies by its refusal to accept unquestioningly the premises of past interpreters.

Before the First World War, Lincoln had become more than an American national figure. His reputation and prestige grew so steadily that the Lincoln message of disinterested yet personal democracy as an ideal for all the world's people stirred interest in him to international proportions. In 1910 Herbert Croly was the first major interpreter to focus attention upon this fact. In his book *The Promise of American Life* Croly included a short essay entitled, "Lincoln as More Than an American." The volume became a political classic, on which Croly built a reputation as one of the most influential writers in America. Croly's writing in this book, and as an editor of the *New Republic,* stimulated the movement for national self-examination. He focused particular attention on Lincoln as a symbol of integrity and human excellence, a moral giant who "was not only good-natured, strong and innocent," but also a genius who "had made himself intellectually candid, concentrated, and disinterested, and morally humane, magnanimous, and humble." Croly's own ideal, according to the publicist Oswald Garrison Villard, was "the liberation of the American personality from its provincialism, its narrowness, its self-satisfaction. . . ." In Lincoln, Croly saw the ideal of a self-taught man who stood for the opposite of narrowness and who was an almost unconscious example to the world of the best which America had to offer. Herbert Croly performed a real service for Lincoln studies in making so significant an observation. He did not become a Lincoln biographer, but his deep convictions made him an unusual interpreter.

In time, foreign interest in Abraham Lincoln resulted in the writing of biographies by non-Americans. Only a few of them, however, display any outstanding grasp of the Lincoln themes. A brilliant exception is a book by the Englishman Godfrey Rathbone Benson, Lord Charnwood. Written during the First World War for a British audience not assumed to know much about the Great Emancipator, Charnwood's *Abraham Lincoln* (1916) is one of the clearest analyses ever attempted. It possesses an almost noble rhythm that makes it rank as literature rather than as eulogistic or polemical writing. The volume represents the very opposite of the intense factual approach attempted by many of its American contemporaries. Charnwood, like Croly, saw Lincoln as an international symbol of democratic idealism, as a universal statesman. His literary skill kept him from cluttering the pages of his work with the routine minutiae of Lincoln's life. His book sought out the reasons behind Lincoln's actions and lifted the whole field of Lincoln studies to an international plane which later writers would keep in view.

But the quest for even the most minute details concerning Lincoln's life proved insatiable. Sometimes writers psychoanalyzed Lincoln. Sometimes they made him out to be a religious deviant. He became the subject of advertisements— one such book was entitled *Abraham Lincoln on the Coming of the Caterpillar Tractor.* A parade of books appeared on the "heart" of Lincoln, the "whole" Lincoln, the "true" Lincoln, on *The Women Lincoln Loved,* and on old Abe and God. Few facets of Lincoln's career were not diligently pursued, especially in the 1920s and 1930s. Many of the books and pamphlets actually distorted history as much as they clarified it; they confused generations of readers. As a result today's layman must engage in considerable grading, sifting, and culling in order to use the vast Lincoln literature intelligently. A person interested in Lincoln must, regrettably, almost seek counsel and instruction as to what works are reliable. Almost every American writer of recent times, believing that he knew something about Lincoln, has been tempted to write on the subject, yearning to lay bare some new fact or detail as yet unculled by others.

In 1920, for example, the respected parson William E. Barton, intrigued by the ancestry of Lincoln, particularly the possible illegitimacy of Nancy Hanks, Lincoln's mother, published *The Paternity of Abraham Lincoln: Was He the Son of Thomas Lincoln? An Essay on the Chastity of Nancy Hanks.* Barton moved from the clarification of Lincoln's legitimacy to various other books on Lincoln, including a two-volume *Life of Abraham Lincoln* (1925). His work illustrates the meticulous methods of an untrained but diligent amateur. Barton did indeed correct numerous errors made by earlier biographers, mostly genealogical. He was among the first to question the authenticity of the Ann Rutledge legend. Barton freighted his narrative, however, with such picayunish detail that a lusterless and episodic book, albeit laudably accurate, resulted. Barton, for example, expends much effort telling the reader about Lincoln's use of the word "that" thirteen times in the Gettysburg Address!

In 1928 one of the most pervasive and influential biographies of Lincoln was written by a statesman who had earlier appraised the career of Chief Justice John Marshall in four massive volumes. To his unfinished book, *Abraham Lincoln, 1809–1858,* Senator Albert J. Beveridge brought a legalistic training and outlook. He planned this study as part of a narrative history of the United States from its constitutional origins to the Civil War. Beveridge also brought to his task a good knowledge of politics, and he invited criticisms from numerous scholars. Beveridge hoped to produce a "true" portrait. Before the senator could complete this project, however, he died; thus his book does not extend beyond the Lincoln–Douglas debates, although this portion of it comprises two volumes. Despite the meticulousness with which Beveridge conducted his research, his work has been superseded by less severe, more believable, and stylistically more felicitous writing. Beveridge accepted much more uncritically than later biographers doubtful evidence presented by Herndon and other Lincoln contemporaries. Beveridge's rigorous method and nationalist biases shine through his pages, although he professed to seek objectivity in dealing with one of the most difficult historical subjects in our national history. Modern scholarship has made Beveridge's brittle judgments seem especially outdated. For at least a decade, however, Beveridge's remained one of the standard biographies of Lincoln.

Probably the most popular of all works about Lincoln is by

the literary craftsman Carl Sandburg. His importance as a Lincoln biographer rests primarily upon the six volumes that comprise *Abraham Lincoln: The Prairie Years and the War Years* (1926, 1939). Cast in a poetic mold, this great work has been referred to by Robert E. Sherwood as "a monument that will stand forever" and by Paul M. Angle as the only book among the thousands which deal with Lincoln that can be called "incomparable." A product of the same Illinois country in which Lincoln was reared, Sandburg sought to portray the fabric of Middle Western society and life in epic proportions. In the preface to a recent edition Sandburg explains how he came to expand the original scope of his work:

> The Lincoln lore of that time and place was of the man in his Illinois background and settings. When for thirty years and more I planned to make a certain portrait of Abraham Lincoln it was as the country lawyer and prairie politician. But when I finished my *Prairie Years* portrait, Lincoln the Man had grown on me so that I went on to write *The War Years*.

Without question Sandburg's work has shaped more of the thoughts and feelings of Americans about Lincoln than any other book. There is a lifelike artistry and realistic detail in Sandburg's style which, when combined with his sensitive, human appreciation of his subject, produces an incomparable result, at once perceptive, intuitive, and at least poetically definitive. Sandburg's lyrical sense of imagination may at times offend the literal-minded historian but it re-creates for his readers much of the atmosphere of the times in which Lincoln lived, with color, drama, and pathos full blown.

In the thirty years since Sandburg first published *The Prairie Years* "fiercely intense research" has characterized Lincoln scholarship. To use Sandburg's own words: "In no thirty-year period since the death of Lincoln has so rigorous and thorough an examination been given the facts and myths of the life of Lincoln." Increasingly this investigation has been carried on by professional historians. In one of his most thoughtful volumes, *The Gateway to History,* Allan Nevins states: "The biographer appeared on the stage of letters hand in hand with the historian; hand in hand they walk there still." Nevins points out that for every man who reads a history of the Civil War, there are at least ten who read lives of Lincoln, Jefferson Davis, Grant, or Lee. Certainly J. G. Randall's volumes on Lincoln are more widely read than his more specialized writings on the Civil War and Reconstruction periods of American history. Professor Randall has been called the most profound of all the Lincoln scholars. In a series of volumes, *Constitutional Problems under Lincoln* (1926), *Lincoln and the South* (1946), and *Lincoln the Liberal Statesman* (1947), Randall pieced together and organized the findings of hundreds of specialists. He prepared a synthesis that incorporated their critical judgments in this greatest work, a multi-volume biography, *Lincoln the President* (1945–55), the last portion of which was completed by his student and colleague Richard N. Current. Randall was known professionally as a "revisionist." Scorning the intricate quibbles of past pedantry, he sought to give a fresh yet sympathetic recounting, in the light of modern research, to each event treated, however familiar. He reanalyzed the Lincoln–Douglas debates, investigated wartime politics, and tried to strip emancipation "of its crust of misconception." Randall also rejected many of the sensational findings of earlier biographers regarding Lincoln's parentage and love affairs. Furthermore, he thought the Civil War a tragic and needless catastrophe stumbled into by a "blundering generation" lacking in the tolerance and patience of a Lincoln. Randall utilized a major portion of his work to air the "needless-war" thesis. Primarily a political biography, the Randall–Current work does not flinch from passing judgment upon both the times and the man. Lincoln emerges unscathed from its pages as a folk hero fully worthy of the image he created.

It was perhaps natural that the critical analysis of modern historians on the Lincoln theme should continue strongly. They brought to their work recognized and indispensable tools of inquiry and good training for the verification of moot points. Two of Randall's students, Current and David Donald, have contributed further to the filling-in of the Lincoln portraiture. Donald, in a re-examination of Lincoln's law partner, entitled *Lincoln's Herndon* (1948), and in *Lincoln Reconsidered* (1956), continued the quest for a reliable, definitive judgment concerning Lincoln's place in history. Current, especially in his editing of Randall's *Mr. Lincoln* (1957) and in *The Lincoln Nobody Knows* (1958) engaged in much the same quest.

Just as Professor Randall's work has been hailed as full of scholarly reliability and Sandburg's has been considered a literary monument, so is Benjamin P. Thomas' *Abraham Lincoln* (1952) generally regarded as the best one-volume life ever written. It is direct, fast moving, a model of economy in its clear and lively style. Thomas, who like Randall devoted much of his life to things Lincolnian, fashioned a biography for both the expert and the layman, a book that emerged as the most effective standard one-volume Lincoln biography of his generation. In this absorbing synthesis Thomas successfully digested not only the vast learning and lore of other scholars; he also incorporated indispensable new sources from the Robert Todd Lincoln Papers, once used by Nicolay and Hay but opened to the public only in 1947. As an editorial adviser he also profited greatly from immersing himself in the magnificent primary *Collected Works of Abraham Lincoln,* published soon thereafter by the national Abraham Lincoln Association.

Still others have brought successive biographical presentations of Lincoln to a level at which a veracious portrait begins to emerge. Among them are Louis Warren, who has treated Lincoln's youth, John Duff, who has dealt with Lincoln the lawyer, Ruth Painter Randall, who has investigated Lincoln's marriage, family, and sons. T. Harry Williams has examined

Lincoln and His Generals (1952), as has Kenneth P. Williams in *Lincoln Finds a General* (1956).

In his *Lincoln Reader* (1947), an anthology, Paul M. Angle presents only part of the findings of no less than sixty-five authors who have dealt with Lincoln. Further full-scale biographies devoted exclusively to Lincoln would possibly serve no useful purpose. Probably no new significant details are likely to emerge. Re-examination and reinterpretation of facts, however, will without question go on. The many themes that crisscross the Lincoln era remain challenging, and the problems which confronted the man were massive, complex, even unfathomable.

Those Lincoln studies which have gained a permanent place on library bookshelves have in common their humanizing of the past. Good biography breathes life into history, particularly for readers who lack the background to understand so confusing a period as Lincoln's crisis-torn administration. The well-researched and superbly written biography enriches one's personal grasp of humanity and lights up the landscape of the past. Biography has some of the appeal of fiction, in emphasizing the place of individuals, incident, and locale in human events. Lincoln's major biographers do not portray the whole history of his era but they often depict its most interesting aspects.

One regrettable tendency, however, emerges from all this Lincoln writing. Much of it overshadows the careers of lesser men, as if only an eminent national hero can reflect the spirit of an age. If, as Allan Nevins has said, biography is valuable as portraiture and as a study of character in history, it should encompass a whole gallery, not only the canvasses of major figures. Lesser men sometimes mirror a past age as well as the Washingtons or the Lincolns.

Only occasionally is a volume written about a figure like Maurice Baxter's *Orville H. Browning* (1957), which gives us an invaluable picture of the society in which Lincoln moved. James C. Malin's rather turgid *John Brown and the Legend of*

Fifty-Six (1942) is nevertheless also rewarding concerning a segment of our national history that greatly shaped Lincoln's role. Willard L. King's book on David Davis (1960) is an attractive work which, like similar books, fills large gaps. Yet most biographers pick the most widely known as their subjects, and Lincoln is too often their target.

In a recent study Professor Harry B. Stevens points out that biographies of four main historical figures—Lincoln, Washington, Jefferson, and Franklin—have been as numerous as those written about the next forty biographees combined. There seems little peril, then, that the handful of books published annually about lesser figures can possibly detract school children from the secure, heroic position of the "stock characters" of our history books.

Concentration on the major figures has its drawbacks. As Michael Kraus sees it, in the public mind the Lincolns and Washingtons can do no wrong and their rivals can do no right. Distortion of history sets in, and myth-making supplants historical objectivity. We take our heroes and bend them to our wishes. Soon tradition becomes so imbedded that even a serious error is hard to correct without giving offense, especially to those whose patriotism is all-knowing and militant. An author's already-great problem of avoiding bias is thus further complicated, especially when he deals with the Lincolns or the Washingtons about whom legends, based upon family or partisan and sectional pride, exist.

A striking example of how an event can be expanded upon over the years is to be found in Stefan Lorant's book, *Lincoln, A Picture Story of His Life*. During a visit to the room in the Petersen House at Washington where Lincoln died, Lorant was shocked to find it only fifteen feet long and ten feet wide. Historically, pictures of the death scene had portrayed the room as a grandiose chamber. Lorant's research demonstrated that artists had kept increasing the number of people at the death scene. From the twelve originally present, the number of bedside mourners grew to twenty-four, then to twenty-six;

finally one illustrator added in everyone who had called at the door, placing forty-six into a room that could not possibly accommodate more than a dozen persons. If such distortion of basic events in the life of a public personality can occur, one can imagine how much more vulnerable to error is the whole realm of ideas about him.

Despite the many publications concerning Lincoln, there still exist almost as many mistaken concepts as there are accurate ones. An example is the exaggerated importance given to Lincoln's alleged love for a soul mate other than his wife. Both the television and cinema medias continue to utilize details classified as questionable by the most reliable biographers. The Ann Rutledge "romance" continues to be the subject of dramatic and television performances despite its many obscurities and contradictions.

A second persistent misconception in the public consciousness is the overemphasized rail-splitting background of Lincoln. Actually Lincoln was closely associated with men of culture in Illinois. He may have mirrored a roughhewn exterior, as Herndon shows, but he also reflected, through self-education, an inner dignity that few frontier politicians achieved. Some of his first political opponents even made fun of his attempt to fill the role of gentleman. Though Lincoln, the successful gentleman-lawyer, does not quite fit the current stereotype, in 1844 his opponents put him down as a political candidate of pride, money, and aristocracy. He married into an aristocratic family and associated primarily with well-born people in spite of the humble occupations of his first years. Lincoln was not only a country lawyer but one of the outstanding lawyers in the country. He handled important cases, practicing before federal courts in Illinois, and was counsel in a Supreme Court of the United States case in 1849. One could even speak of Lincoln as a corporation lawyer. He demanded and received a fee of five thousand dollars from the Illinois Central Railroad. In 1855 he was also one of several attorneys in the McCormick Reaper case (*McCormick* vs. *Manny*

& *Co.*), representing rivals of the company. Yet his picturesque career on the Eighth Judicial Circuit helped cement the
legend of Lincoln as a country lawyer. He was an extremely
subtle lawyer and won ninety-four decisions in one hundred
and five cases. At the age of forty-nine he was already
nationally known because of his notable debates with
Douglas. At fifty Lincoln was far from a failure as some
writers continue to allege. In 1859 he was the leading Whig
and then the leading Republican in Illinois.

Lincoln had been part of a growing pioneering America.
His six picturesque years at New Salem, the four years in the
Illinois legislature and his two Congressional defeats had
transformed him into a knowledgeable, perceptive politician.
Somehow there should exist in the public consciousness an
image of the versatile, open-minded intellectual Lincoln who
was forever unfriendly toward closed opinions and dogma.
Such a Lincoln did not merely prattle about democracy in the
Fourth of July tradition but was both its critic and its defender.
This Lincoln, as early as age twenty-nine, gave a sharp
warning against disorder, angry passions, mobs, the burning
of churches, murder, and lynching. This was not merely the
awkward country bumpkin of popular image. Behind an out-
ward half-shod elegance there stood a man who set himself
above the crowd and who put strong emphasis upon the
toughness of reason as opposed to local prejudice. Lincoln's life
story illustrates how he outgrew the restrictions of his origins
and yet clung to a practical philosophy that stemmed from
grass roots.

It is obvious that Lincoln has been many things to many
men. From Herndon's day to the present, writers have chosen
to emphasize his conservatism or his liberalism, his wartime
expediency or his personal peculiarities. No one of us has a
monopoly on the wisdom of great men. It is admittedly
difficult to separate fact from fiction, myth from reality.
Lincoln's very illusiveness makes it possible to cite his words
on each side of innumerable questions. We do, however, grow

exceedingly fond of firmly-imbedded symbols; and even of fables. Widely accepted stereotypes blur clear interpretation as we enshrine our heroes in a stifling aura of dignity to which they themselves might have objected.

To most persons Lincoln remains, in Roy Basler's words, America's major "prophet, savior and martyr." Despite all the nonsense written about him he is still, for most of us, the greatest of our presidents. Lincoln's humanity perhaps best explains why he is the one president whose stature remains international and the one about whom there has been the greatest biographical interest.

By successive applications of all the tools in the biographer's panoply—industry, insight, imagination, the development of a rigorous methodology—we have drawn nearer each year to a reliable understanding of Lincoln as both man and statesman. What had seemed at first sight a simple biographical task turned out to be the most complex and difficult piece of portraiture in our national history. Fortunately, the line of biographers from Herndon to Sandburg to Randall has helped to conquer many if not all of the difficulties which threatened to obscure Lincoln's true greatness.

APPENDIX

The Contributors Comment upon Their Work

❦

FAWN M. BRODIE was born in Ogden, Utah, September 15, 1915. She received a B.A. from the University of Utah in 1934, and an M.A. from the University of Chicago in 1936. She is married to Bernard Brodie, the author of several well-known books on military strategy, and is the mother of three children. In addition to magazine articles, she has written two biographies, *No Man Knows My History, the Life of Joseph Smith, the Mormon Prophet* (Knopf, 1945), and *Thaddeus Stevens, Scourge of the South* (Norton, 1959).

The biographer is, much more than the historian, peculiarly at the mercy of his chosen subject. He is bound on the one hand by the historian's ideal of truth, and if he is a properly indefatigable researcher there is no detail so obscure that he will not somehow hunt it down if only to file it properly among his notes. On the other hand, he is bound also by the novelist's exacting requirements of style and dramatic narrative, which make the selection of his material out of all the voluminous notes one of the major tasks of the writing. A good biography must maintain the pace and suspense of the novel, and be accurate history in the bargain.

In more recent times the biographer may be judged also by his skill in dissecting and analyzing his subject's motivations. If wise, he will avoid the clinical jargon of the psychoanalyst, but if he runs away altogether from the immense legacy of Freud and other modern contributors to our understanding of mind and emotions, he is likely to end up writing a biography that is neither penetrating nor subtle, and may be quite wrong-headed.

A biographer is often attracted to a particular subject for personal reasons. He will not spend four to ten years in a bedeviled search for facts unless the king, president, poet, or courtesan he is writing about has somehow fired his own fantasies. It may be that a conflict in the life of his subject coincides with one of his own conflicts; if he falls in love with, or "in hate with" his character, it may possibly be because there is an elemental resemblance between his subject and someone close to him in his own life.

Without this original attraction, whether of love, hate, or both, there is simply insufficient motivation for the immense amount of work required to do a good and original job. Nevertheless, the biographer must be particularly careful not to let his own conflicts influence unduly his descriptions or analyses of those of his subject. Moreover, he is as rigidly bound as the historian by his facts. If he begins romancing, the result may be a contribution to literature but not to history.

It so happens that the two figures in American history about whom I have written have been immensely controversial. Both Thaddeus Stevens and Joseph Smith posed the same technical biographical problem: how to write the story of a man acting upon and reacting to the world around him without losing the man in the larger stream of history. To write the biography of Joseph Smith one had to write also the history of the early Mormon Church. With Stevens the context was even more pressing. His life spanned a period of more than three-quarters of a century, which included the Civil War and the early years of Reconstruction, in all of which he was deeply involved. There was the sheer physical bulk of the Lincoln material to be dealt with, the years of debates in the *Congressional Globe,* the overwhelming mass of other government documents and newspaper material, to say nothing of the endless rows of boxed manuscript material in the Library of Congress. After the essential facts were gathered, one had to face constantly during the writing the problem of striking a proper balance between the Stevens stories and the background material required to illuminate them properly. Moreover, one had to re-create the passion and intensity of the Radical Republican revolution while duly considering not only the attacks of the men who opposed it at the time but also the attacks of the modern revisionist historians, some of whom have been curiously intent on minimizing the horrors of slavery and blowing up the horrors of the Reconstruction.

Fortunately, from a biographer's point of view, the life of each man built up to a dramatic climax and then swiftly ended. There were no anticlimactic years of decline in either case to lessen the impact. The rifle bullets of a masked mob cut down Joseph Smith at the window of the jail in Carthage, Illinois, when he was thirty-eight. The climax of Thaddeus Stevens' life—the impeachment and trial of Andrew Johnson —came when he was but five months short of death, and his final speech, which he was too ill even to read himself, was perhaps the most revealing document of his life.

NORMAN CORWIN began his professional career as a newspaperman. He then turned his attention to radio and became a writer, director, and producer for the Columbia Broadcasting System. He was named chief of special projects of the United Nations Radio during its formative years, and created a series of broadcasts which have been translated and produced on most of the radio systems of the world. Mr. Corwin has been a recipient of the One World Flight Award, established in memory of Wendell Willkie, and a grant from the American Academy of Arts and Letters. His excursions into the world of Lincolniana include the first production of *The Lonesome Train* cantata and a script on Ann Rutledge. In recent years he wrote and directed two stage plays which toured the United States and played on Broadway. The first was a theatrical evening based on the works of Carl Sandburg, and the second was a dramatization of the Lincoln–Douglas debates, called *The Rivalry*.

In writing *The Rivalry,* my dramatization of the Lincoln–Douglas debates, my hardest job was to distill the dramatic essence of each man's position, for, in their original form, the debates are very long, discursive, and doggedly repetitious. The trick was to foreshorten, splice, integrate, and juxtapose material without sacrificing the quality of authenticity. Sometimes a sentence by either contestant in one debate would prove better than another by the same man on the same topic in an earlier or later debate, although the surrounding context might be common to both instances. In such a case, I always tried to choose the line which best expressed the candidate's intention. It is easy to see why, therefore, the brief flurries of tête-à-tête exchange, the infighting and repartee, do not occur in the play exactly as they did in the debates.

The job of getting material for characterization was relatively easy in the case of Lincoln. Carl Sandburg has told me that more biographies have been written of Lincoln than of any other world figure save Christ and Napoleon. Douglas has been the subject of much less study. In a way, this worked to the advantage of the play. Since Douglas' change of heart from fierce antagonism to gallant support of Lincoln is not common knowledge, it provided an element of surprise and disclosure to the closing events of the play.

Mrs. Douglas was another matter. The bibliography on her is paper-thin: a few passing references, a few photographs showing her dark beauty, a few compliments by male admirers, strewn like bouquets across her almost invisible trail. The very absence of material on Adèle attracted me. It gave me the opportunity to invent her scenes by using a kind of triangulation of small reference points. My choice of Mrs. Douglas as the narrative mortar of the play—a very old and time-honored device in playwriting—commended itself over the idea of using Mrs. Lincoln, who seemed to me too obvious and unpromising a figure. Mrs. Douglas was beautiful, Mrs. Lincoln was not. Mrs. Douglas was present at all the debates, while Mrs. Lincoln was not; and so on, down through a whole list of check points.

The writing of the play was never simple. It went through many revisions and vicissitudes before the main element— the debates themselves—was right, or as right as I could make it. In this process I had the signal help of George Brandt, the producer *in situ* of an earlier, unproduced, inchoate version of the play, who urged, pushed, and shoved in the directions finally taken.

SHERRILL HALBERT is a United States district judge. A native Californian, he is the son of pioneer parents. His grandfather, Dr. Joel B. Halbert, although a slaveowner, was a staunch supporter of the Union cause and President Lincoln. Judge Halbert has been active in civic affairs and public life. In addition to holding memberships in numerous literary and historical societies, he is presently on the Board of Advisors of Sacramento State College, on the Board of Trustees of McGeorge College of Law, a trustee of the California Historical Society, and a member of the Board of Directors of the American Society for Legal History.

Abraham Lincoln found his beau ideal in Henry Clay. I cannot remember when Abraham Lincoln was not my beau ideal. When I was a student in high school, an English assignment required me to write a biographical essay. Acting with the confidence of youth, I selected Lincoln as my subject. I was unable to find a suitable biography in the school library, so I used my "spending money" to purchase the one-volume work by John G. Nicolay. This volume has become the cornerstone of my Lincoln library.

The effort spent writing this essay gave me my first real appreciation of the magnitude of my subject. This was an awareness which caused me to fix for myself a rule never again to write anything about Abraham Lincoln unless it could be done in a careful and considered fashion. With this rule as a restraint, the leading of a busy life has, to a very great degree, prevented me from writing much outside of legal briefs as a lawyer and opinions as a judge. Then came an invitation to address the annual meeting of the American Society for Legal History. At first I hesitated, but finally I decided to meet the challenge. The result was a speech on the suspension of the writ of habeas corpus by President Lincoln, the greater part of which is printed in this volume.

In preparing the text of this speech I had to read and study many books that revealed something of the times and events covered. Some of these books contained source material; others were simply what their authors wrote on the subject. The latter allowed me to compare my findings with those of the authors, in the hope of eventually arriving at the facts. Fortunately, many pamphlets on my subject were written and published at the very time the events under consideration were taking place. These pamphlets, with the public records and reported law cases, afforded me more contemporary material than an author usually has available to him.

Before starting to write I assembled many pages of notes with a reference to the source of each. With the notes assembled, I prepared an outline and started to write. Having neither the ability nor the confidence of a professional writer, some pages were written and rewritten literally dozens of times. Whether my product indicates the care and consideration which my rule requires it to have, I leave to the reader to decide.

HAROLD HYMAN was born in New York in 1924. He served with the Marine Corps in the South Pacific during the Second World War, studied at UCLA as an undergraduate, and took his Doctorate of Philosophy at Columbia University. Mr. Hyman is the author of two books dealing with the loyalty oath in American history and is a recipient of the Sidney Hillman Foundation Prize Award and a Citation of Merit of the California Writers' Guild. He is an associate professor at UCLA and is presently at work on a biography of Edwin M. Stanton, to be published by Alfred A. Knopf.

A century-long encrustation of stereotypes obscures the realities of the Lincoln–Stanton relationship. I needed a sledge hammer and a scalpel to get at what seems to me to be a closer approximation of the truth.

The blunt instrument served to test the reliability of contemporary accounts of the two men, which historians for decades have accepted as valid. Rereading these accounts, I tried to determine if the narrator had firsthand opportunity to observe the incidents he described. Next, I checked on whether he set down his description soon after the event, or much later, after the vagaries of memory had taken their toll. Further, I sought to ascertain the observer's reputation for accuracy among persons who knew him well. And last, I was determined to employ incidents in my story only if their factuality was attested to by at least two other persons.

For example, in Donn Piatt's *Memories of Men Who Saved the Union,* the author, a lifelong friend of Stanton's, describes the Reaper trial. He has Stanton swear that if Lincoln remained on the case, then he would resign from it. It sounded convincing, and was certainly picturesque. Ever since, historians have repeated the Piatt anecdote, and have concluded from it that Lincoln and Stanton were incompatible personalities.

Applying my "hammer," I found that Piatt was not on the scene at the Reaper trial. He not only reported at secondhand, but did not put pen to paper until more than two decades after the event he described. I became aware that among his contemporaries Piatt had the reputation of a namedropper and incurable exaggerator, who loved to magnify his associations with men greater than himself. Lastly, no other reporter sustained Piatt's version.

If it takes the hammer to crack the weight of falsehood, then a finer instrument is needed to reconstruct the truth. The historian's function is always twofold. On the one hand, he must criticize, test, and demolish the fabric of hearsay and myth. Then, he must rebuild, from the best materials he can gather and from the resources of his intelligence and imagination, what he hopes will be a true account.

My research brought me into contact with Stanton descendants, Lincoln collectors, and primary source material in the form of new manuscripts. These manuscripts, which included a large number of Stanton's own letters and those of his relatives and associates, offered insights from which my story was built. Out of such effort I have tried to portray both Lincoln and Stanton in more human and credible terms.

There is no eternal law which the historian is forbidden to

attack. On the contrary, by professional obligation he is pledged to snoop in dusty corners, striking out with hammers and probing with scalpels. He knows that no sooner will he have submitted his findings to the public than others will seek to employ these weapons against him.

MORT REIS LEWIS is a television writer and producer and has created many programs in the historical field, including the NBC series "Stroke of Fate." He was president of the Civil War Round Table of Southern California, vice-president of the Lincoln Sesquicentennial Association of California, and is a member of the Advisory Council of the National Civil War Centennial Commission and chairman of its Television Program Committee. He has published many articles on Lincoln and is considered an authority on Lincoln's humor.

The beginnings of my interest in Lincoln's humor can be traced to the moment at which I won a book of Lincoln speeches for my successful defense of the virtues of Warren G. Harding in schoolroom debate. I devoured the contents of my prize, and from that moment on I was a Lincoln man. In later years, when writing skits and jokes for radio and stage comedians, as well as for Broadway revues, and influenced, no doubt, by the nature of my work, I began to appreciate the importance of humor to Lincoln.

I had acquired a knack of "switching" jokes—something necessary to the professional survival of any comedy writer who had to provide one hundred jokes or so a week to demanding employers. This knack has been of invaluable help in tracing the genesis of funny stories Lincoln told—in recognizing the originals of jokes he "switched." That he did this there can be no doubt, if one compares some of the stories he told with ones we know he read. His friend of the Eighth Circuit, Henry Clay Whitney, wrote that Judge Samuel Treat had lent Lincoln a copy of *Joe Miller,* and that Treat had "found Lincoln narrating the stories contained therein around the circuit, but very much embellished and changed, evidently by Lincoln himself." Lincoln, of course, had "switched" the *Joe Miller* jokes—brought them up to date, perhaps even given them a current impact by substituting the names of acquaintances or notables in his "new" stories, for those used in the hoary compendium. This is a trick all comedy writers will recognize. Monologists have employed it from time immemorial.

When I came upon Ulysses S. Grant's account of the president's telling him the humorous fable about the vainglorious monkey which collapsed under the weight of his own tail, I was naturally curious to know where Lincoln found the original of his parable. Later, I read that the president's source was the works of Orpheus C. Kerr. I proceeded to reread my own copies of the three-volume edition of Robert H. Newell's *The Orpheus C. Kerr Papers,* some 1049 pages in all, but without success. Then, thinking that perhaps, as often happens, the source had been incorrectly given, I went through my Petroleum V. Nasby, Artemus Ward, Private Miles O'Reilly, and a number of other humorous authors Lincoln was wont to read, in the hope of finding a clue to a source other than Orpheus C. Kerr. Perhaps a month afterward I located a book called *Versatilities,* by one of Lincoln's favorite humorists, Robert H. Newell (Orpheus C. Kerr). Investigating this book of verse, I found the satirical "A Fable for Strategists," undoubtedly Lincoln's source for the story he told Grant! This is, of course, a very minor discovery, but it is the kind of thing that makes research in the Lincoln humor field interesting.

Curiosity, and a willingness to dig are perhaps as necessary in my particular field of Lincolniana, as in those considered more important. Equally true is that evaluations must be made on the basis of knowledge and experience. Lincoln's humor is serious business.

WILLIAM MARSH is a descendant of one of the Pilgrim Fathers who settled Hartford, Connecticut, in 1636. He has had a lifelong interest in American history, and particularly the political and military history of the Civil War. He is not a professional writer,

but his recent semiretirement from business has given him more
time to devote to study and the composition of articles such as the
one which appears in this book.

Many years ago, when I lived in Tennessee and Maryland,
I had the privilege of visiting the scenes of many of the
major military engagements of the Civil War. My interest in
this subject has endured throughout the intervening years.
The particular story of General Henry Wager Halleck appealed to me largely because the story seemed mysterious
and incomplete. No biographer had ever thought him a worth-
while subject for a book, and, almost entirely overlooked by
historians, he received only scant mention in the vast literature of the Civil War. In addition, whenever he was mentioned, it was with uncompromising scorn. *Stupid, incompetent,* and *hated* were the words most widely used to describe
his official conduct. Few men in public life have been made
the object of such virulent attack. I had found, in my reading, no solid evidence to justify such treatment, and the story,
frankly, piqued my curiosity.

In my search for Halleck material I only did what every
other researcher must do—try to locate original, unpublished
papers. To broaden my knowledge of the general background,
I consulted a number of standard historical works and biographies. The Library of Congress, a number of state libraries,
and several state and local historical societies were co-
operative and very helpful. The most difficult problem encountered was in locating living descendants of the Halleck–
Hamilton–Cullum families. This took many months of hard
work, but the result was gratifying; I was given access to
family records not obtainable from any other source.

I think what prompted me to undertake this study in the
first place was my desire to seek out the truth about Halleck
and to try to change, in some way, the public image created
by his enemies. My motive has been to do simple justice to
a man who served his country with distinction, and whose
reputation has suffered undeservedly at the hands of his contemporaries and historians.

DAVID HUMPHREYS MILLER is a writer, artist, television commentator, and specialist on the Civil War, American Indians, and the West. He is the author of several books on American history, including *Custer's Fall, The Indians' Side of the Little Big Horn Story* (1957), and *Ghost Dance* (1959). He has spent over twenty-five years among the Sioux, Cheyenne, Crow, Blackfeet, Kiowa, Comanche, Apache, Hopi, and Navaho tribes of the United States, as well as the Shapra and Jivaro headhunters of South America. An artist of national reputation, he has painted murals for the National Park Service and other nationally known institutions. He is a member of the executive board of the Civil War Round Table and a director of the Hollywood Author's Club. As a television host and commentator on CBS's *Cavalcade of Books,* he is widely known to televiewers on the Pacific Coast.

I was sixteen years old, in 1935, when I left my boyhood home in Ohio to live among the Indian tribes of the Dakotas, Montana, and Wyoming. The oldest of these Indians had been fierce fighters in the past. Among the Sioux were many old warriors who had fought under Little Crow, Red Cloud, Crazy Horse, and Sitting Bull.

Out of skepticism and disbelief in the white man's history books, I determined to get the true story from the Indians themselves of their conflicts with the whites. Since many of these venerable warriors spoke no English and I was anxious to communicate with them firsthand regarding their exploits, I painstakingly learned various tribal tongues as well as the sign language used and understood by all Plains Indians.

I found that my fluency with their native tongues permitted me to become accepted as one of them, and they talked more openly to me than they had to other white men. Black Elk, famous medicine man and survivor of the Little Big Horn fight, adopted me as his son. He named me *Wasicun Maza*—"Iron White Man"—after a prominent Sioux chief who was known to all members of the Sioux Nation. "I want all our people to know you as well as they knew him," Black Elk explained.

Subsequently, I was adopted into four tribes: Sioux, Crow, Blackfeet, and Kiowa (in Oklahoma). This further paved the way for me in gaining the Indians' confidence, and I was accepted everywhere as an "Indian"—even as a leader.

All told, I interviewed seventy-one Indians who had fought Custer at Little Big Horn. But by the middle thirties— over sixty years after the Minnesoto Outbreak—only four old-timers, all Santees, were still alive who had fought under Little Crow. They were Medicine Bear, Big Breastplate, Sacred Blanket, and Red Leaf, brother of one of the condemned Sioux executed at Mankato. Red Leaf was so advanced in years, when I met him, that his grandsons had to prop him up so he could talk to me. The details of the Outbreak were still vivid in the memories of these fighting men, since this had been the outstanding event of their lives.

The Santee Sioux who fought the Minnesotans are all dead now. Many of their deeds seem far from civilized. But credit them, if you can, with purest motives of self-preservation in a hopeless effort to stem the tide of an alien and inimical culture.

JAMES ("JAY") MONAGHAN, whose studies for a Ph.D. in history were interrupted by the First World War, began his career as a professional author with books on big-game hunting and outdoor life. He has continued to write on a variety of subjects, among which are Lincoln and the Civil War. He is the author of *Diplomat in Carpet Slippers,* a study of Lincoln's foreign policy, *Civil War on the Western Border, 1854–1865,* and two biographies: *The Man Who Elected Lincoln,* and *Swamp Fox of the Confederacy.* Mr. Monaghan has been state historian of Illinios, a fellow of the Henry E. Huntington Library, and consultant for the Wyles Collection of Lincolniana at the University of California. He is now at work editing a comprehensive volume on the American West and is writing a book on Australian participation in the California Gold Rush.

In historical writing I try to re-create the people, their surroundings and culture, as accurately as possible, but I prefer not to express a personal preference concerning them. I try to let the characters do all their own talking. This gives life to the scene, and, if the situation is correctly re-created, the reader draws his own conclusion, and it will be much more lasting than one consciously pointed out to him by the author.

I am especially interested in making the characters so real that readers who would have loved or hated them in life will love or hate them as portrayed in the book. It is my hope that readers who are Whigs or Tories at heart will ally themselves with their counterparts when they read my text.

A reviewer once complained that instead of presenting a balanced academic interpretation of the Chicago *Tribune's* pre-Civil War editor, Dr. Charles Ray, I portrayed him with my own bigoted Northern bias. On the other hand, a reviewer of my biography of M. Jeff Thompson complained that I was so objectionably pro-Southern that no one except an unreconstructed Confederate could read it. Both reviewers thought that they were being critical. To me these are among the two highest compliments I have ever received, and I wish the two books might always be read together. It might help us understand the Brothers' War.

The life of every writer of history is bound to be full of experiences. A person who is fortunate enough to live in two or three eras at the same time is never going to be bored. Historical research has enabled me to meet the people of every state in our Union, the hut-dwellers of west Africa, and the Indians on the far islands off Alaska, where I retrieved a Lincoln totem pole. In Australia—the last place in the world anyone would look—I unearthed two remarkable Lincoln items. And let us remember that the grandest experience for every lover of history is inside the covers of the next well-written book.

MARIANNE MOORE is one of the great poets writing in English today. Among her more recent works are the *Collected Poems* (1951); *The Fables of La Fontaine* (translator) (1954); *Predilections* (1955); *Like a Bulwark* (1956); and *O To Be a Dragon* (1959). Miss Moore has been the recipient of numerous awards, including the Dial Award, the Shelley Memorial Award, the National Book Award, and the Pulitzer Prize. Her contribution to this volume grew out of an article written for Ralph G. Newman's collection, *Lincoln for the Ages.*

Abraham Lincoln and history: in what light do they appear to us in 1961? Even presented in elementary textbook incompleteness, Lincoln was to me, as a child, a symbol—not that I knew the word—of a kind of person on whom to rely; compassionate, natural; obedient to conviction regulated by conscience. Not at any time a member of a church, Lincoln believed in God as revealed in the Bible, his life confirming the paradox that he that loseth his life shall save it; a clear mind and firm conscience having constrained him to serve those less equipped.

What of history? Is mankind evolving as an instrument of justice? Subject to indignities of fashion and behavior, we seem to be living in a second Regency period; whereas, materially, we are better off than Joseph was when he sought corn of Pharoah; than in the time of Nero, Henry the Eighth, or Louis the Fourteenth. Lincoln set himself to eradicate slavery and officially did. Yet slavery persists. Whole populations are hungry; murder plots are so numerous that they can no longer be ignored—not in countries to the south of us, but in our back streets and therapeutic parks. Nuclear energy is being applied to peaceful uses. Surgeons perform dazzling rescues, transplanting organs safely—perhaps. Tuberculosis can be arrested; even cancer? We have improved cattle-breeding techniques and developed better barley. We have jets, helicopters, under-water suits, sky-diving suits, space suits. We can bring the theater and the concert to the drawing room —or to privacy. But is all that we read ennobling or entertaining? What is the effect on boys and girls of books we give them?—given us?—written by us? Does the reader deduce, Elizabeth Gray Vining inquires, "that life is good, that truth is worth seeking?"; that it is the heart which conduces to happiness?

Our war to save the union was not waged with words alone; we need West Point and Annapolis; but has not Lincoln taught us something? Are we evolving into stewards of those who need us? Not unless the heart is able to act against itself. We know this; society is not regeneratd *by mass*. It is the changed individual who changes society. Freedom—the indispensable need; that we may work for others' freedom—toiled for without reward; with innocence our defence—kept hardy by a clear mind and tender conscience. Man must control himself if he is to control society.

ALLAN NEVINS is one of America's most distinguished historians. He was professor of American history at Columbia University from 1931 to 1959 and has been an editorial writer for the New York *Post,* the New York *Sun,* the New York *World,* and the *Nation.* Mr. Nevins served with the Office of War Information during the Second World War, and was chief public-affairs officer at the American embassy in London. He is a past-president of the American Historical Association, member of the American Academy of Arts and Letters, the Council on Foreign Relations, and is president of the Society of American Historians. Mr. Nevins has been the recipient of numerous awards and has been twice winner of the Pulitzer Prize. Probably his best-known works are his six-volume history of the period of sectional struggle, his lines of Grover Cleveland and Hamilton Fish, his analytic history (with Frank E. Hill) of the Ford Motor Company, and his *Emergence of Modern America.*

Like all Americans except the aristocratic-minded, Lincoln took democracy for granted; and students of the subject have taken his attitudes on the subject for granted too. It is clear that he gave but slight attention to theories of democracy. He never broke the subject down into its components of social democracy, economic democracy, and political democracy, for only the last arrested his attention. As for social democracy, a belief in essential human equality was so deeply ingrained in his nature that he would hardly have cared to discuss, or even think, about it. He knew that his wife's family, the Todds, thought themselves a good deal better than the Lincolns, and the idea amused him. It probably never occurred to him, in any distinct way, that Charles Francis Adams or Jefferson Davis (that "tother fellow," as he called him) thought themselves better than he; if it had, this idea too would have amused rather than irritated him. In his world every decent, well-behaved human being was as good as every other such being. The question of economic democracy, again, was not acute in Lincoln's time. He made his sympathy with workingmen, as with farmers, quite plain; but the problems wrapped up in the industrial revolution and the rise of great corporations and swollen fortunes were not yet pressing. The maladies and potentialities of political democracy, however, deeply engrossed him.

My essay, I think, is deficient chiefly in failing to do justice to the spiritual element in Lincoln's attitude toward democracy. That element is hard to portray. It lay under the surface in much that he said and did; when it broke through to the light, as in the Conkling letter, the Gettysburg Address, and the Second Inaugural, it was powerful in its impact both upon his own time and upon subsequent generations. Yet it largely eludes description and defies analysis. Attentive readers may find some clue to its origins and nature in the book of the English-born mystic, Francis Grierson, *The Valley of Shadows,* which emphasizes the silences of prairie Illinois—"for out of those silences came the voice of preacher and prophet and a host of workers and heroes in the great War of Secession." They may find other clues in the pages of Sandburg.

My own interest in Lincoln, however, is not analytical or biographical, but historical. Such impressions as I have formed of him, his slow sure growth, his limitations that throw into relief his powers, his patient understanding of popular failures because he sometimes failed himself, and his tremendous gifts of management and eloquence, have disengaged themselves, in bits and pieces, from my six volumes on the period of sectional conflict, beginning with *The Ordeal of the Union,* and ending (for the present) with *The War for the Union.* They lack the coherence of biography, but they perhaps gain a great deal from the background of surrounding events and contemporary personages. To these six volumes others will be added, two of them full of materials touching on Lincoln.

ANDREW F. ROLLE, born in Providence, Rhode Island, is a professor of history at Occidental College. He teaches and writes in the field of American history, with particular attention to the West. His books include *Riviera Path* (1948), written while serving as American vice-consul at Genoa, Italy; *An American in California* (1956), a prize-winning biography; and *The Road to Virginia City* (1960). He is at work on a comprehensive new history of California and another book that deals with Confederates who refused to surrender after the Civil War. He is interested, as well, in the effects of the American West upon foreign immigrants and will incorporate his findings into a forthcoming book entitled *Italy out West.*

My concept of history is basically a fusion of two points of view. First, I believe that the writing of history is a literary art, rather than a laboratory experiment. Secondly, however, I feel that the historian must apply certain tests of verifiability to what he writes. These two concepts underly the Lincoln piece that I prepared for this volume. My contribution unveils the steps by which Lincoln's biographers made him out to be more than life-sized, indeed almost a mythical and symbolic figure.

I believe that the study of history is one of those disarmingly broad, cultural experiences which helps to remove mankind from its savage origins; in short, that it is a civilizing factor. Happily, most historians have lived through that phase of historical inquiry which tended to stress a relentless, interminable quest of brute, objective facts for their own sake. As keepers of the record of mankind, historians must fight the tendency to chop up the study of history, to particularize, to break it into disjointed fragments. Historians have made notable advances not only in presenting history palatably, but in reducing the romantic biases of the past to more reasonable terms. They no longer claim to be fully scientific in the process, but try to get at the problem of reliability through means that have much in common with the writing of good literature. Several generations removed from the Civil War, the historian of today considers the social, intellectual, economic, and literary aspects of man's behavior in that struggle, as well as the patriotic and political impulses.

In looking at seemingly irrational and unexplainable emotional factors in human history, the historian broadens the scope and stature of his subject. At a time when scientific studies command so much prestige, because of their utility, we need to realize more than ever before that practical utility alone cannot answer all of our problems. History is one of those areas of inquiry that attempts a fuller explanation of man's conduct. A knowledge of man's past is absolutely necessary to an understanding of his present and future. History acquaints man with the experience of the race and helps him understand the making of what lies ahead.

JUSTIN TURNER is an investment executive, lecturer, and author. He is a member of the National Civil War Centennial Commission, the American Historical Society, is chairman of the Board of Governors of the University of Judaism, in Los Angeles, co-chairman of the B'nai B'rith Archives, in Washington, D.C., and a trustee of the National Foundation for Jewish Culture. He is a collector of historical manuscripts and a contributor to a wide range of historical journals and reviews.

My interest in the Hampton Roads Peace Conference first arose as a result of my study of Alexander Stephens, vice-president of the Confederacy. It was further stimulated when I acquired the Thomas T. Eckert papers from a member of the Eckert family. The contents of this file, which relate directly to the conference, were preserved intact as a result of their important relationship to Lincoln's report to Congress. On February 7, 1865, Lincoln asked Eckert to furnish him with copies of all dispatches, relative to the peace negotiation, which had been sent by the Secretary of War, or himself, between the 29th of January and the 2nd of February, the day he left Washington for City Point. Eckert complied with Lincoln's request and kept the originals. They remained in the Eckert family until 1950.

My acquisition of the Eckert papers resulted in a chain reaction of reading and research. Looking backward, I studied previous attempts to end the war by way of peace conferences. There were obvious reasons why these attempts had been made and why they failed. I was fascinated with the accounts of Lincoln's chiropodist, Zacharie, and his relations with Lincoln, Banks, and Seward. This led me, in turn, to the study of the influential and interesting Francis Preston Blair, and the lives of his two sons: Francis Preston Blair, Jr., who was governor of Missouri, and Montgomery Blair, who served as Lincoln's postmaster.

My study of the peace commissioners themselves—Stevens, Hunter, and Campbell—showed me that all three men were basically moderates, opposed to secession and the dissolution of the Union. It was easy to see why they had been selected by Jefferson Davis to talk of peace. I hope some day to incorporate the results of this research into a larger work, which will also cover the subject matter of my contribution to this volume.